The Vlgar Frog

REVISITED

digitally remastered from the original ink drawings
which were believed lost for thirty years; new format
with previously unseen pictures by the author

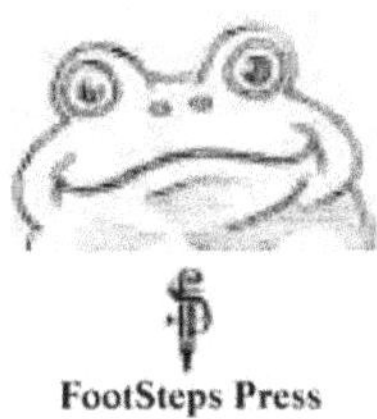

FootSteps Press

The Vulgar Frog
Footsteps Press First Edition
Published in the United Kingdom

First Published By Quartet 1977

ISBN 978-1-908867-04-9

The Vulgar Frog

REVISITED

by

Jonathon X Coudrille

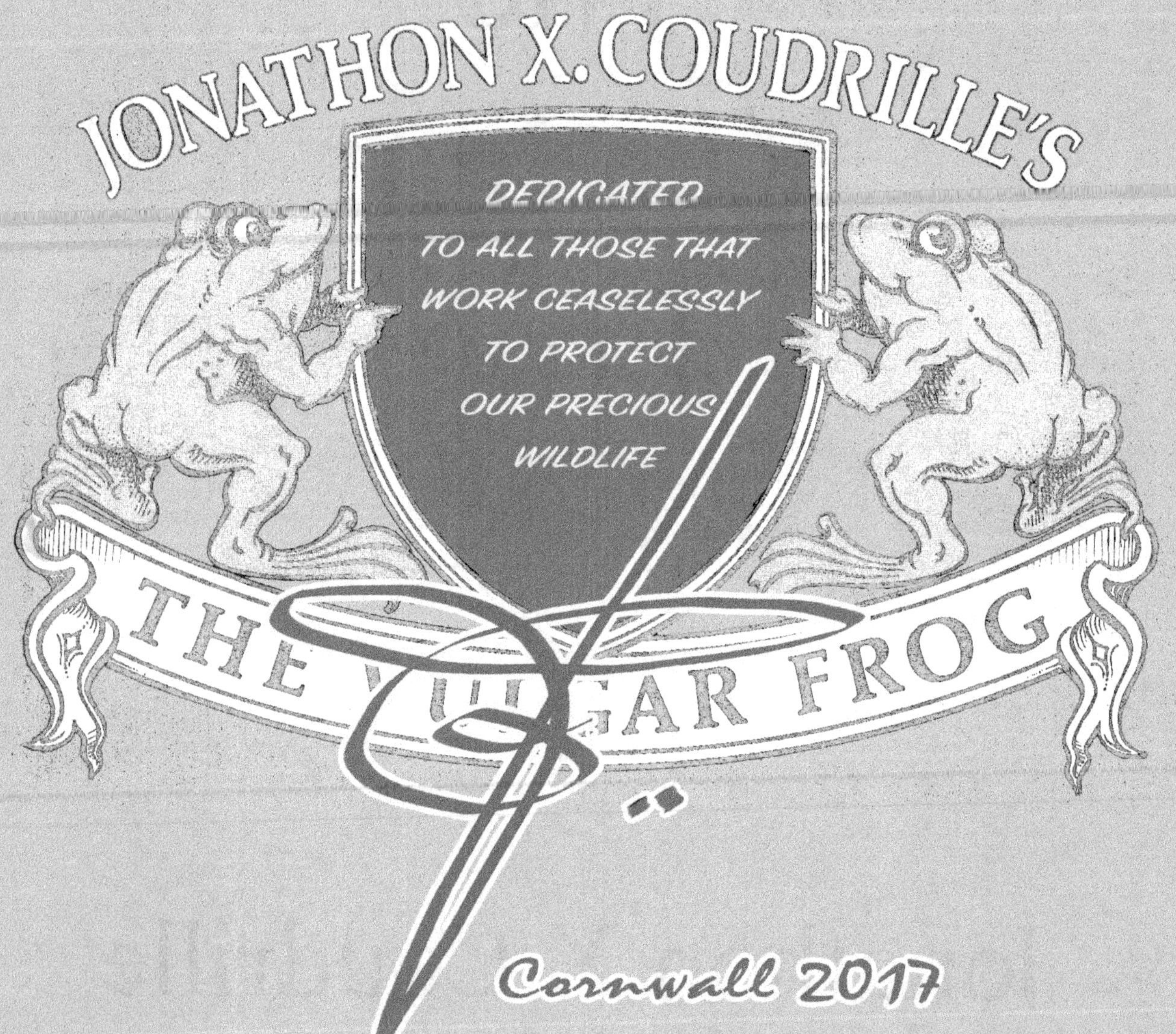

JONATHON X. COUDRILLE'S
DEDICATED
TO ALL THOSE THAT
WORK CEASELESSLY
TO PROTECT
OUR PRECIOUS
WILDLIFE
THE VULGAR FROG
Cornwall 2017

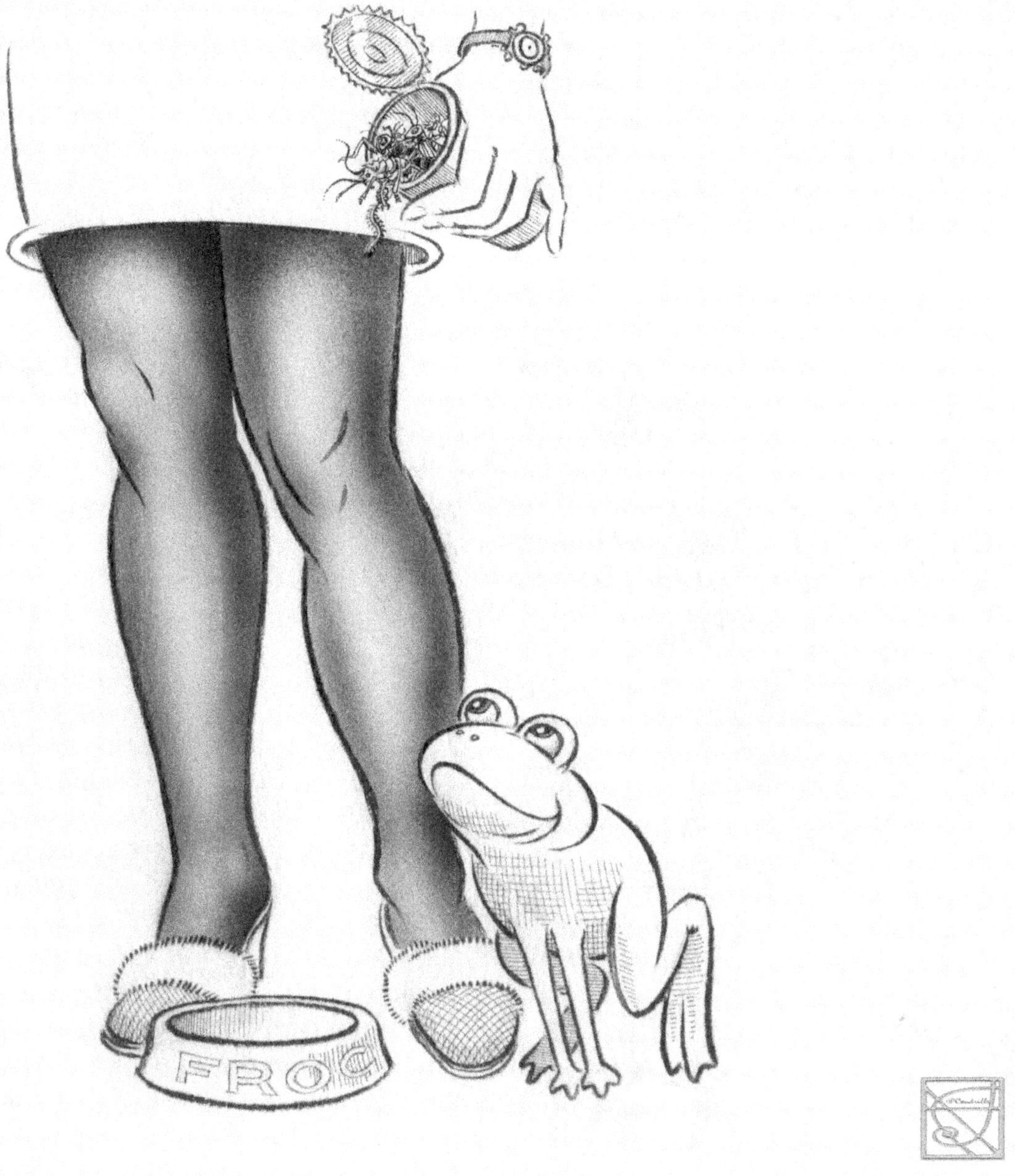

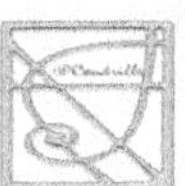

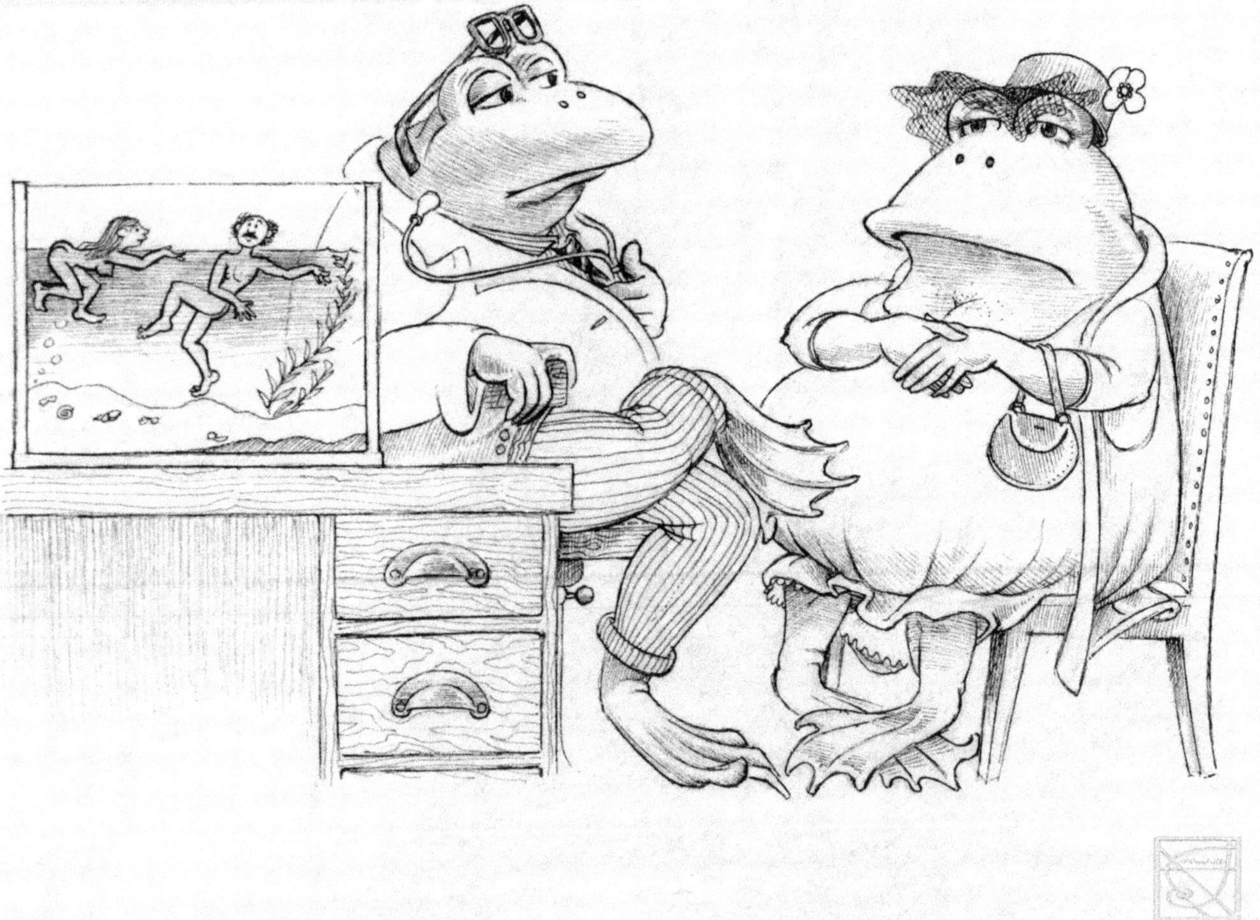

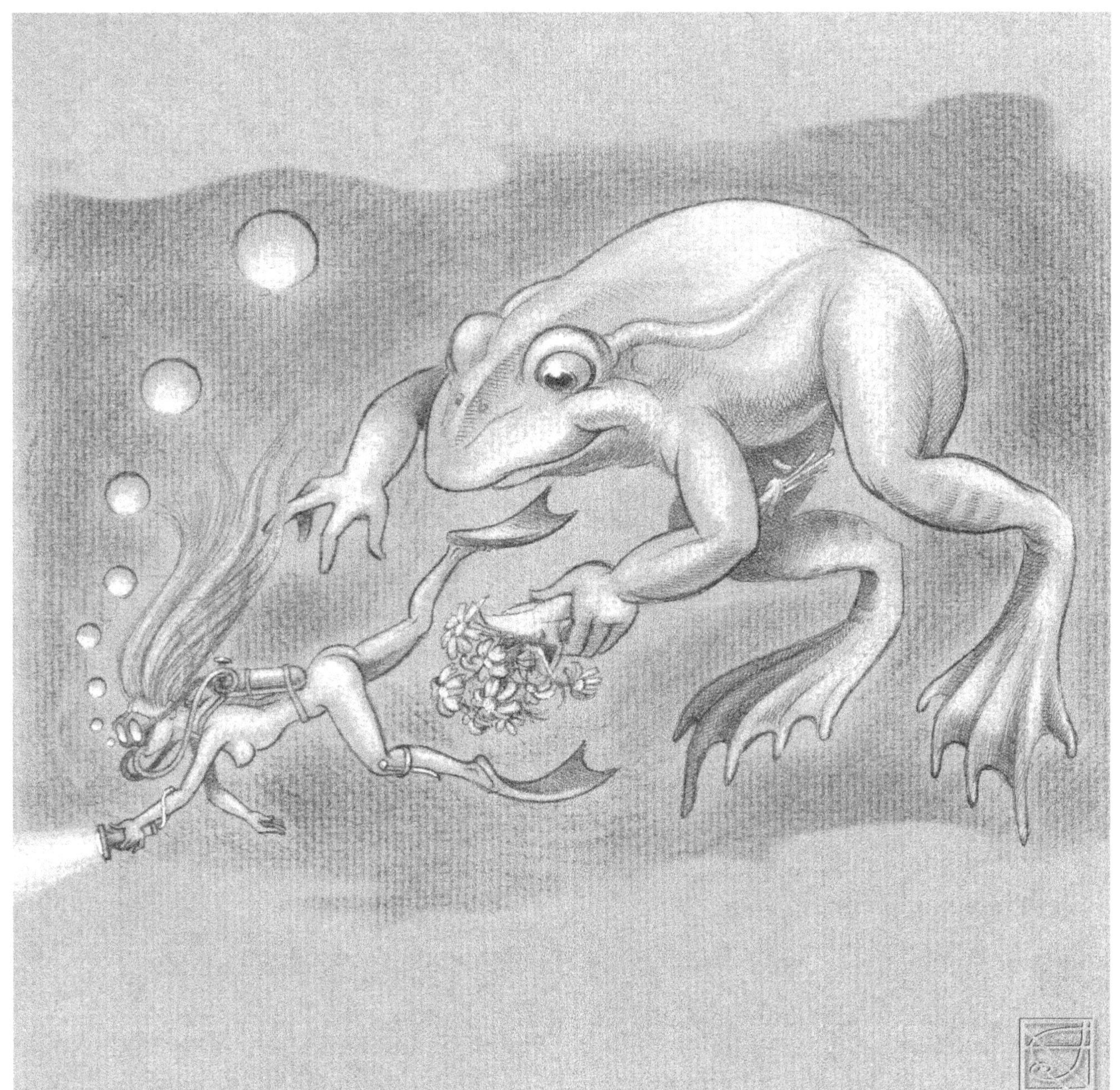

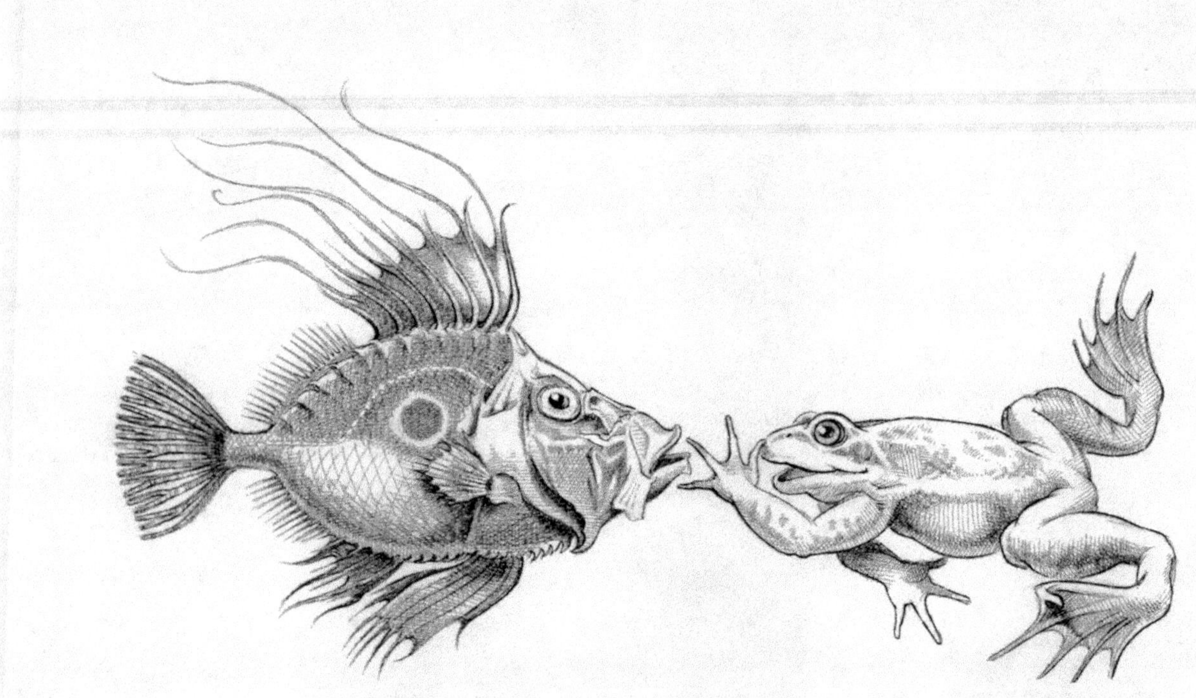

RANA ESCULENTA DISRESPETING ZEUS FABER 1982

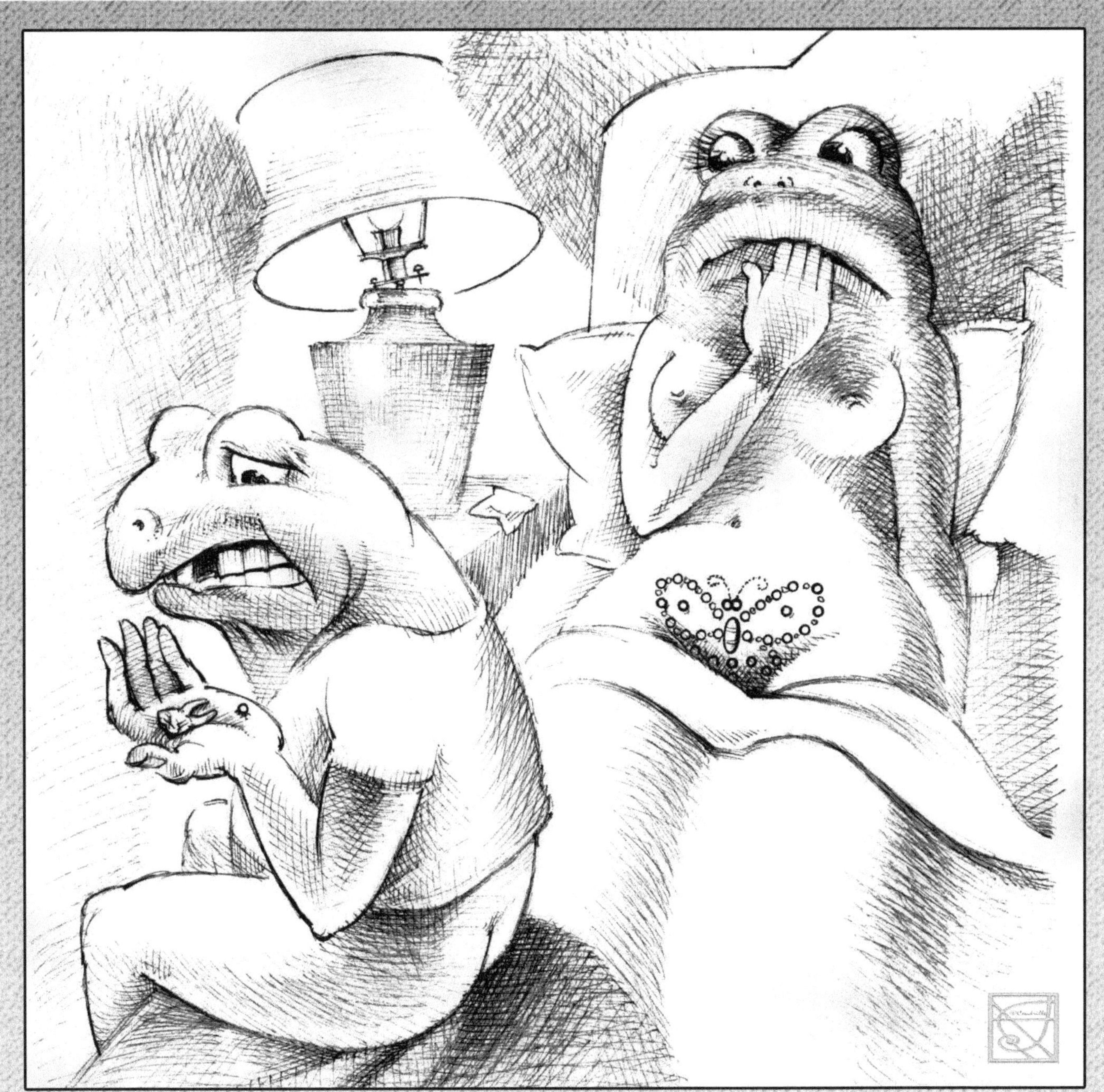

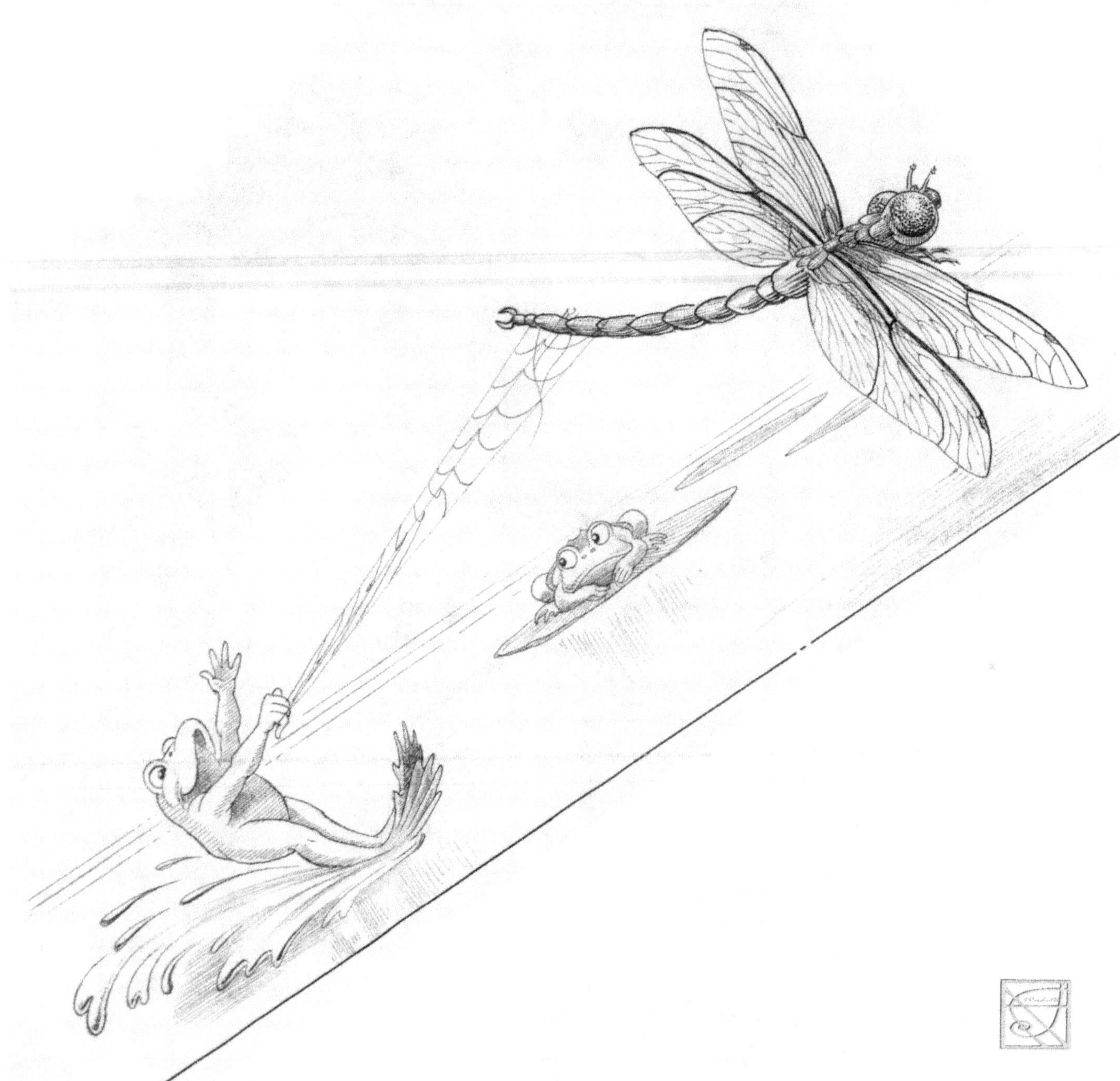

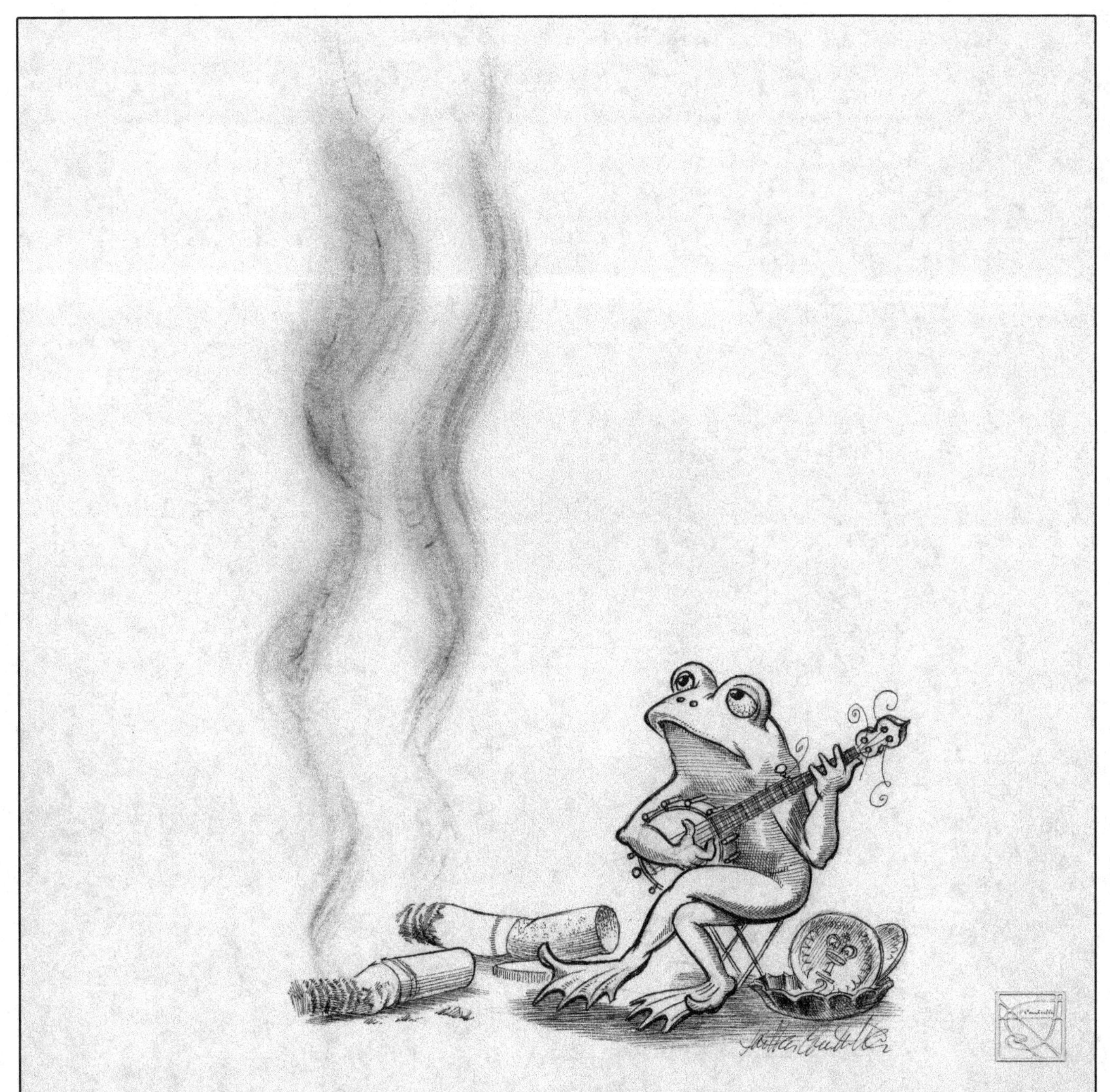

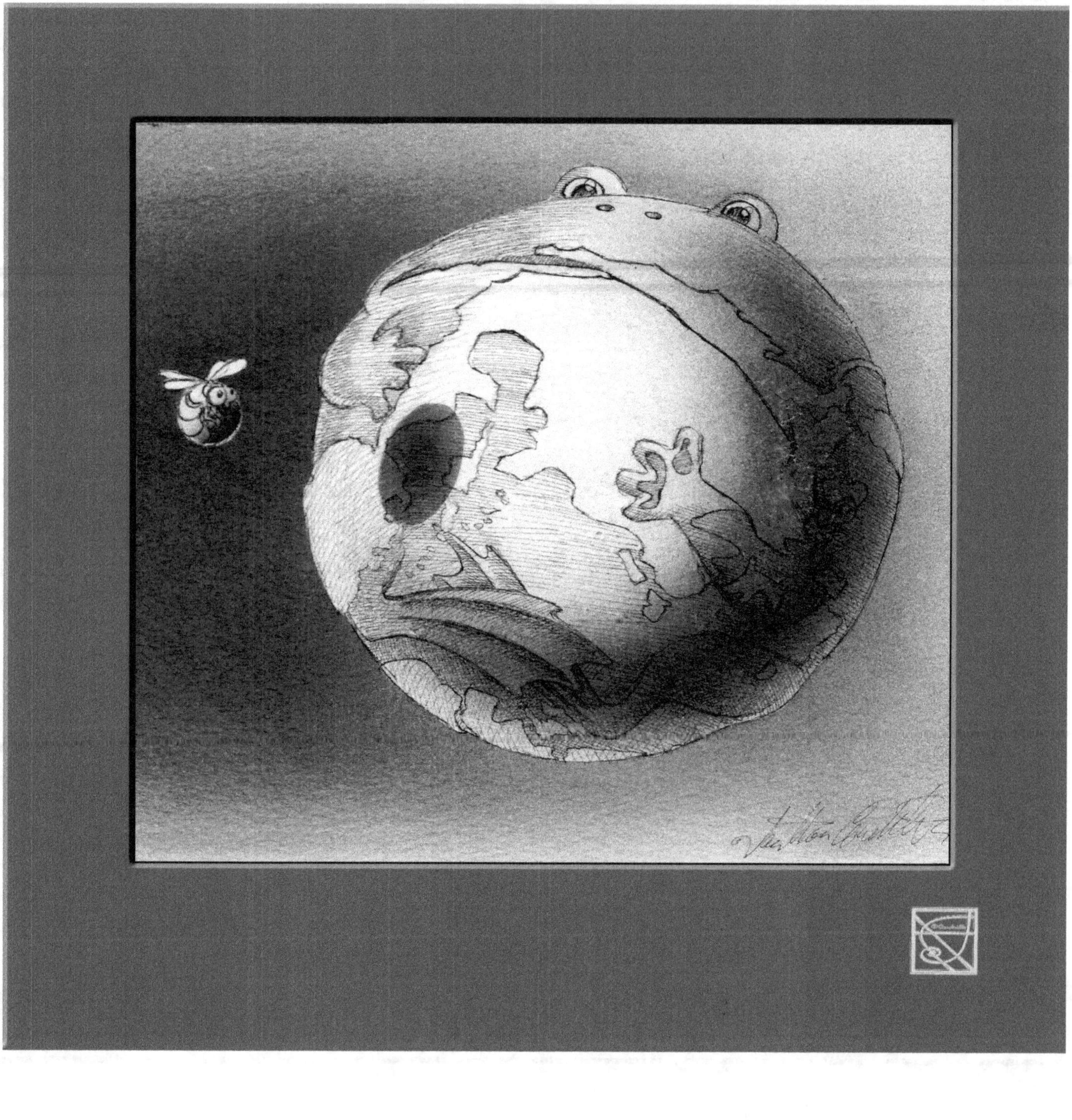

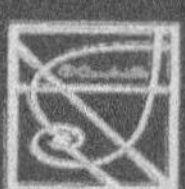

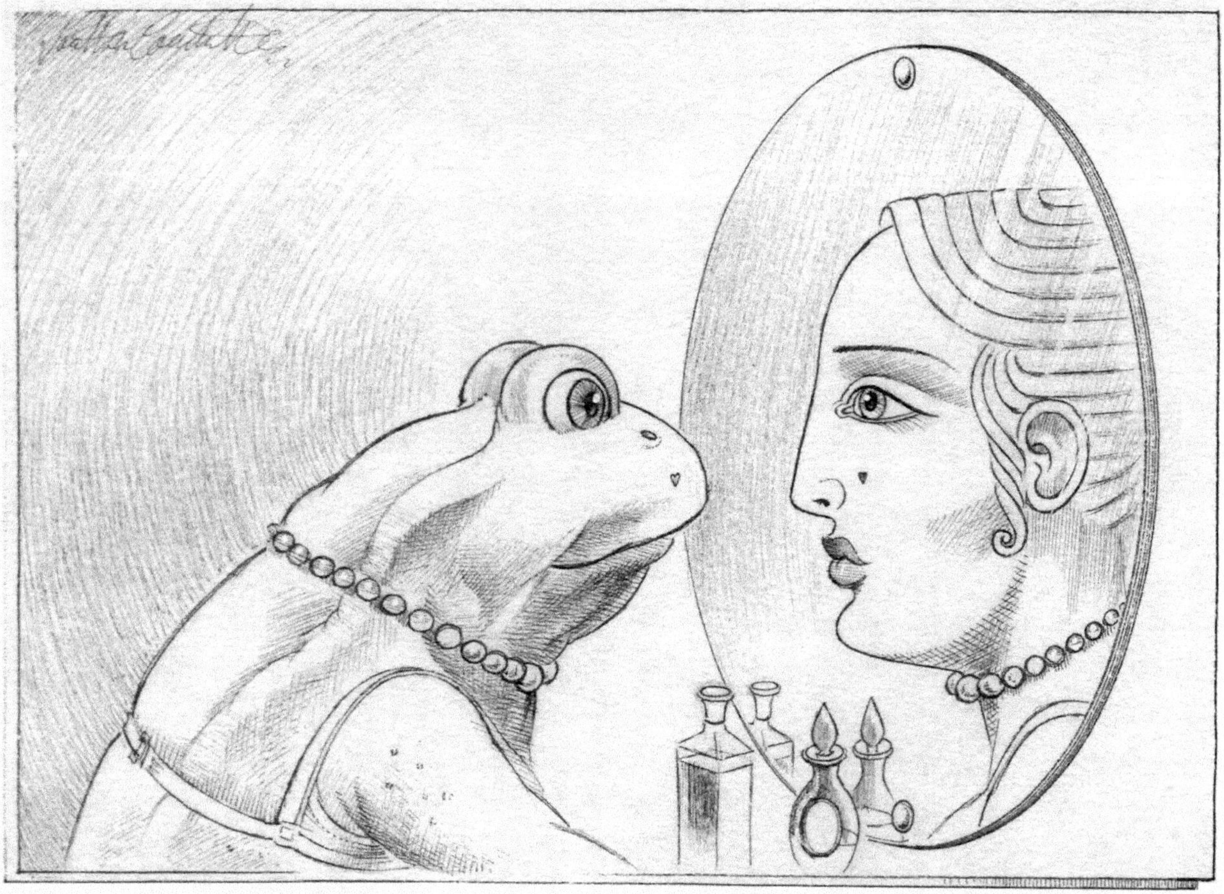

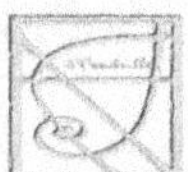

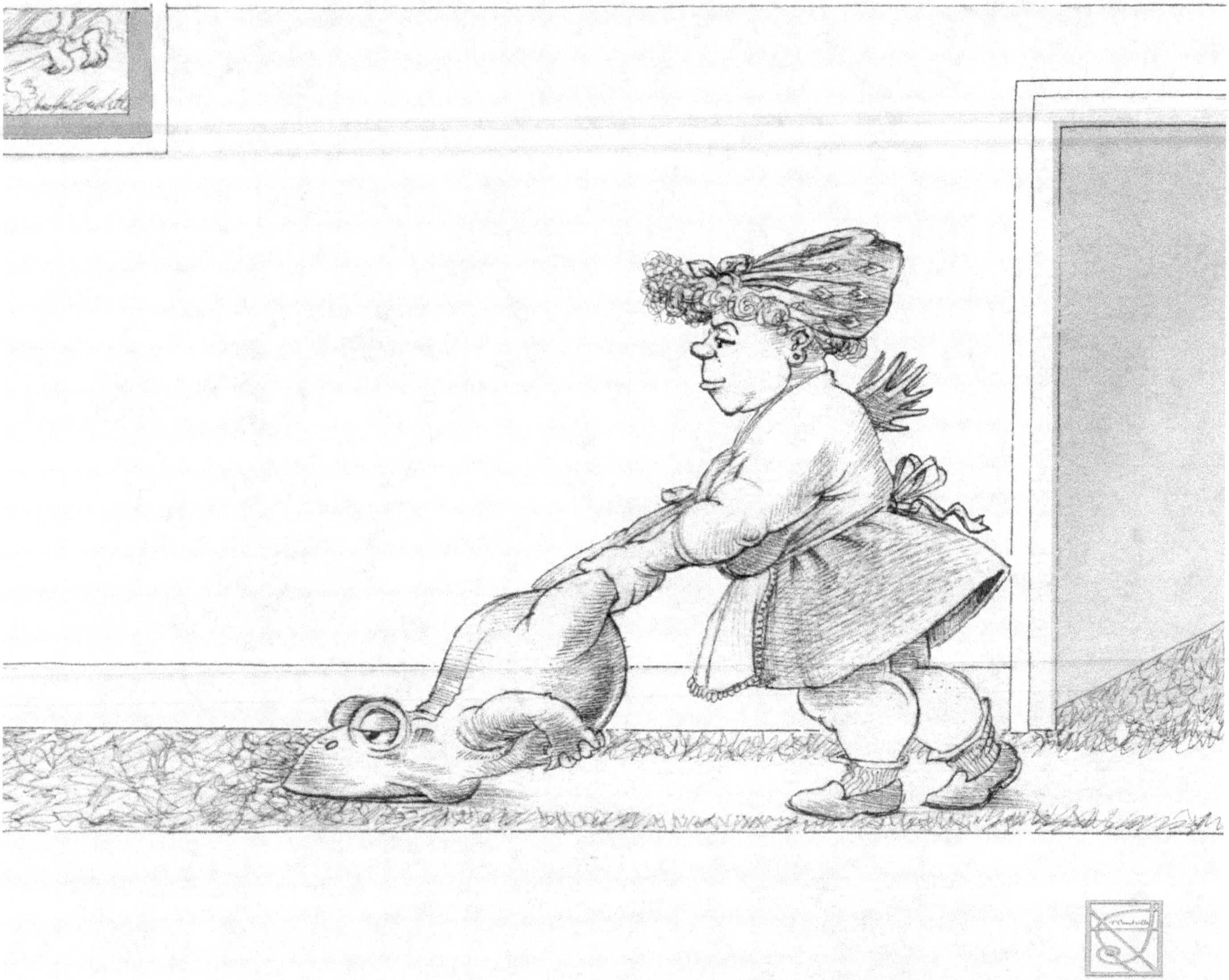

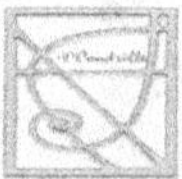

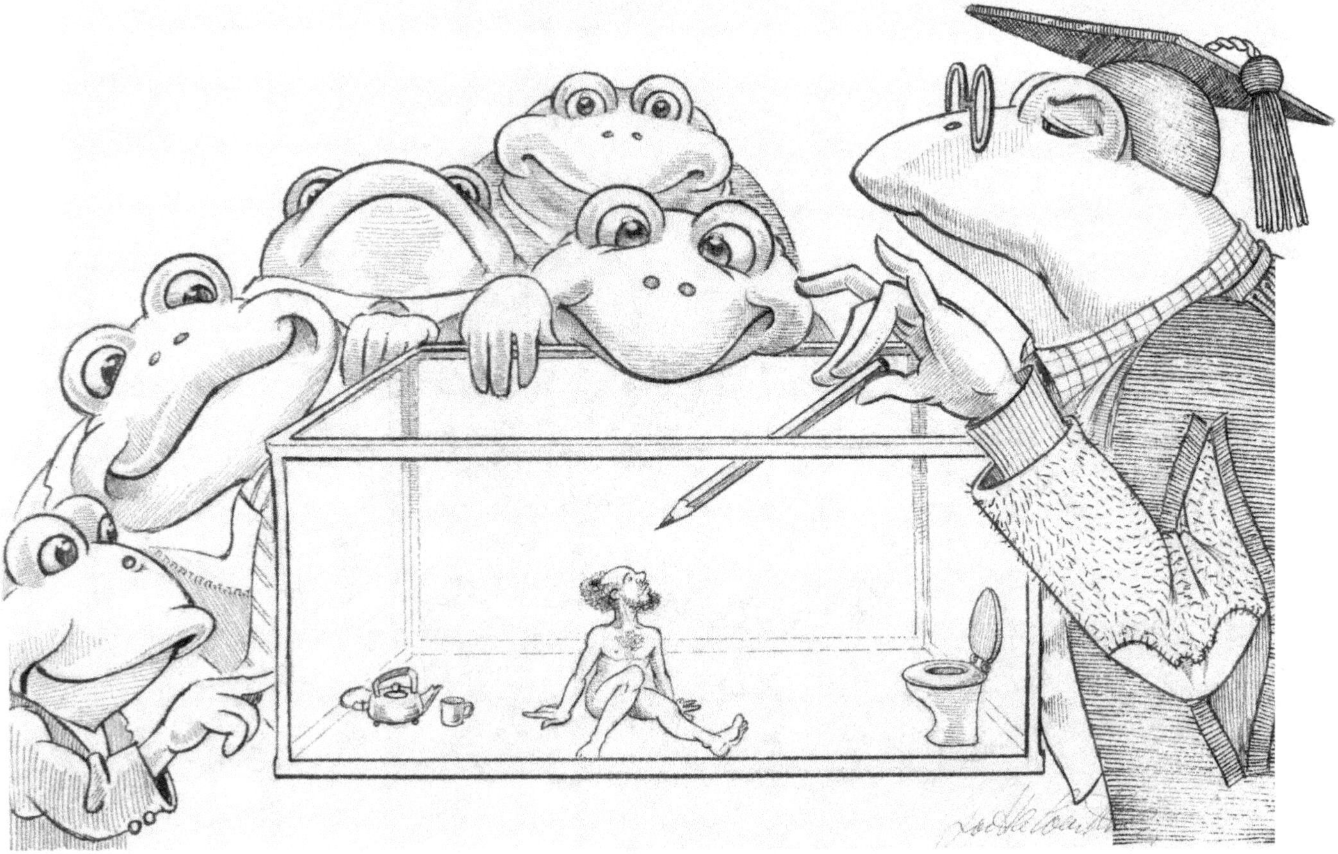

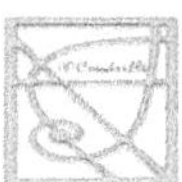

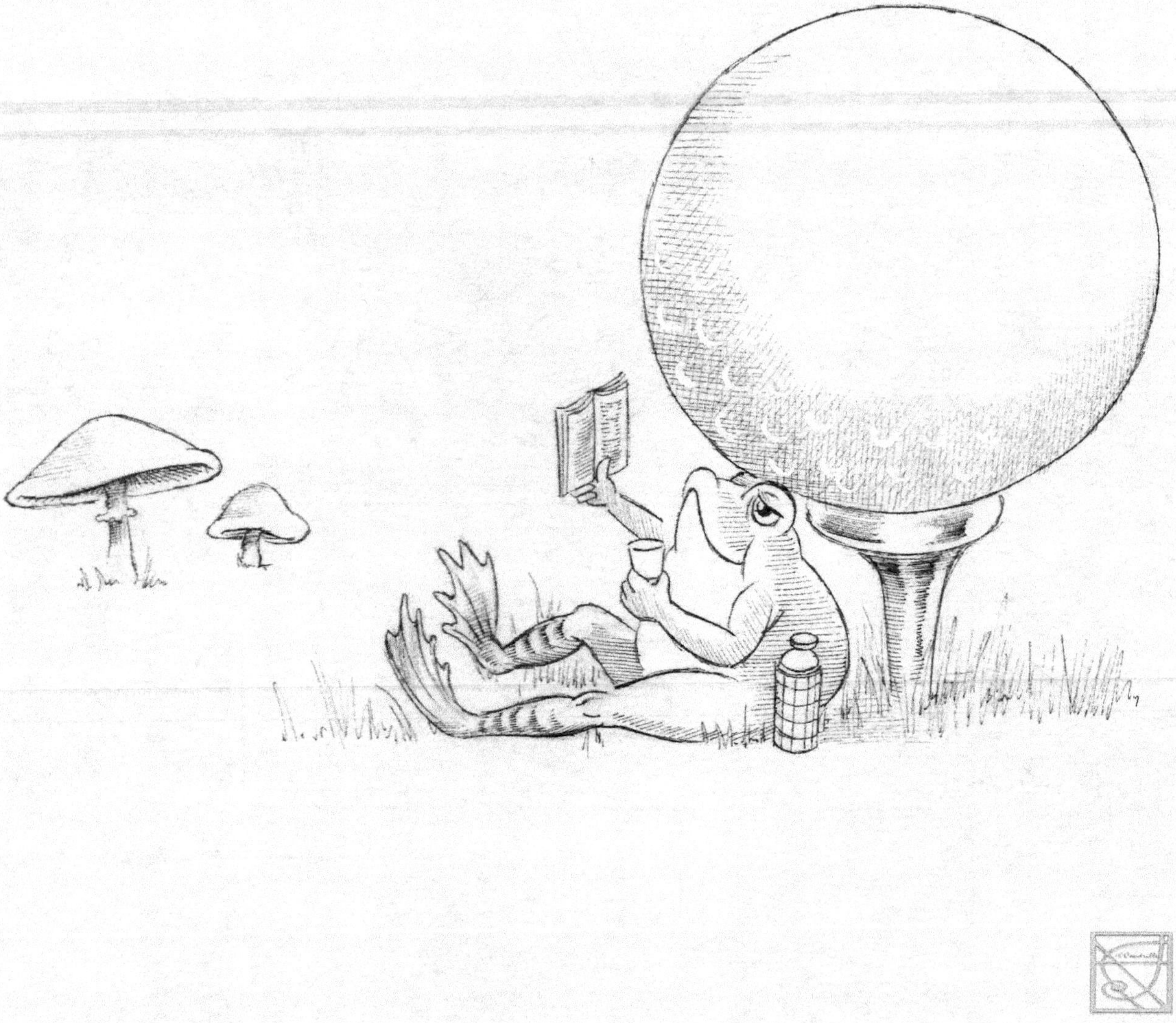

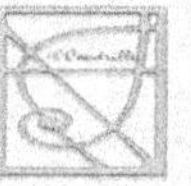

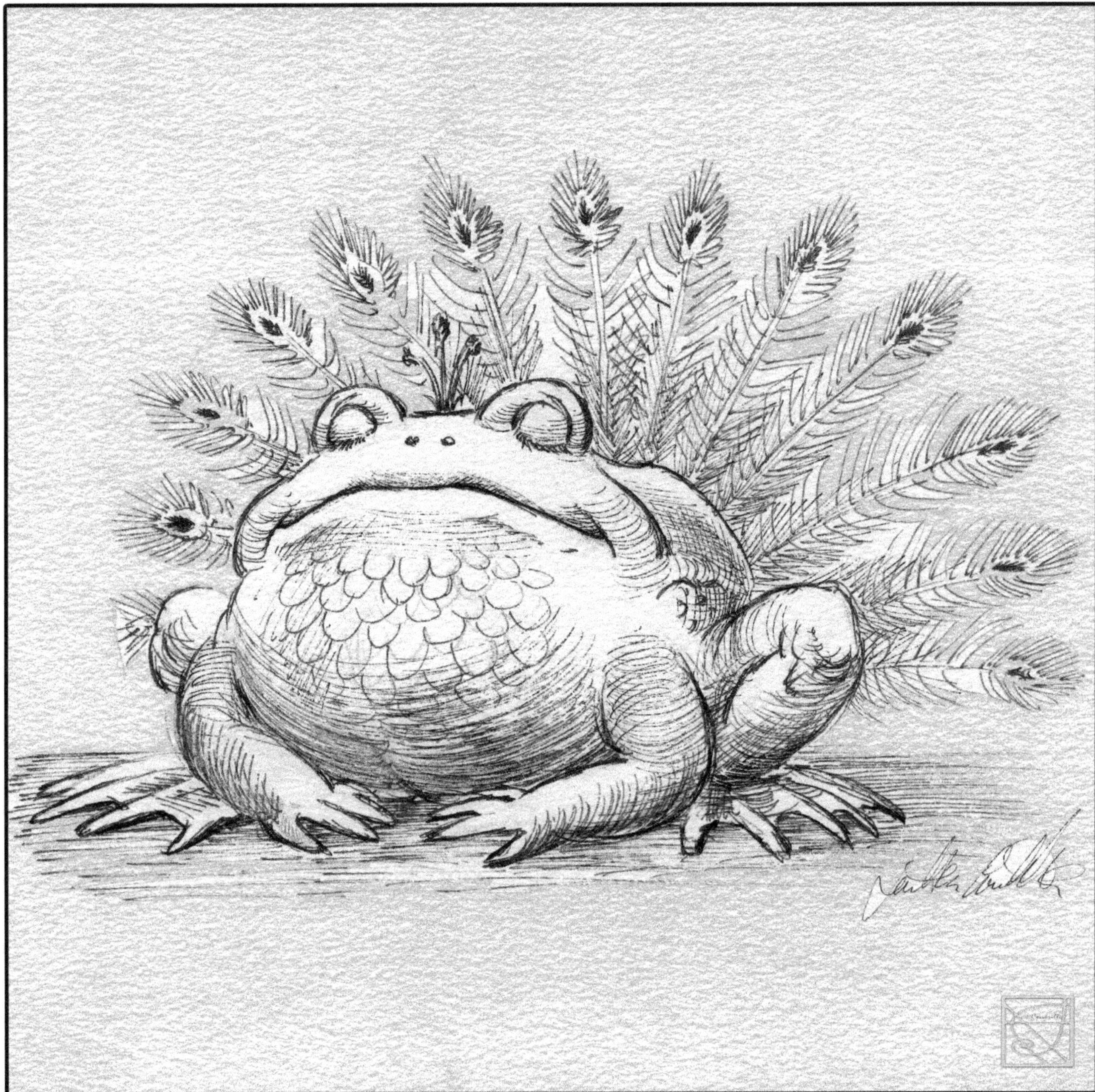

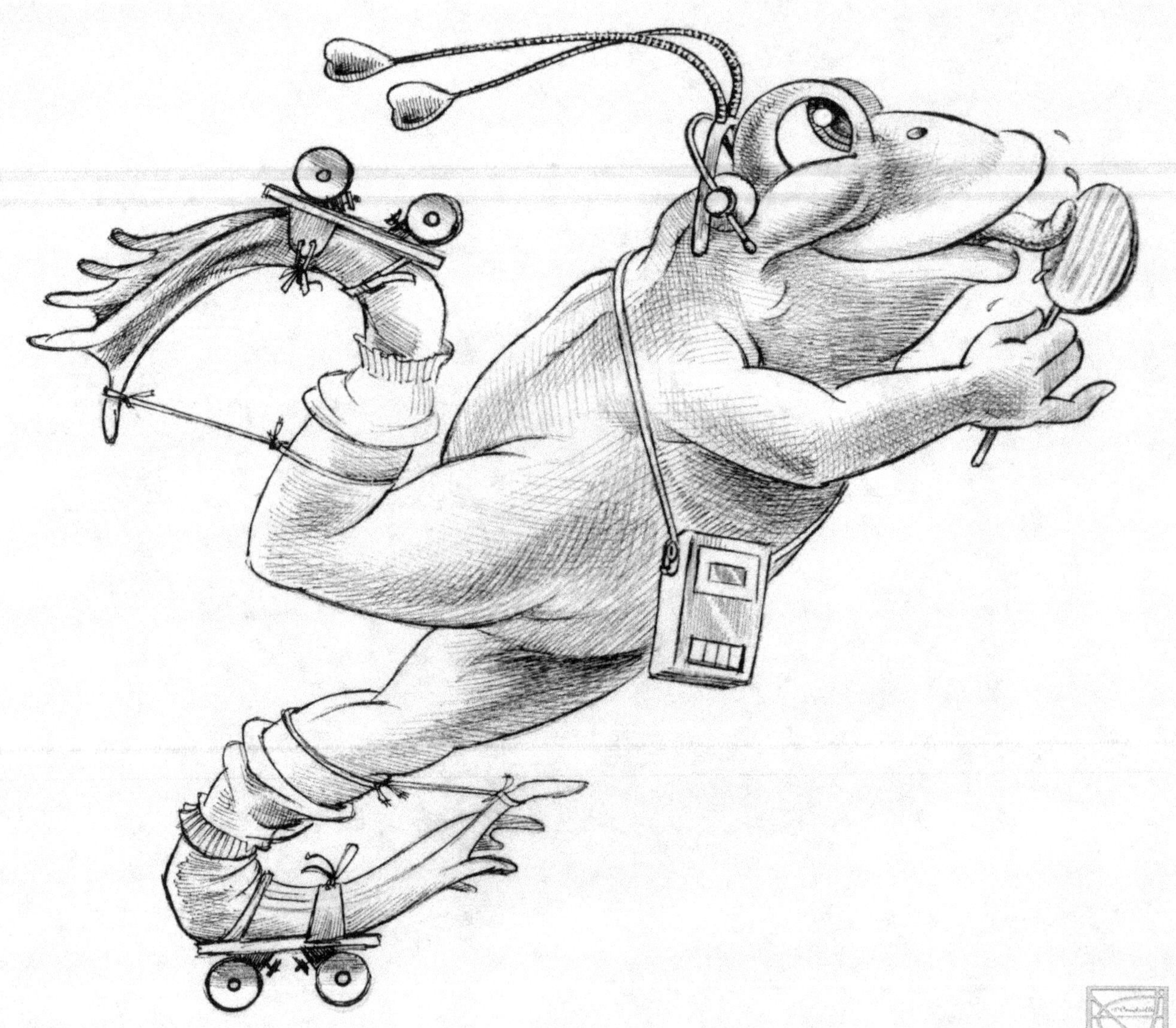

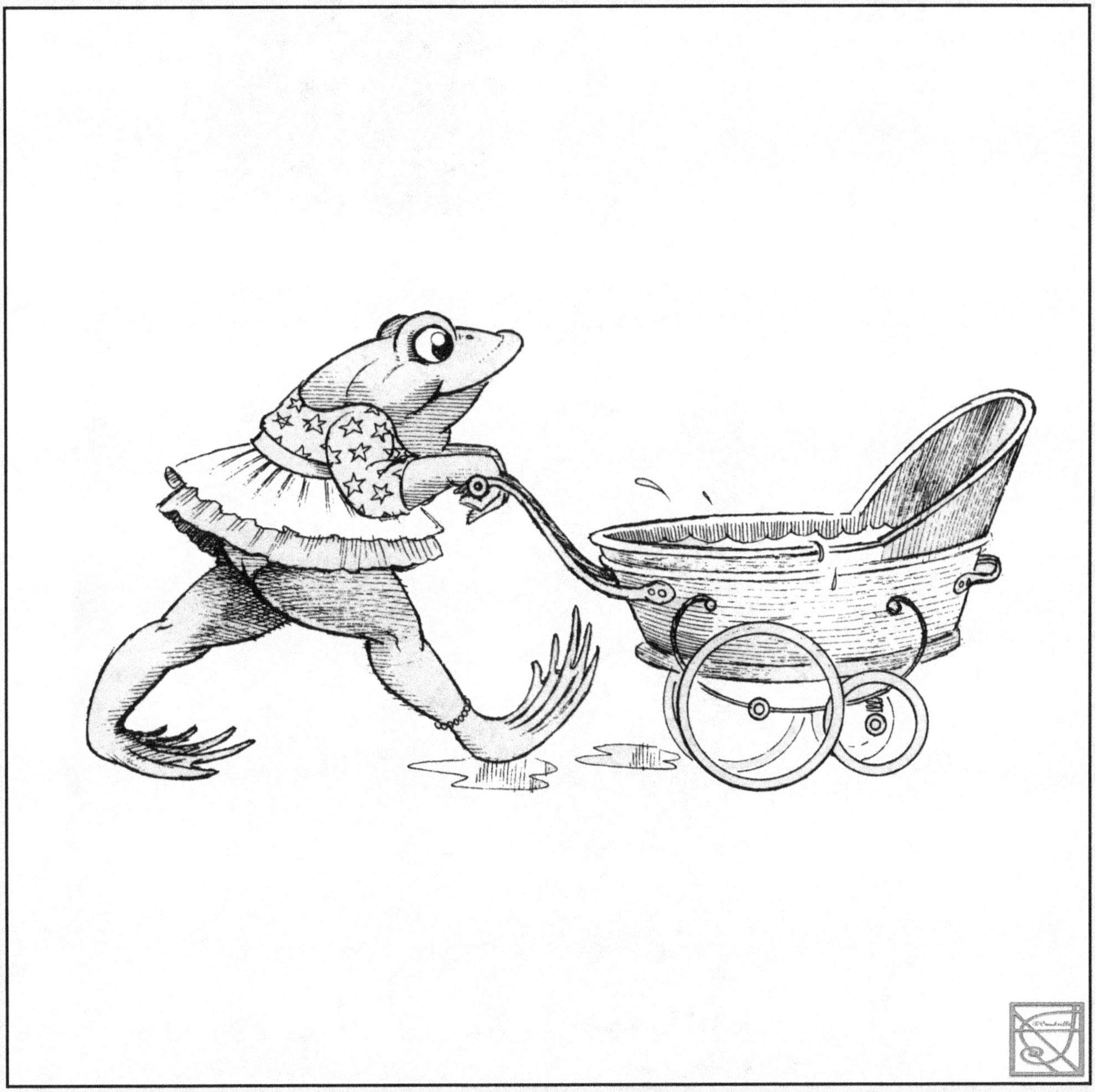

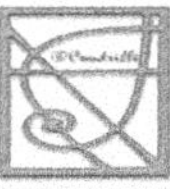

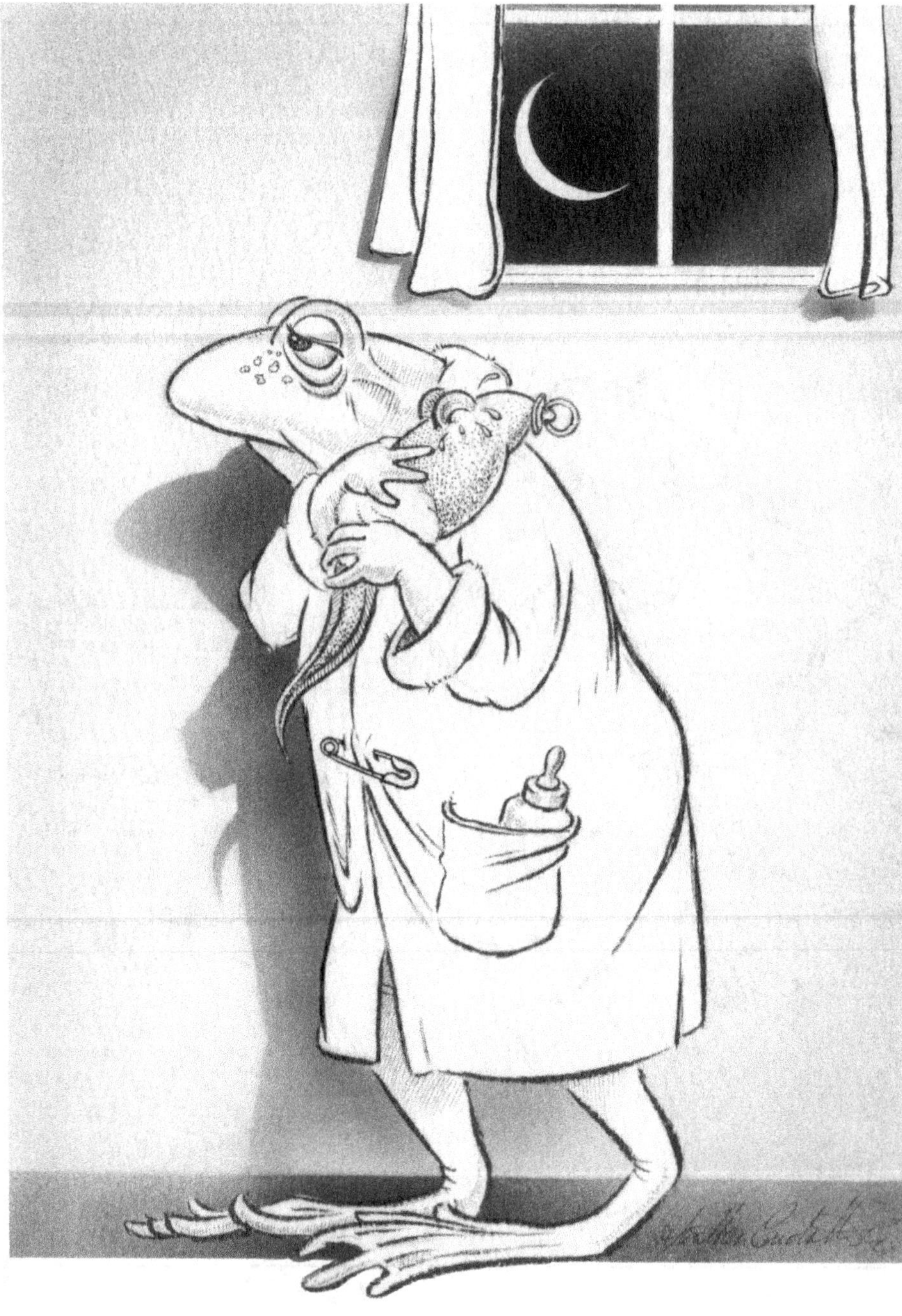

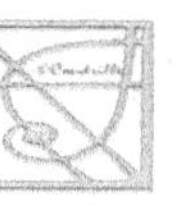

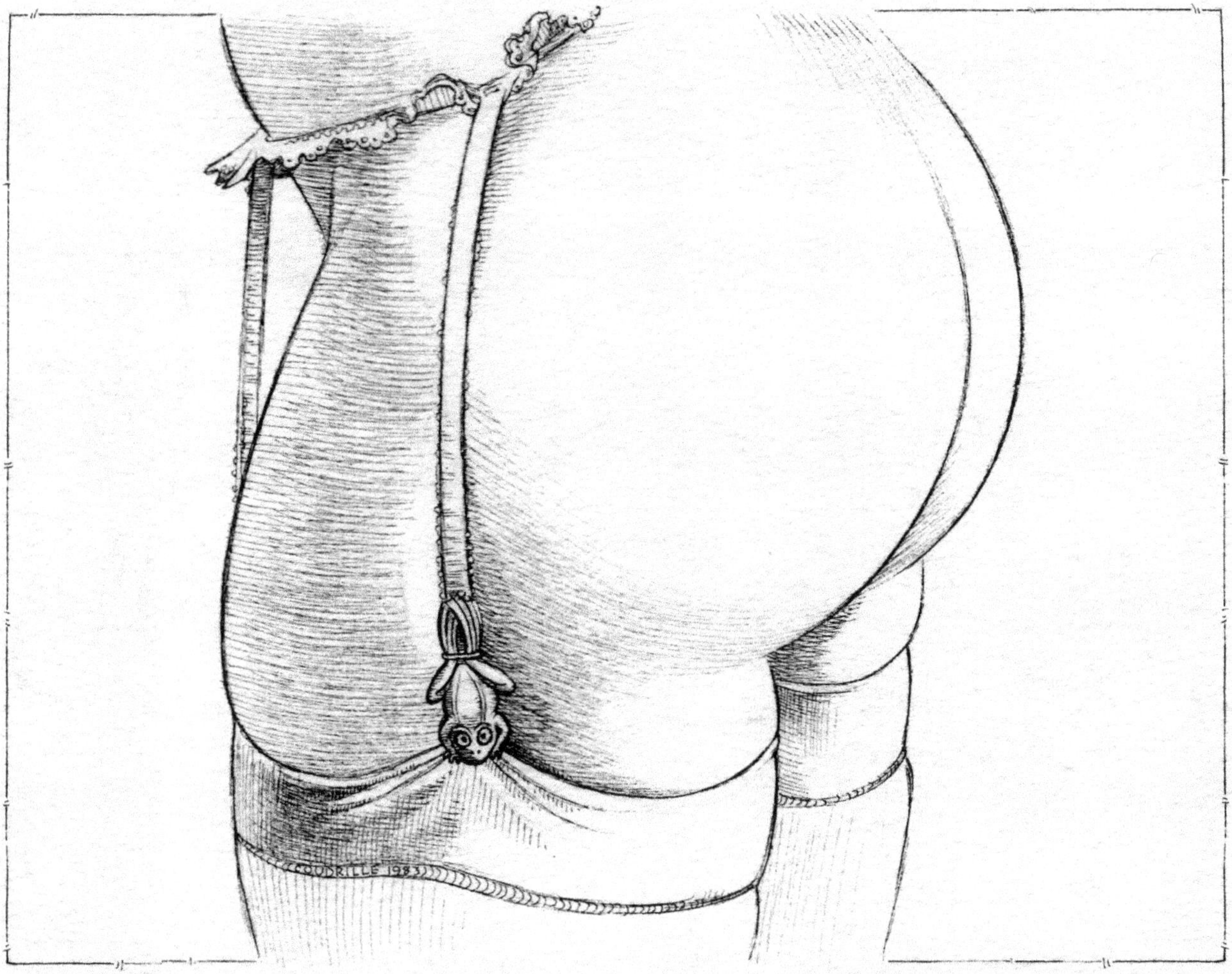

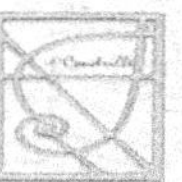

QUADRILLE 1983

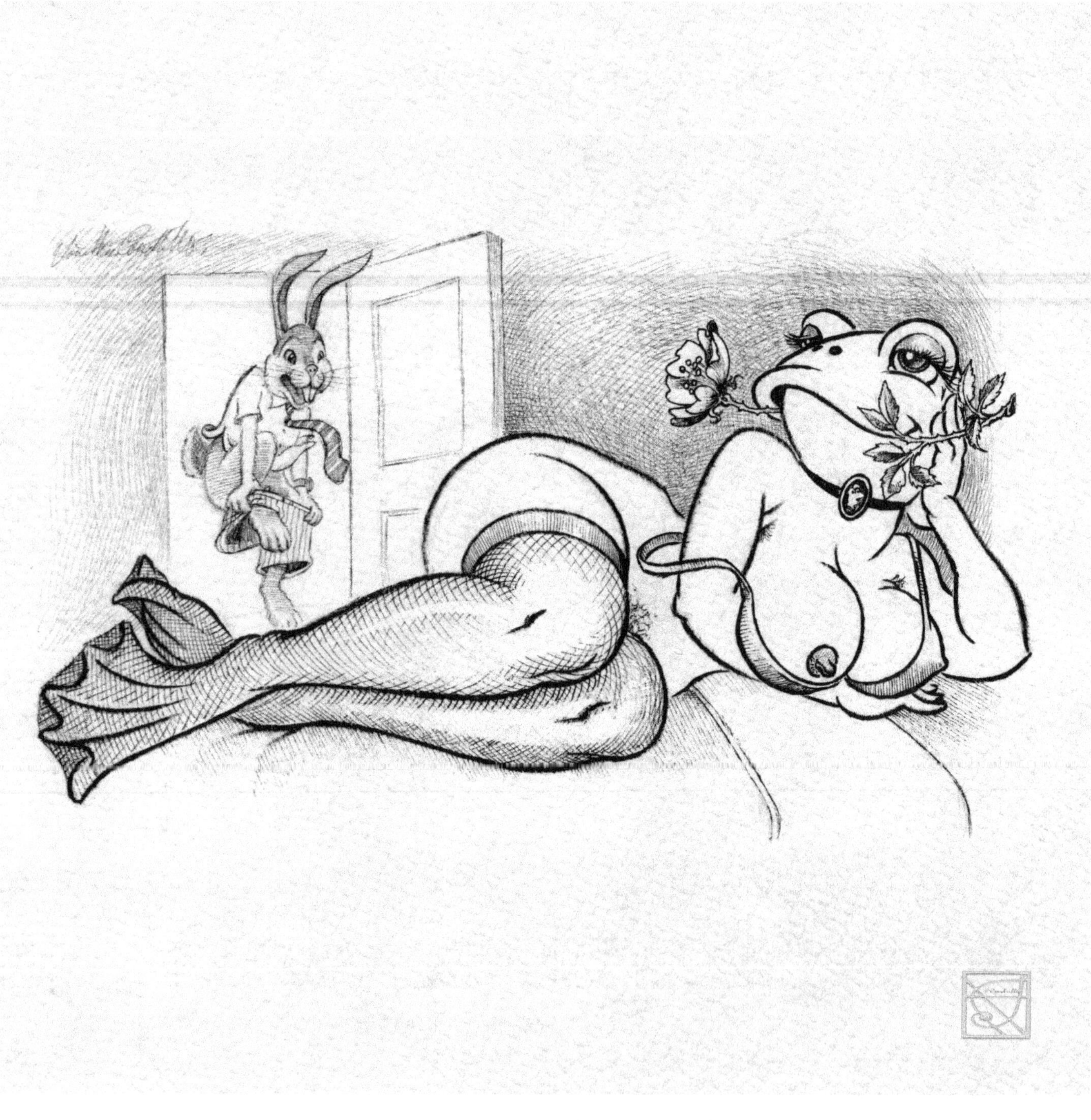

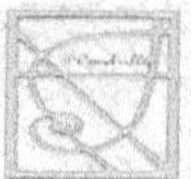

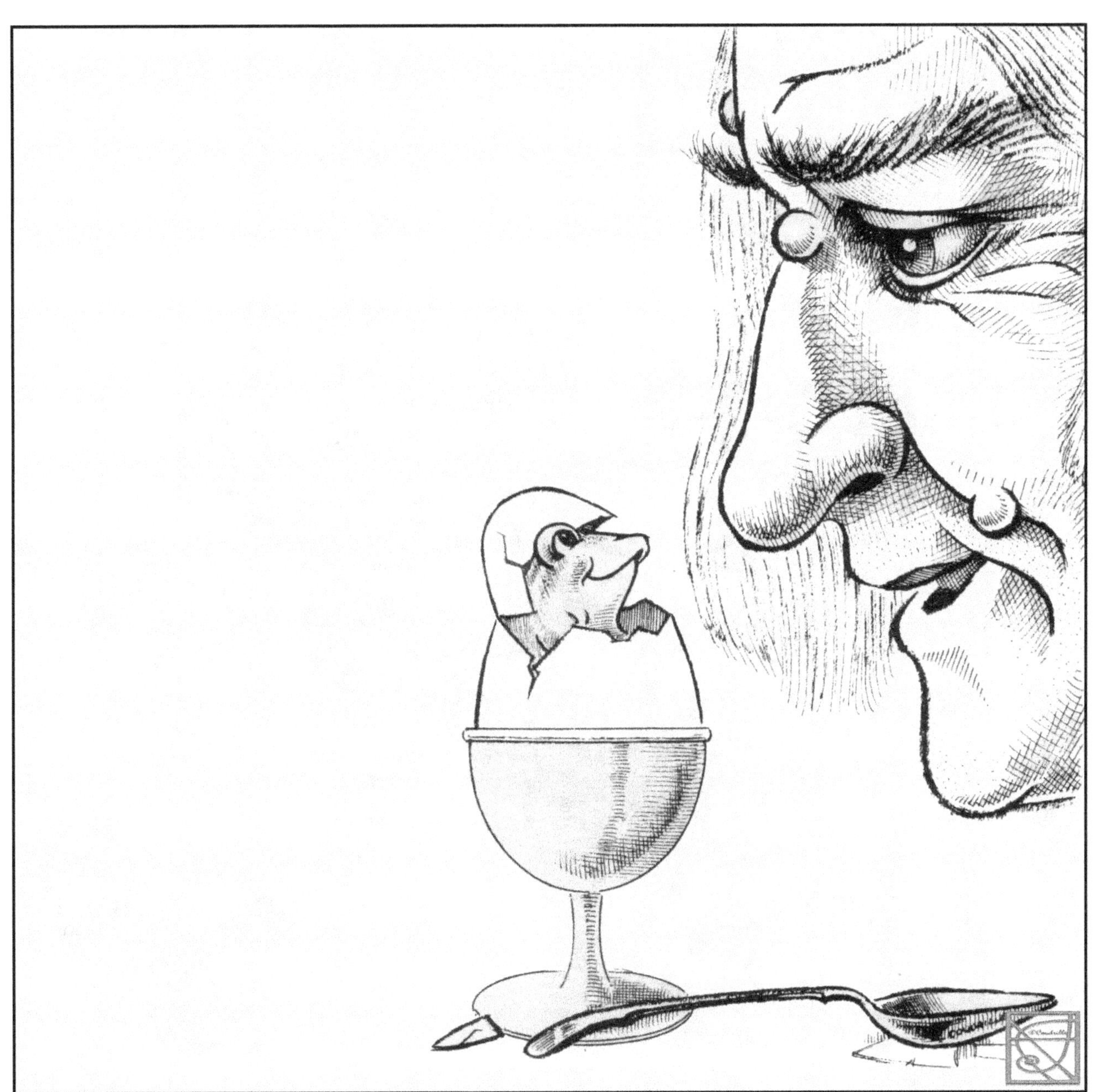

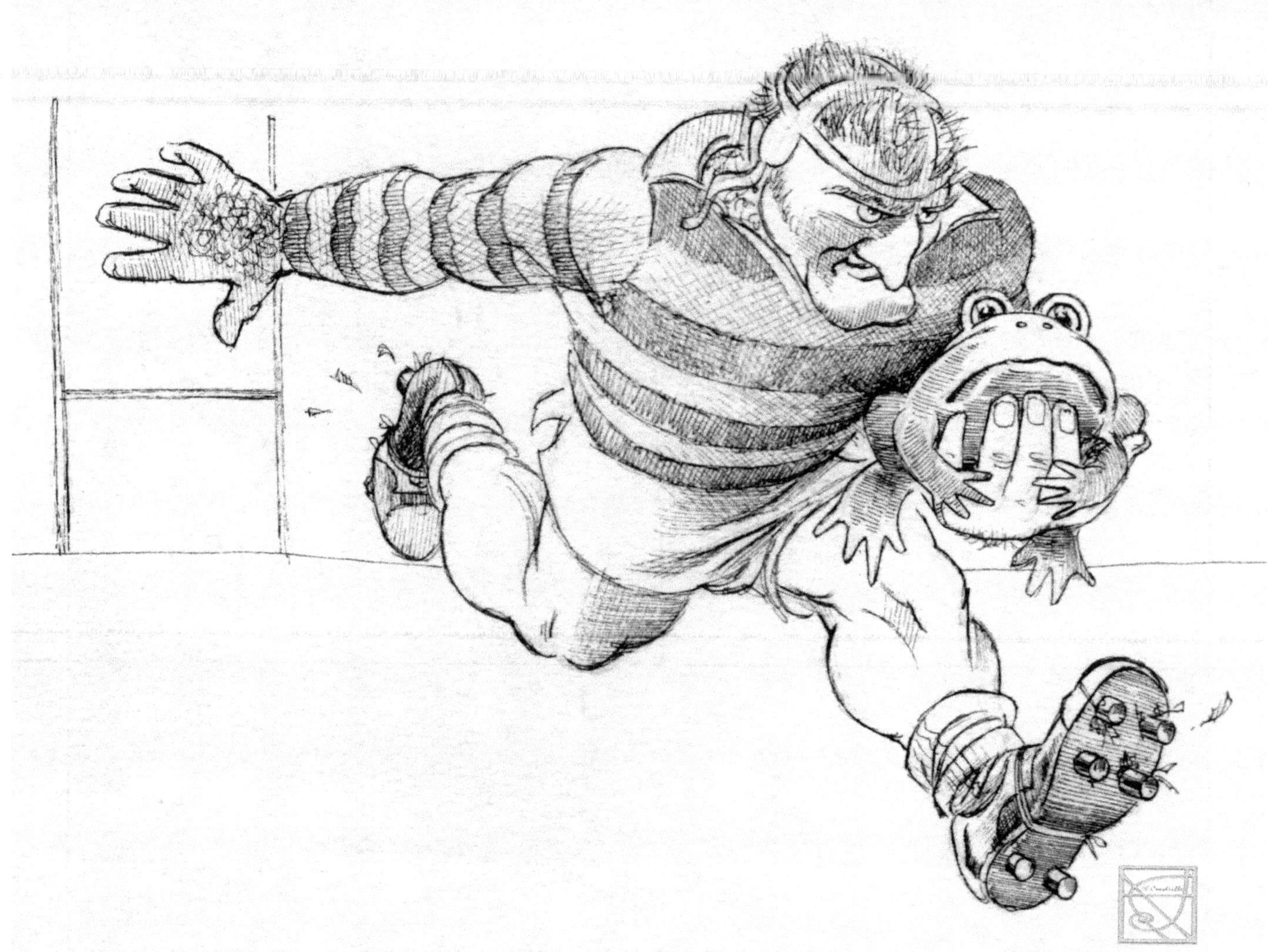

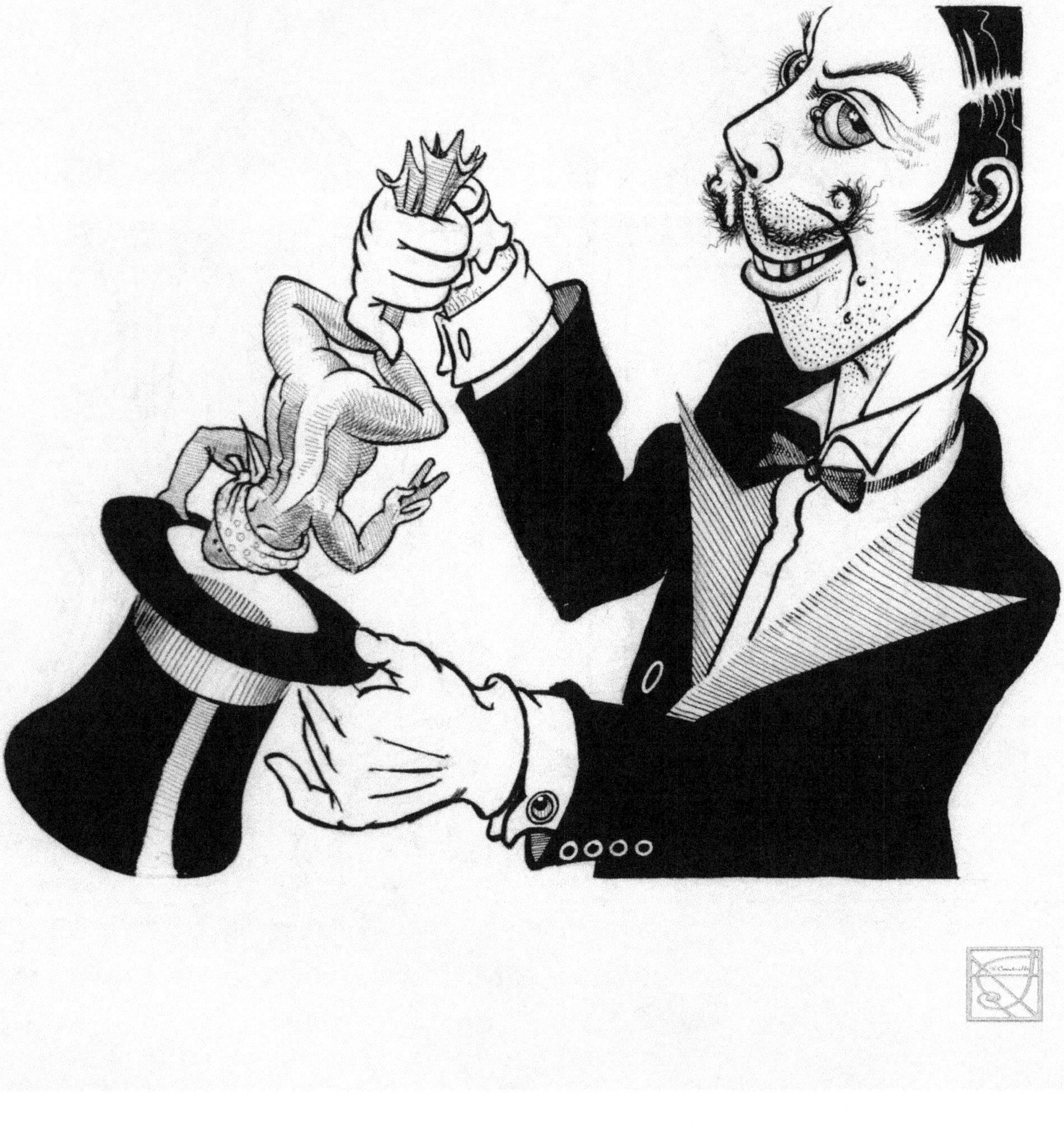

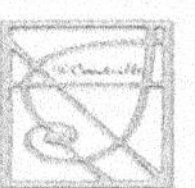

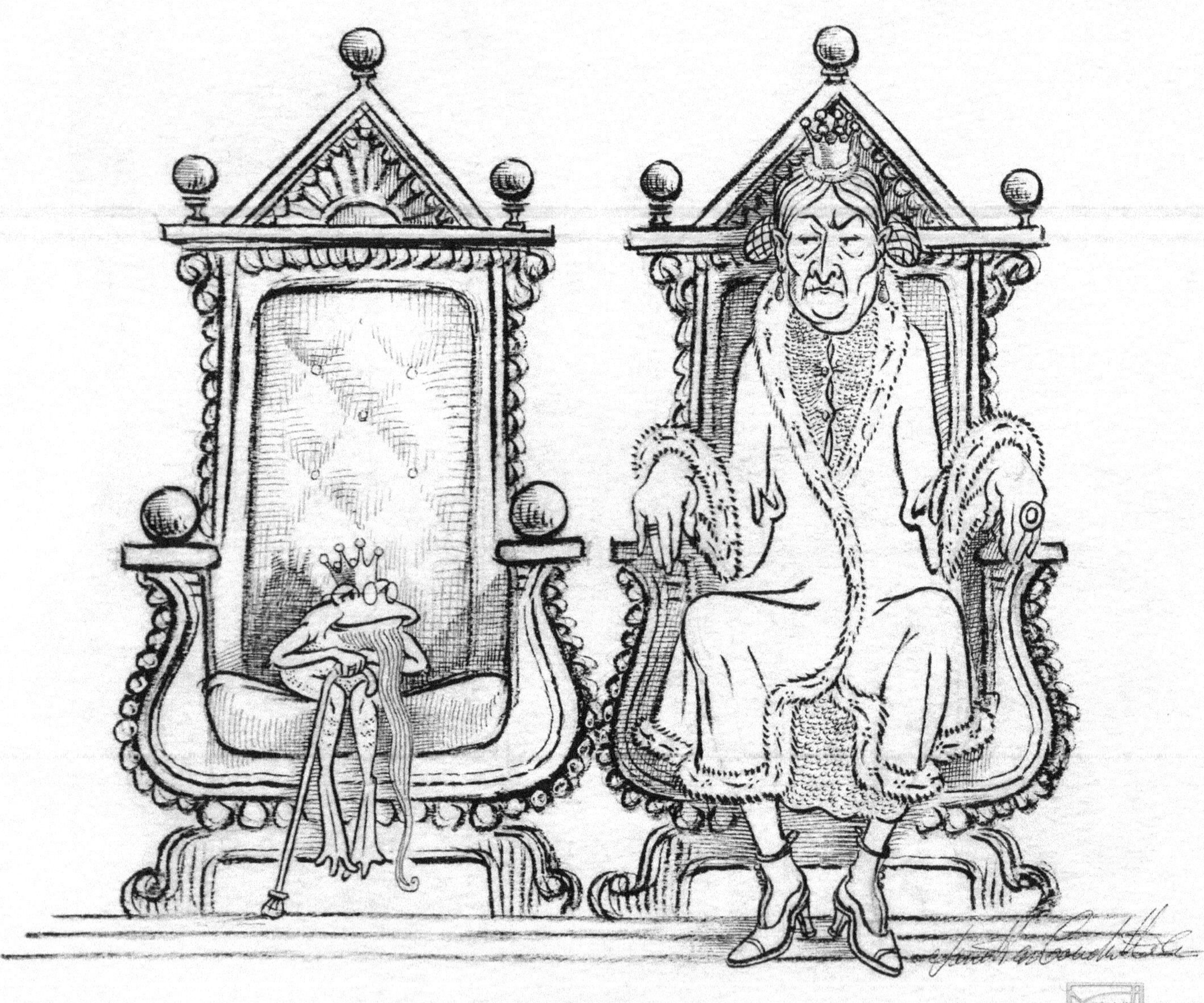

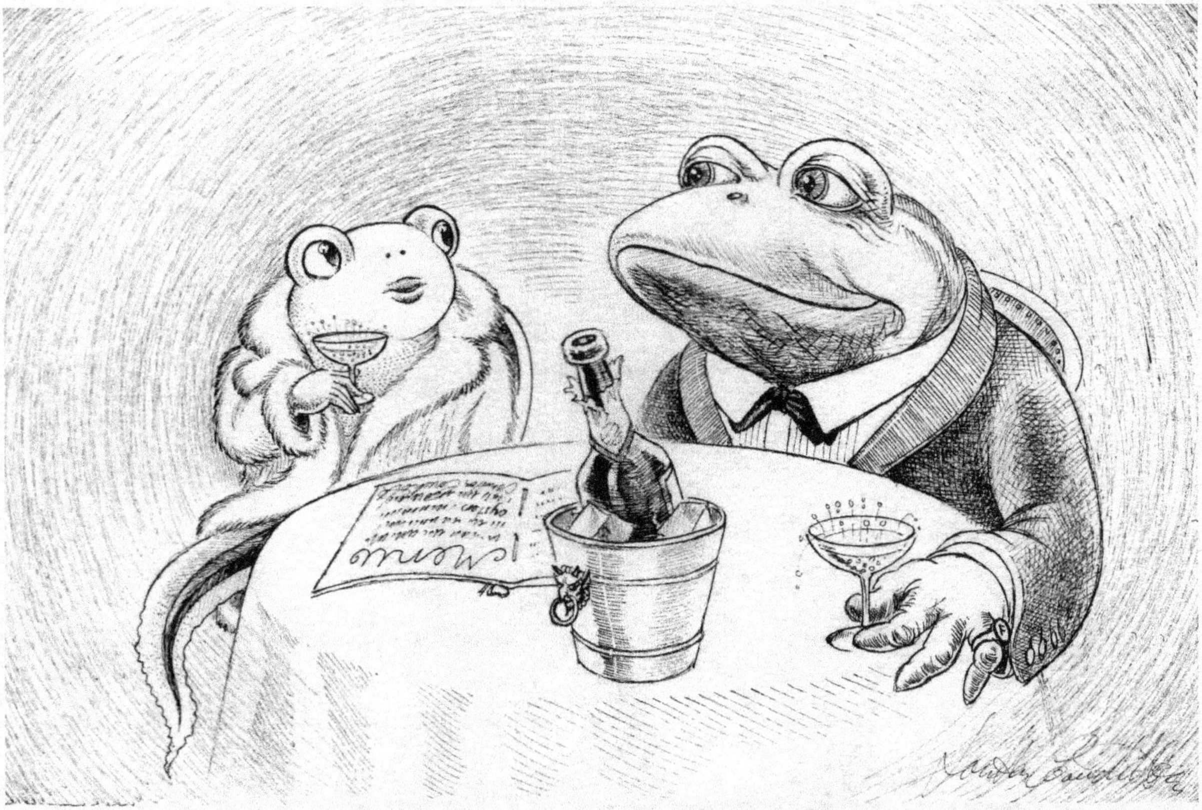

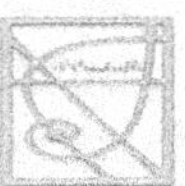

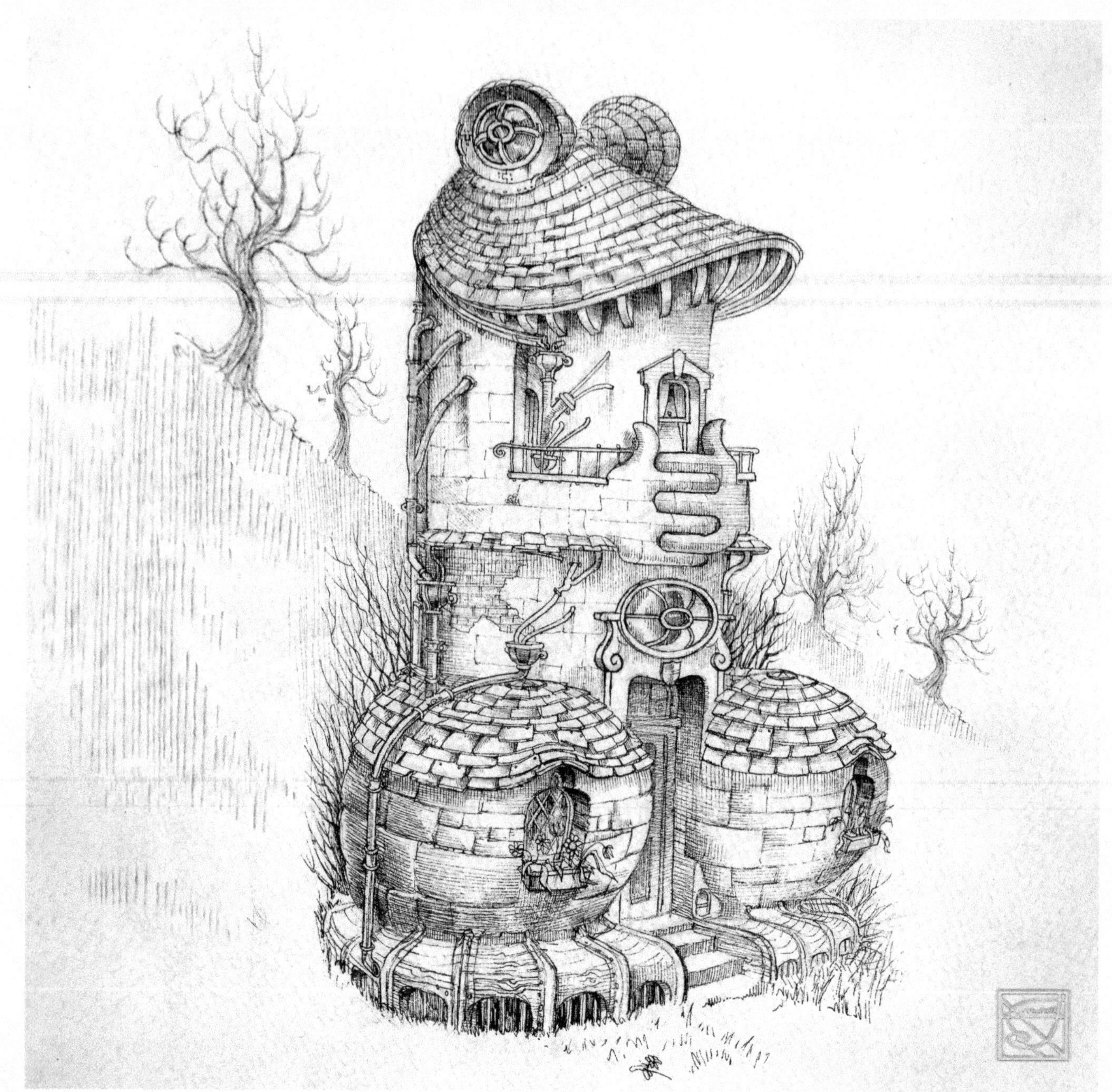

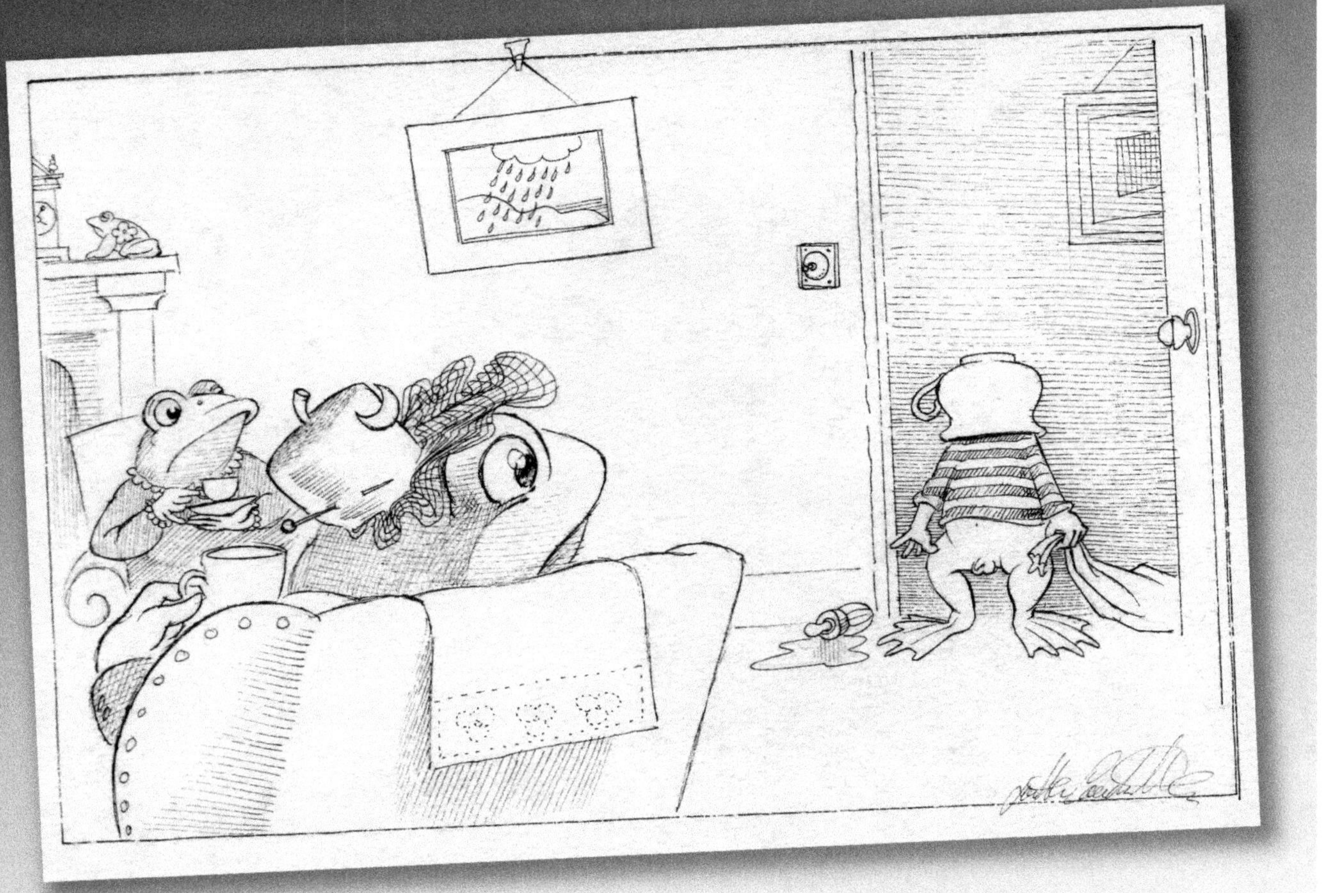

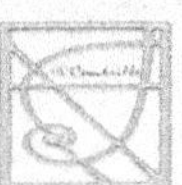

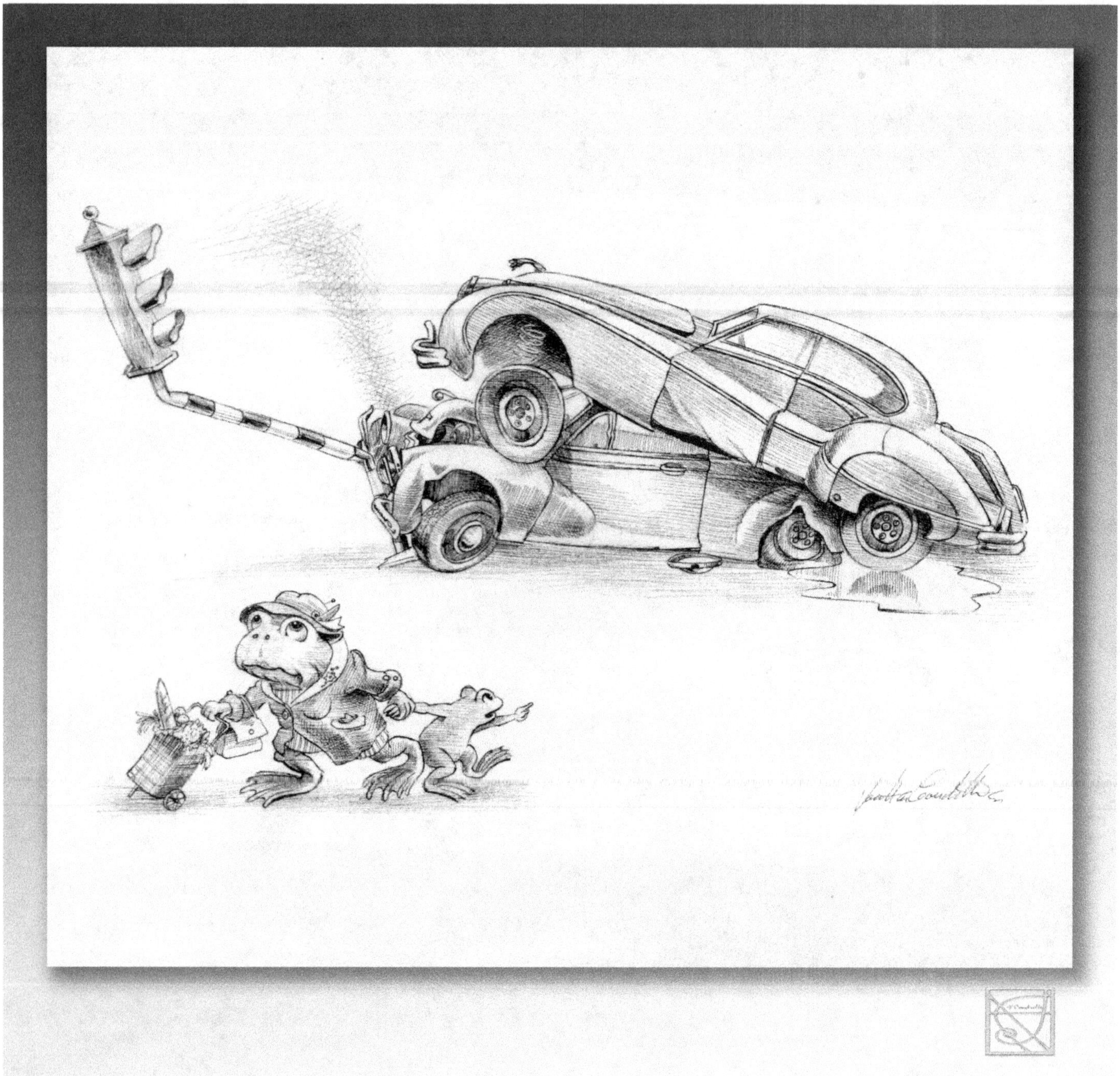

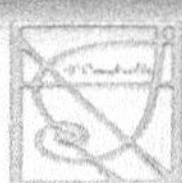

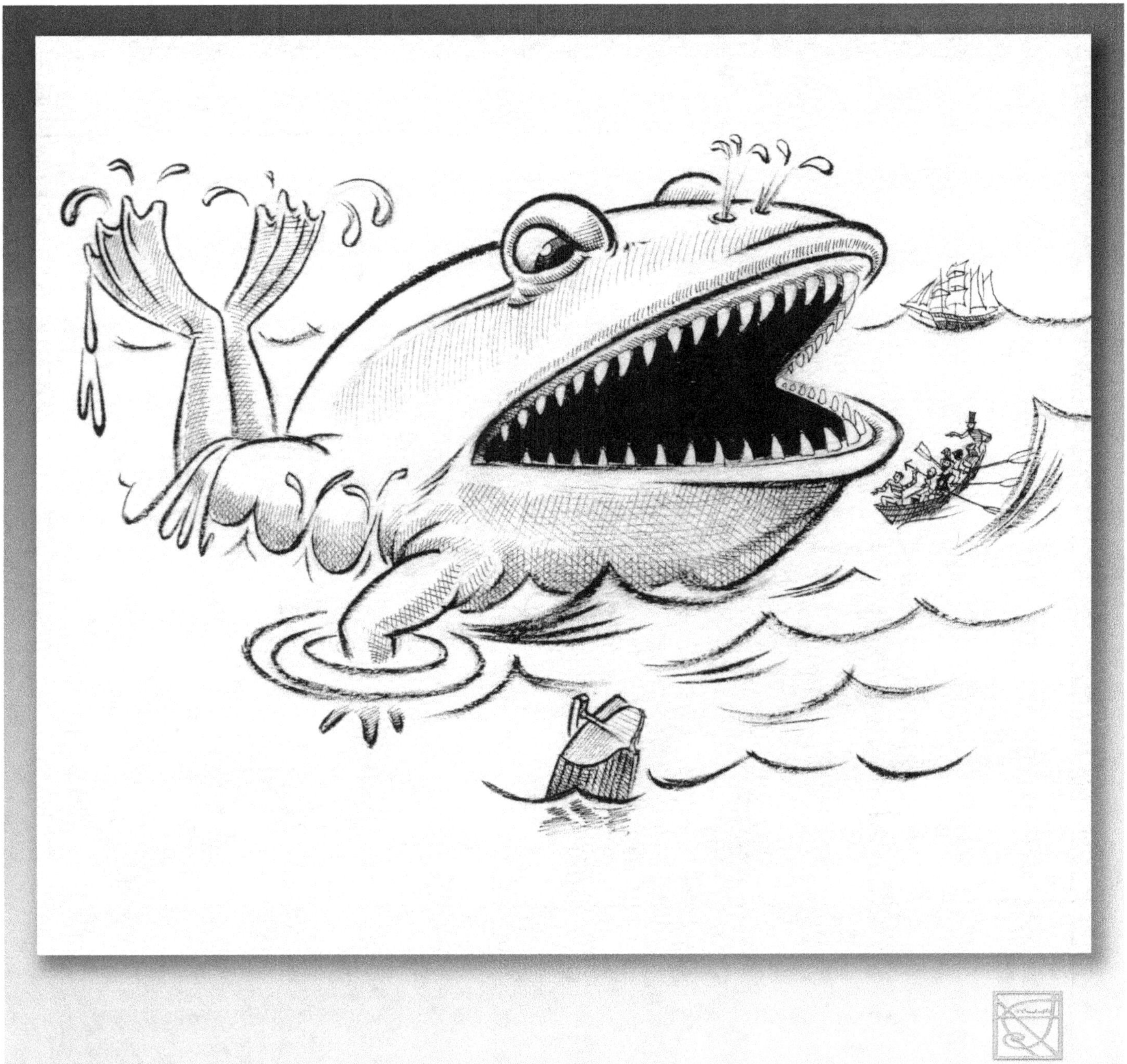

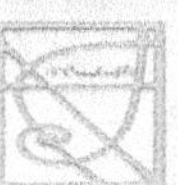

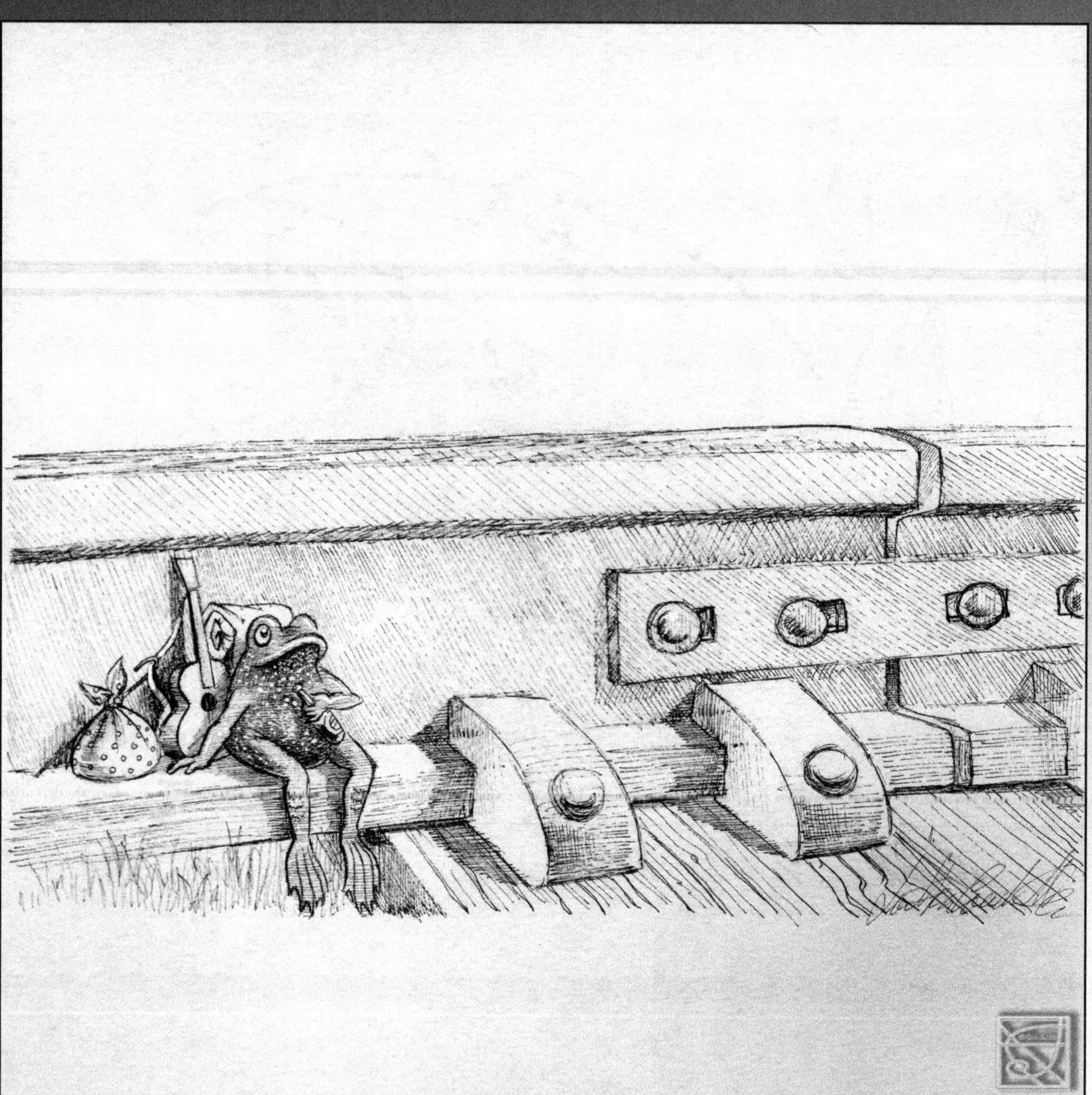

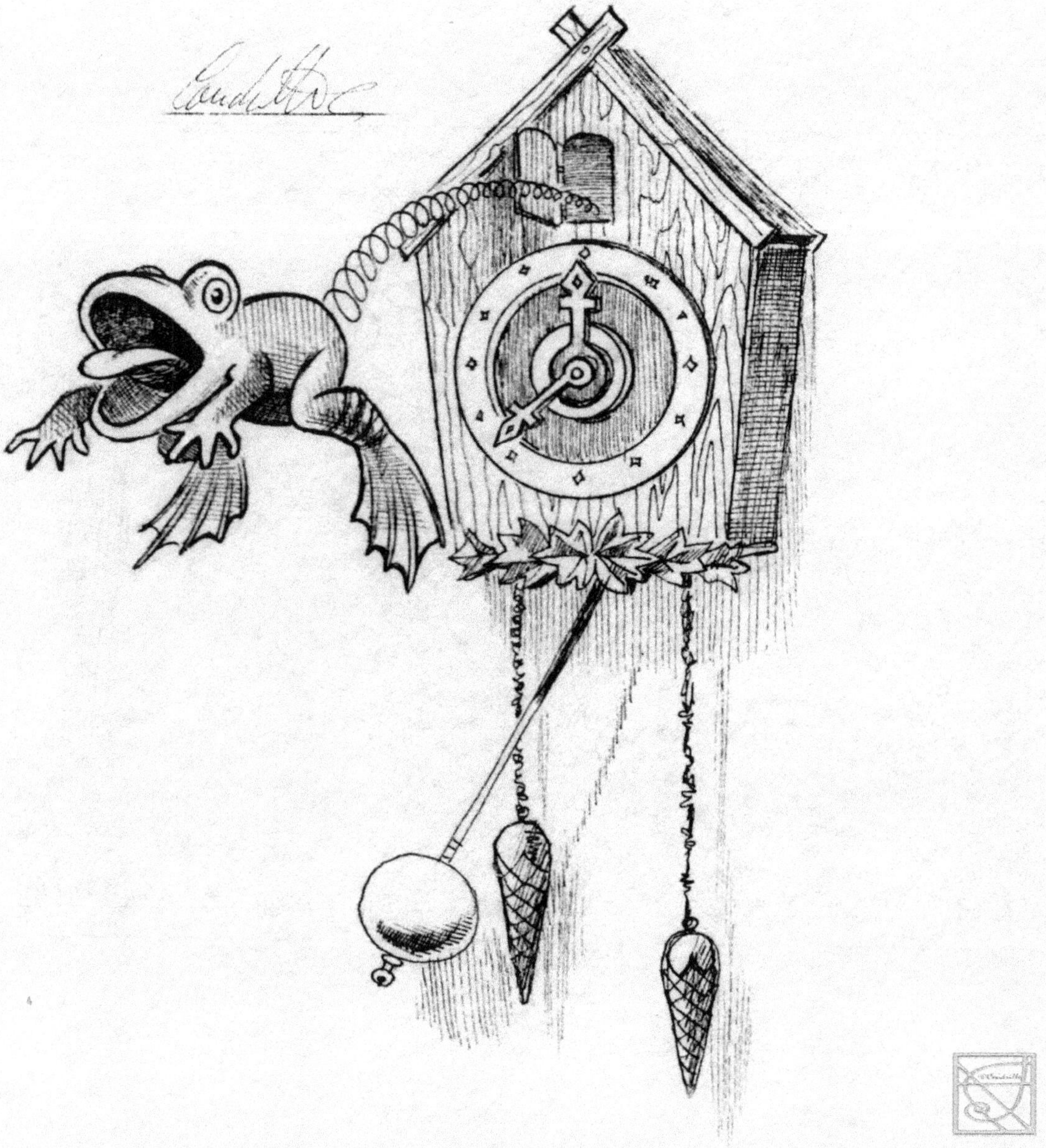

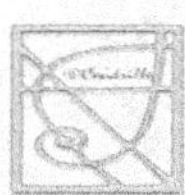

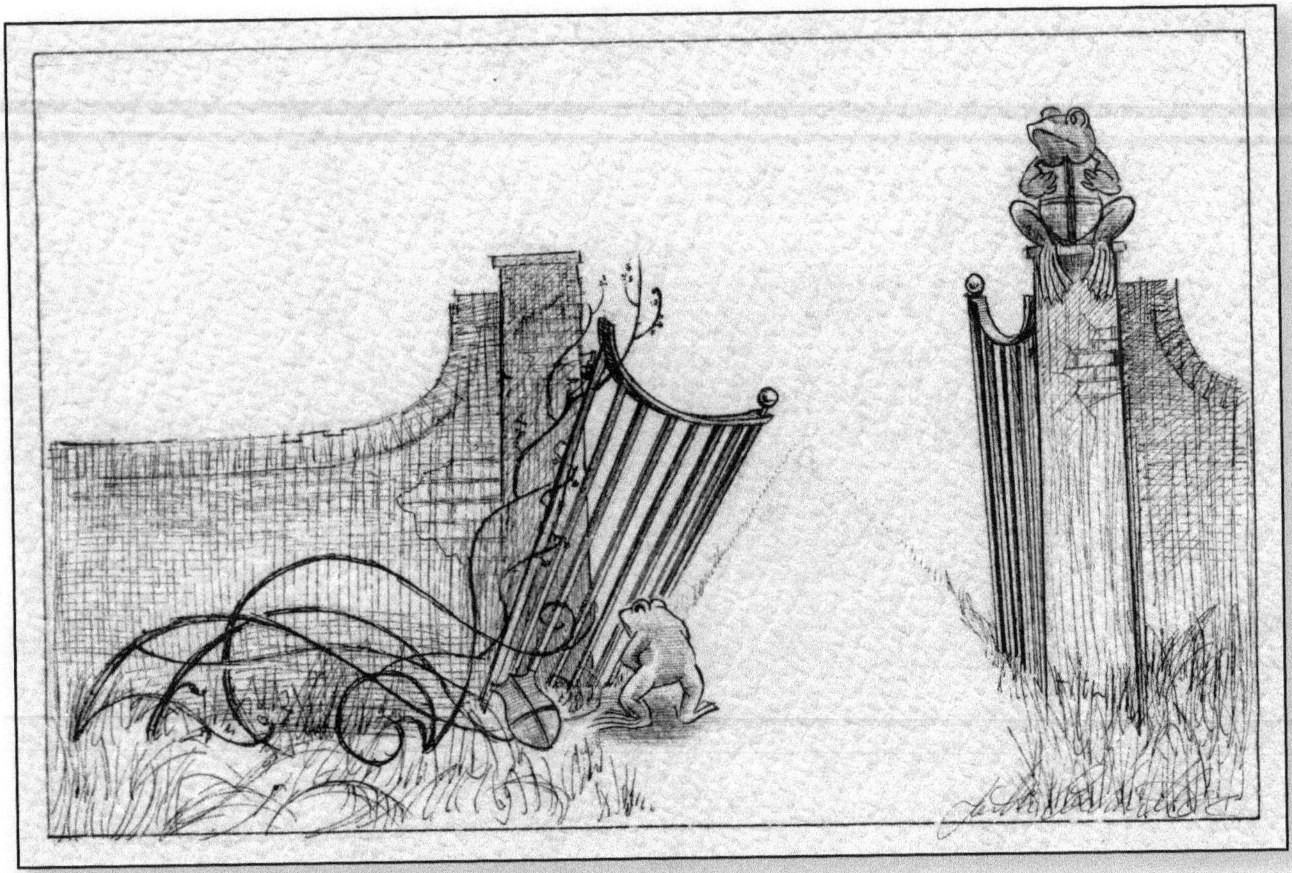

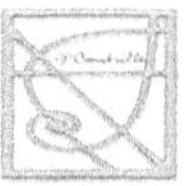

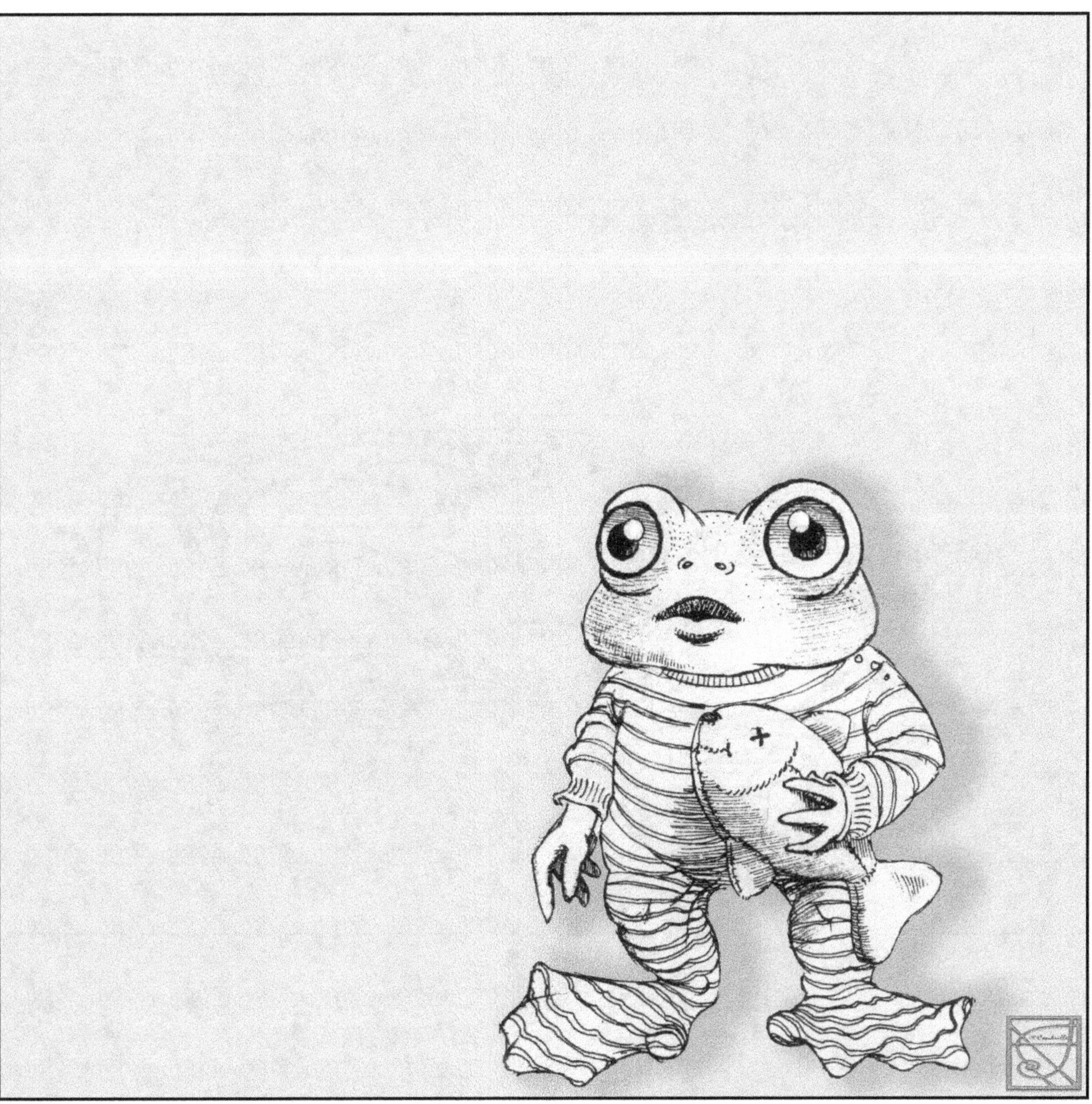

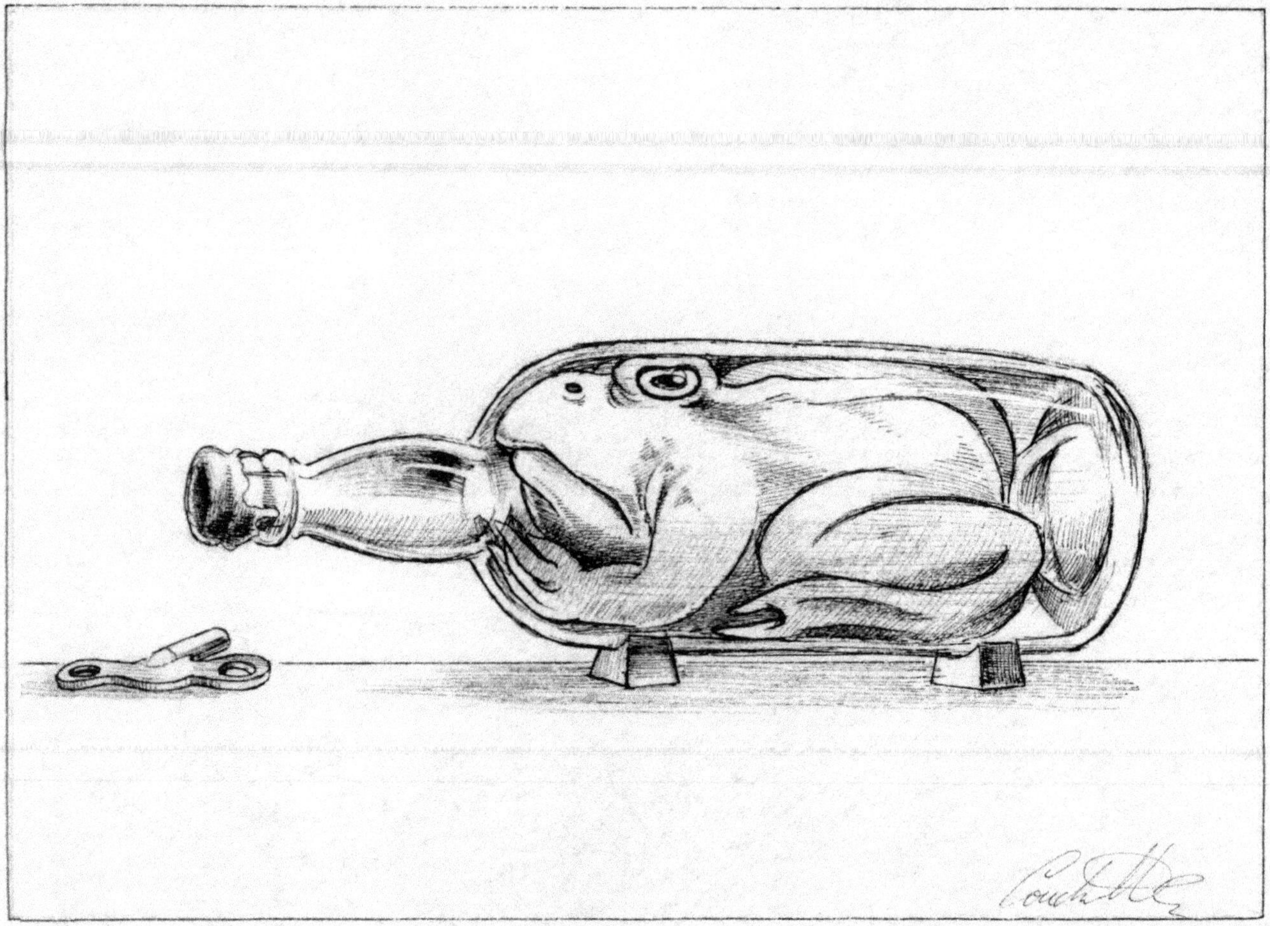

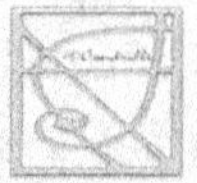

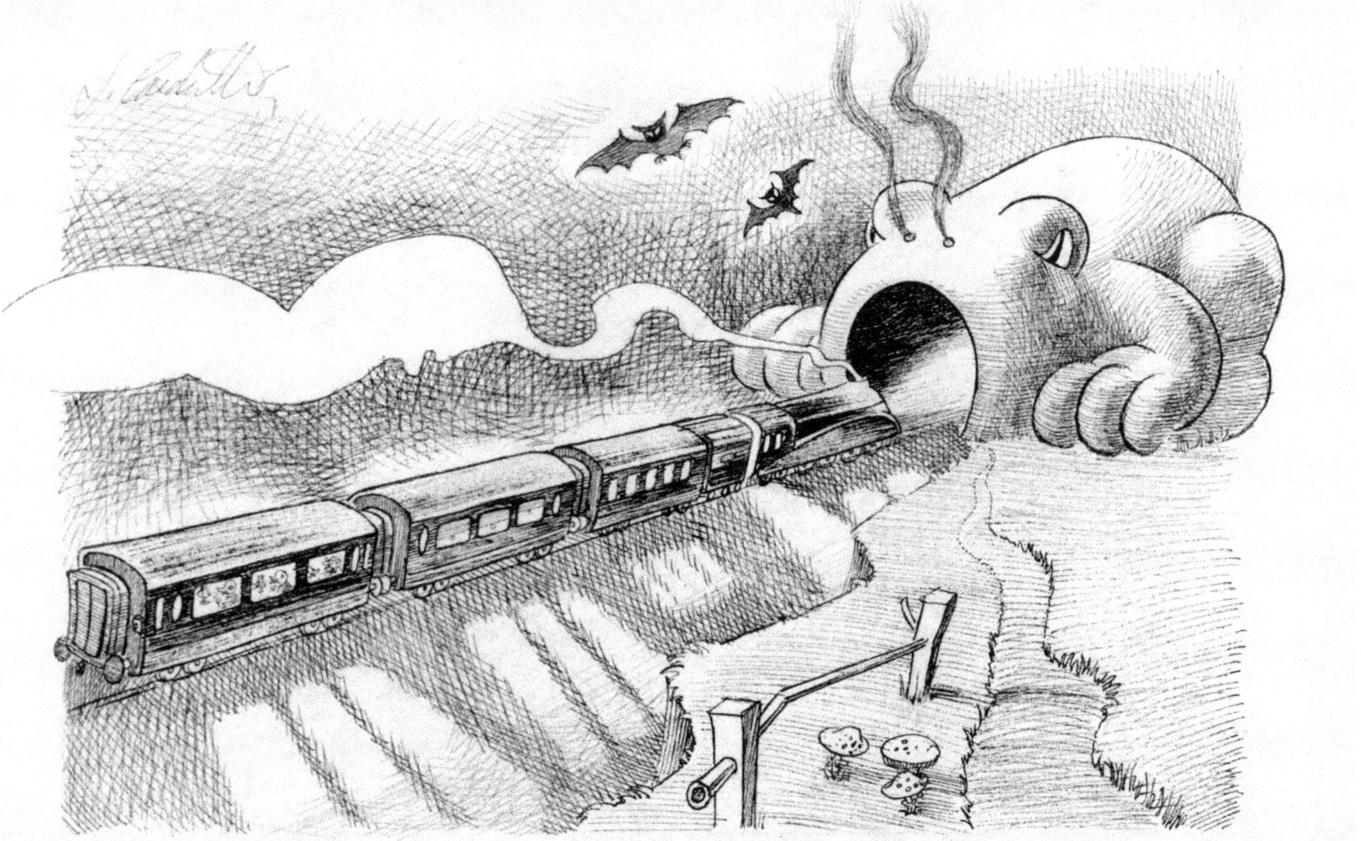

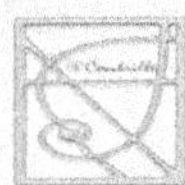

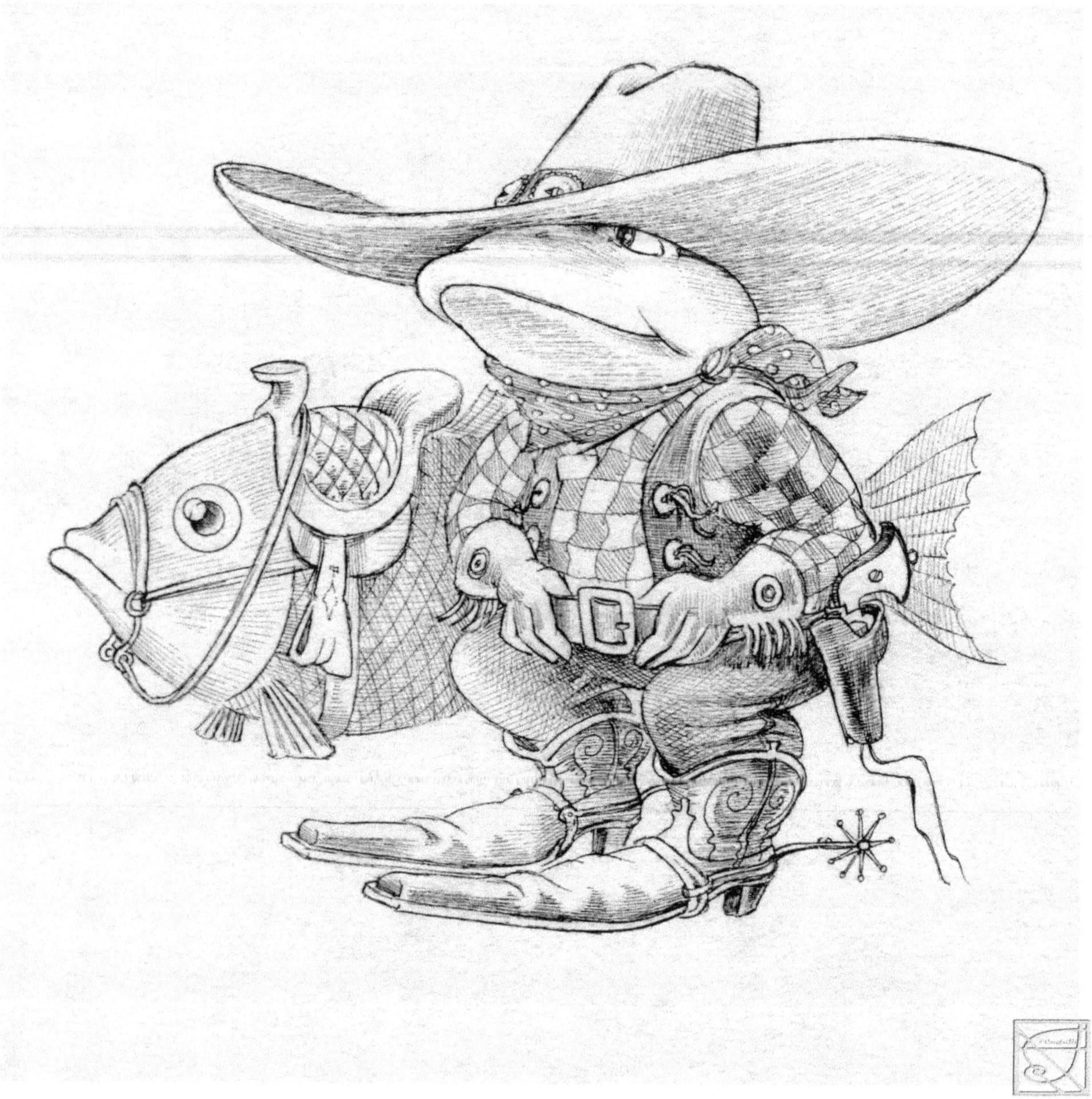

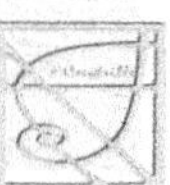

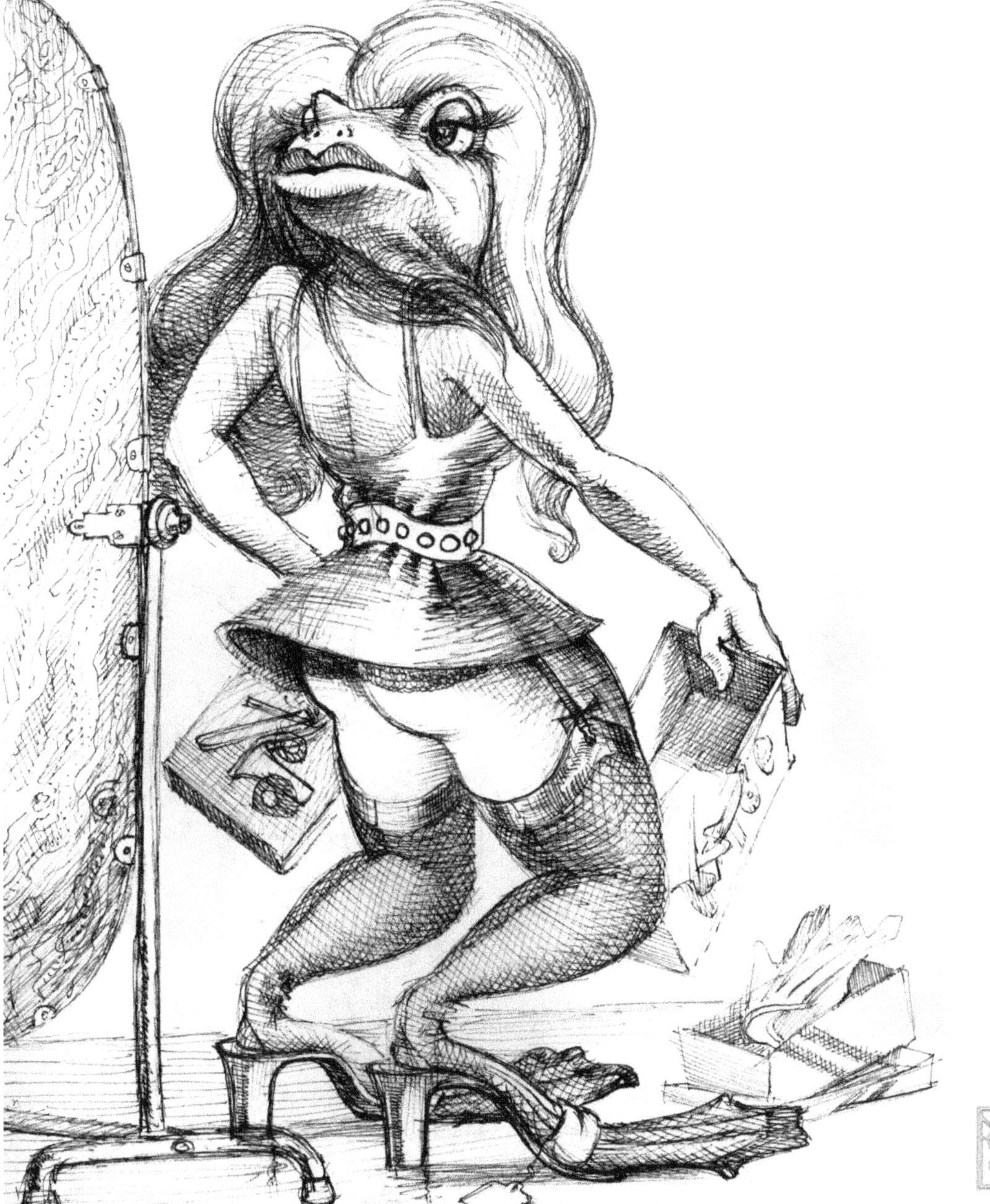

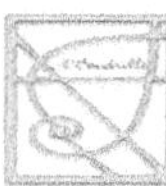

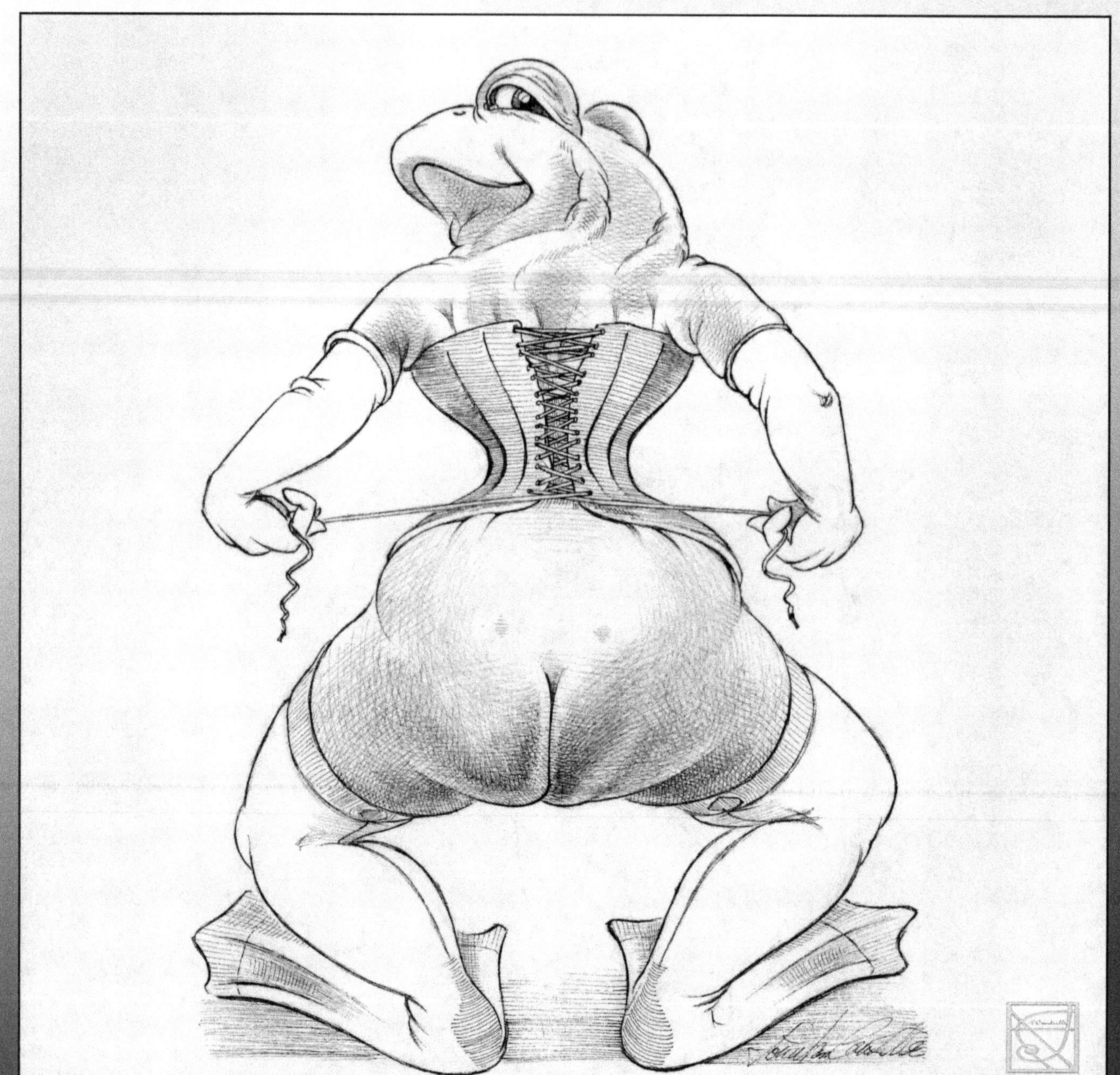

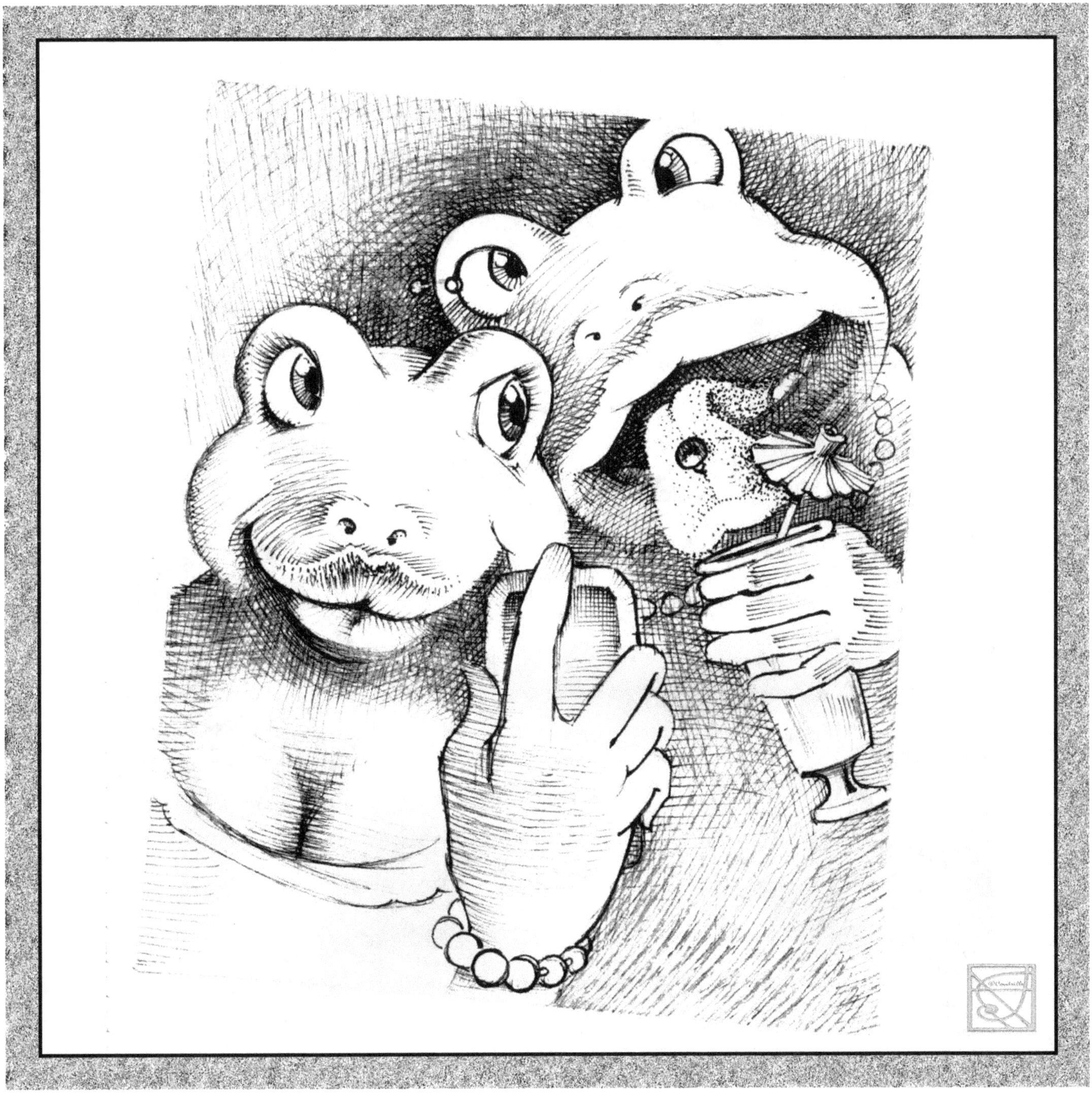

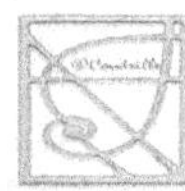

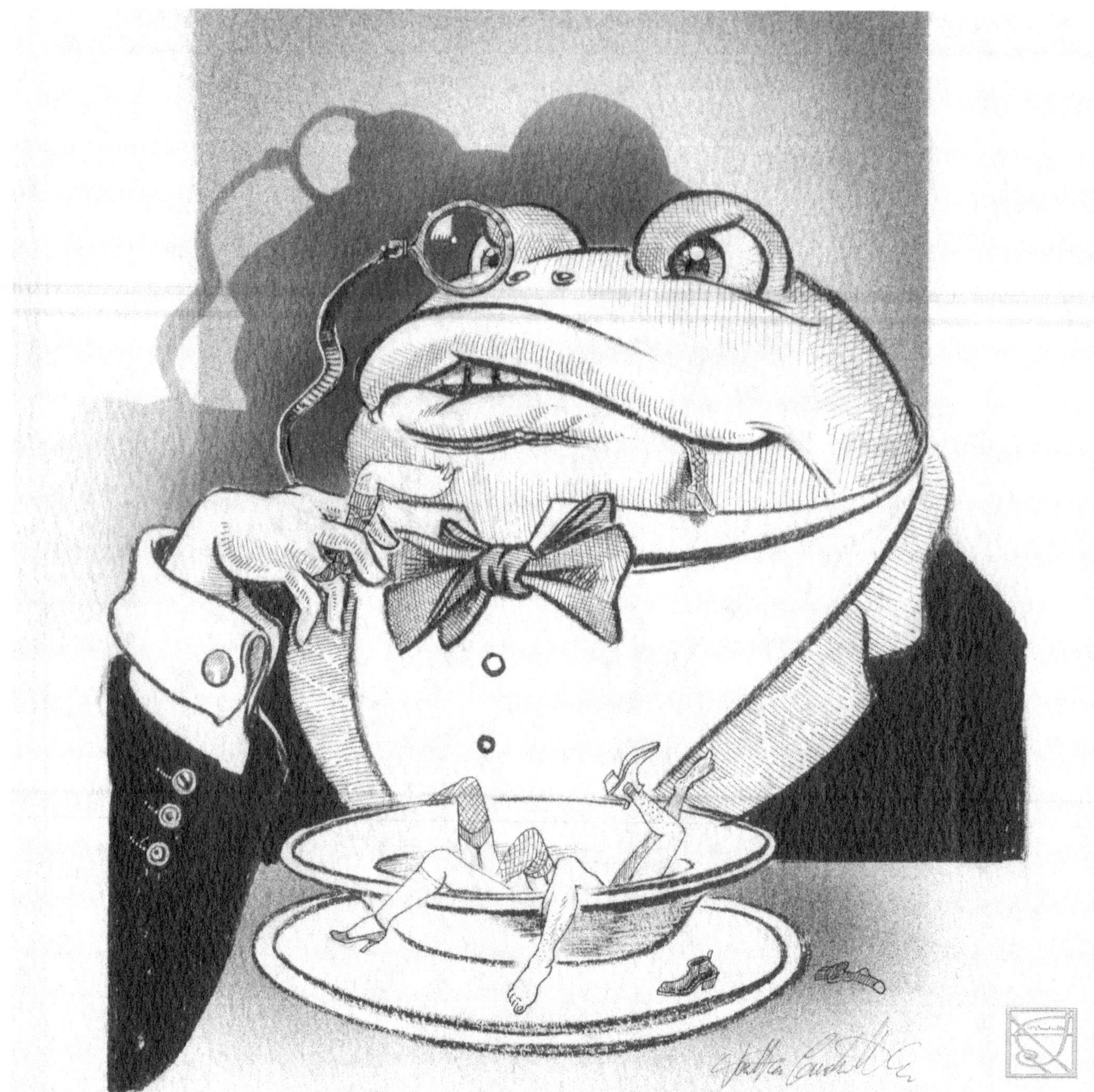

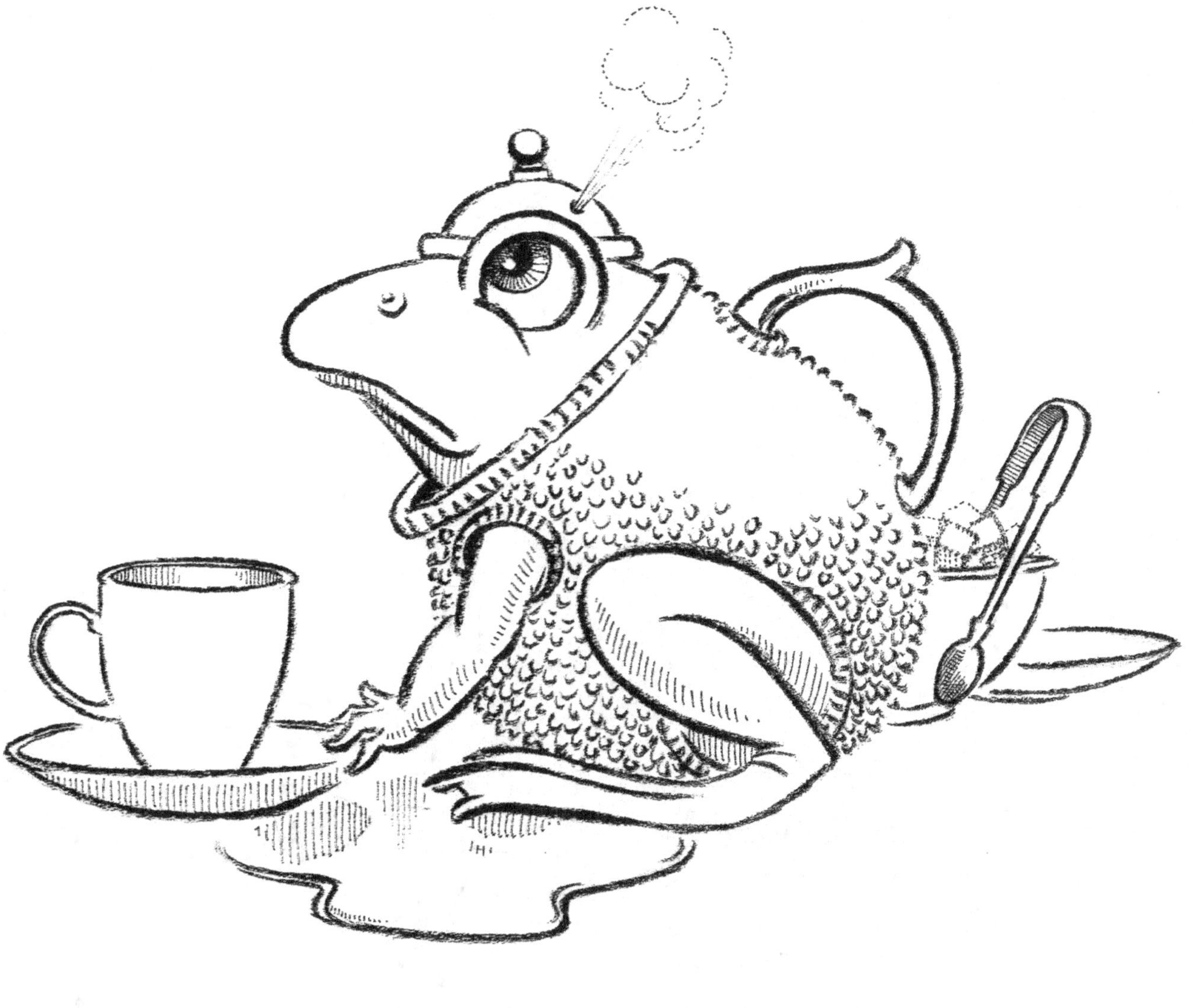

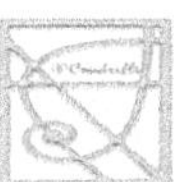

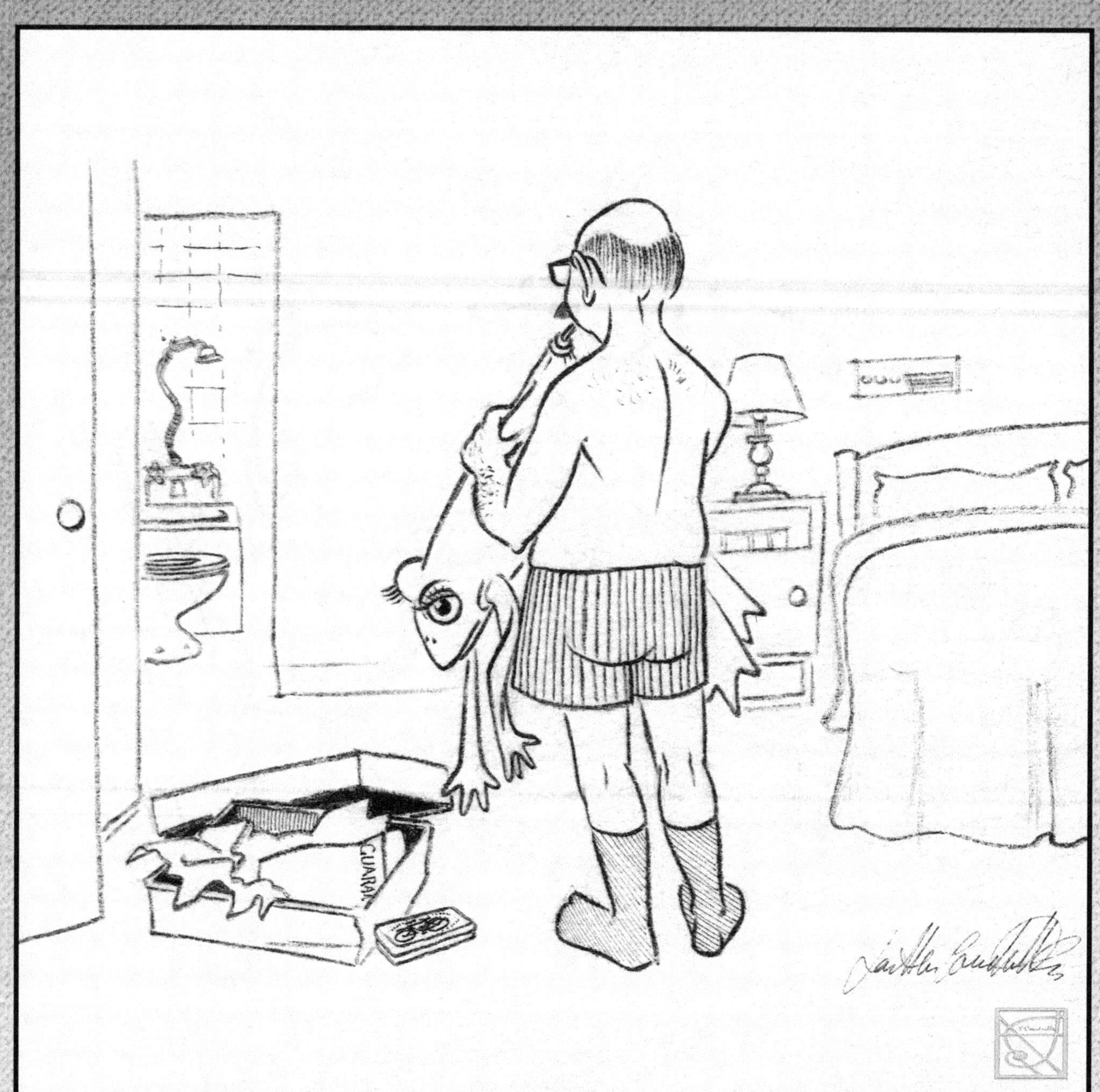

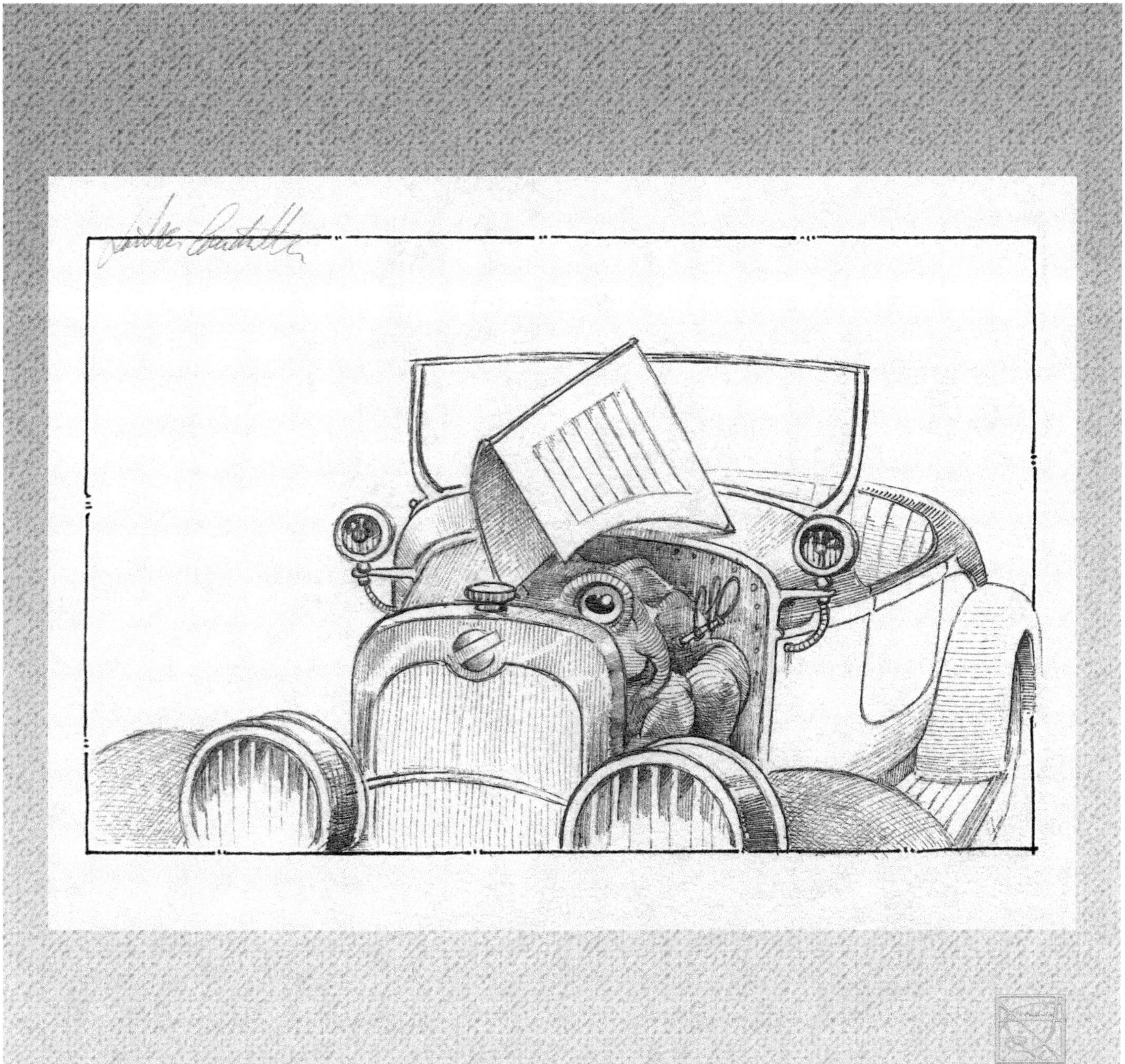

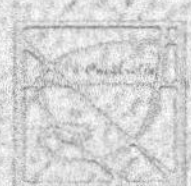

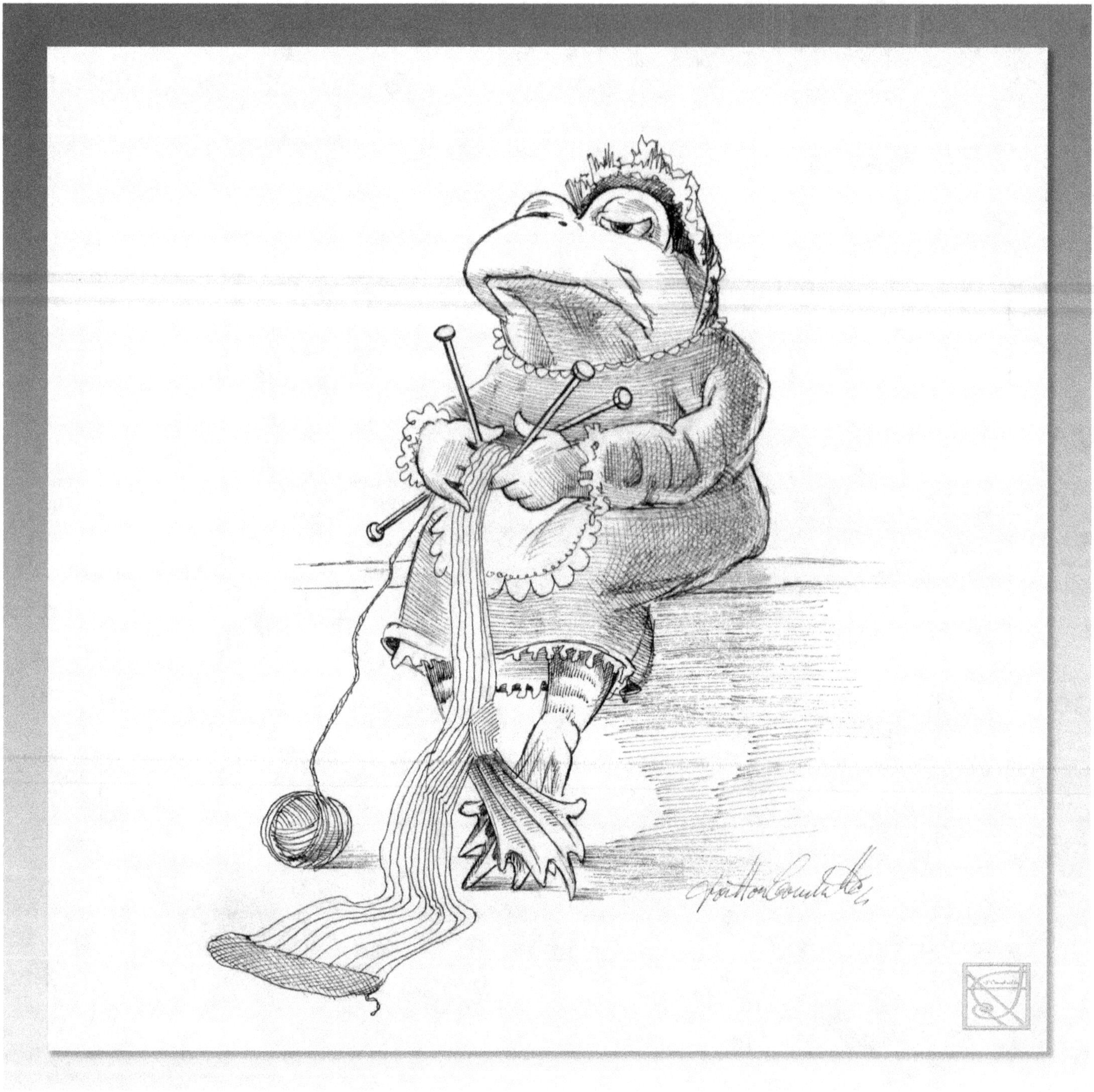

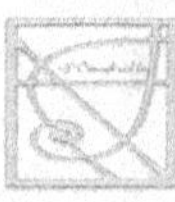

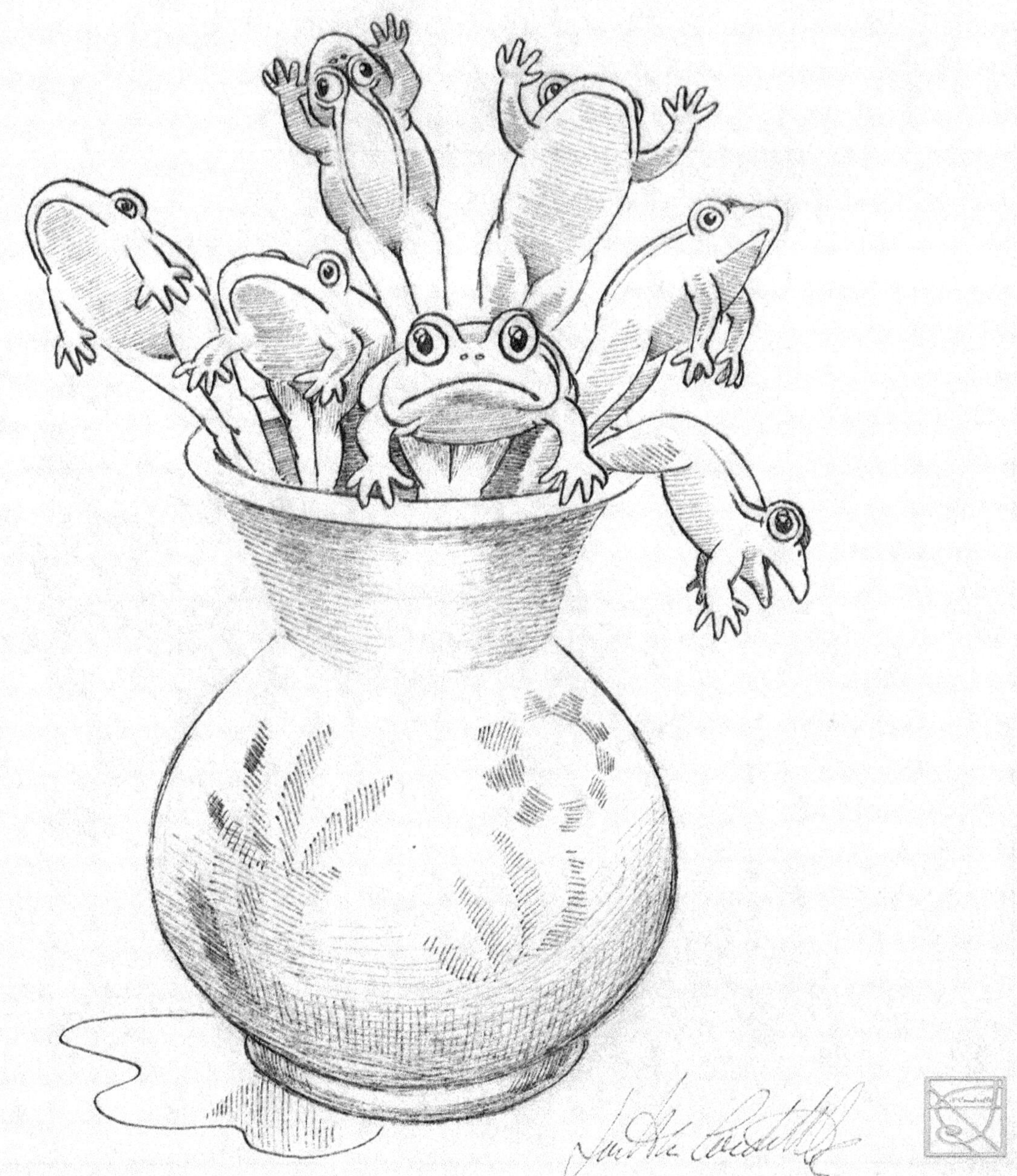

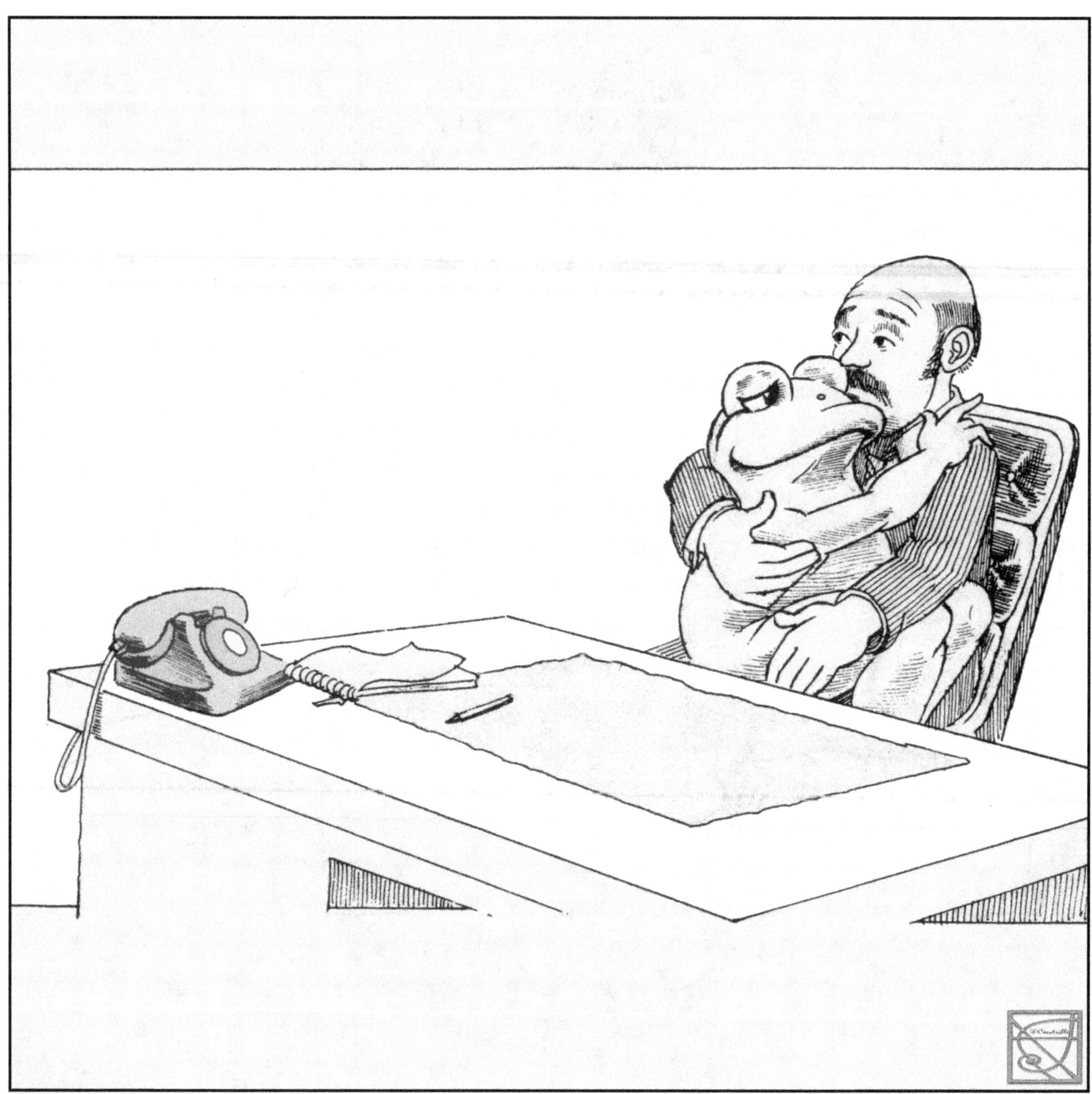

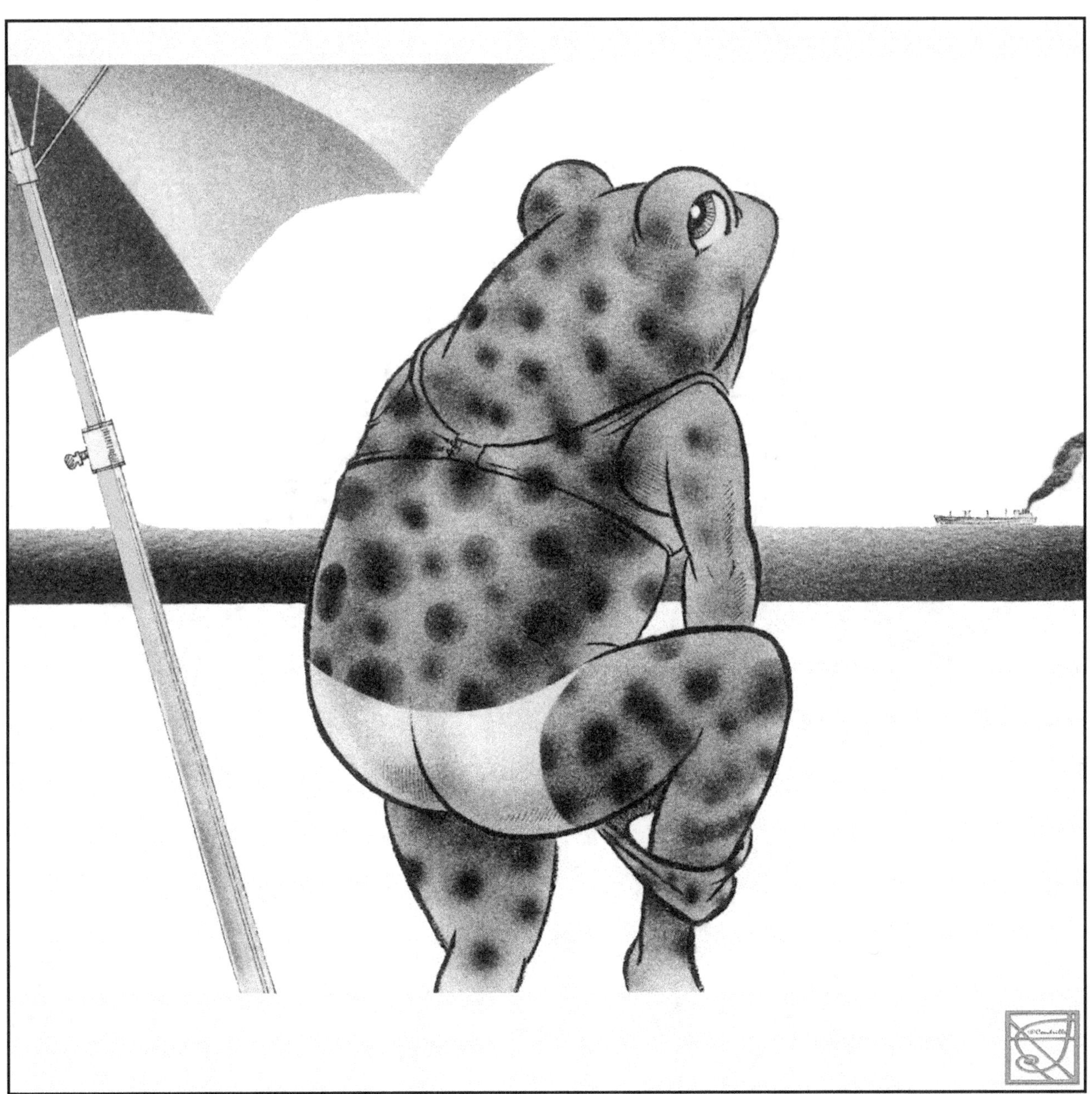

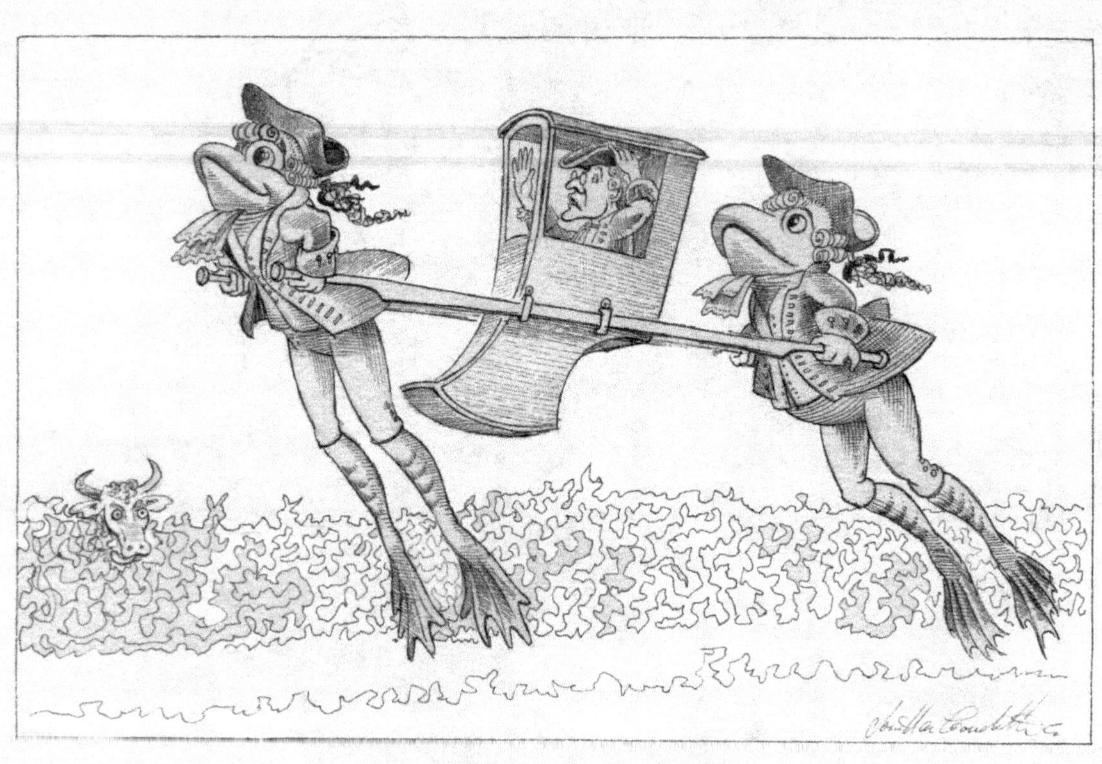

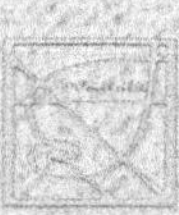

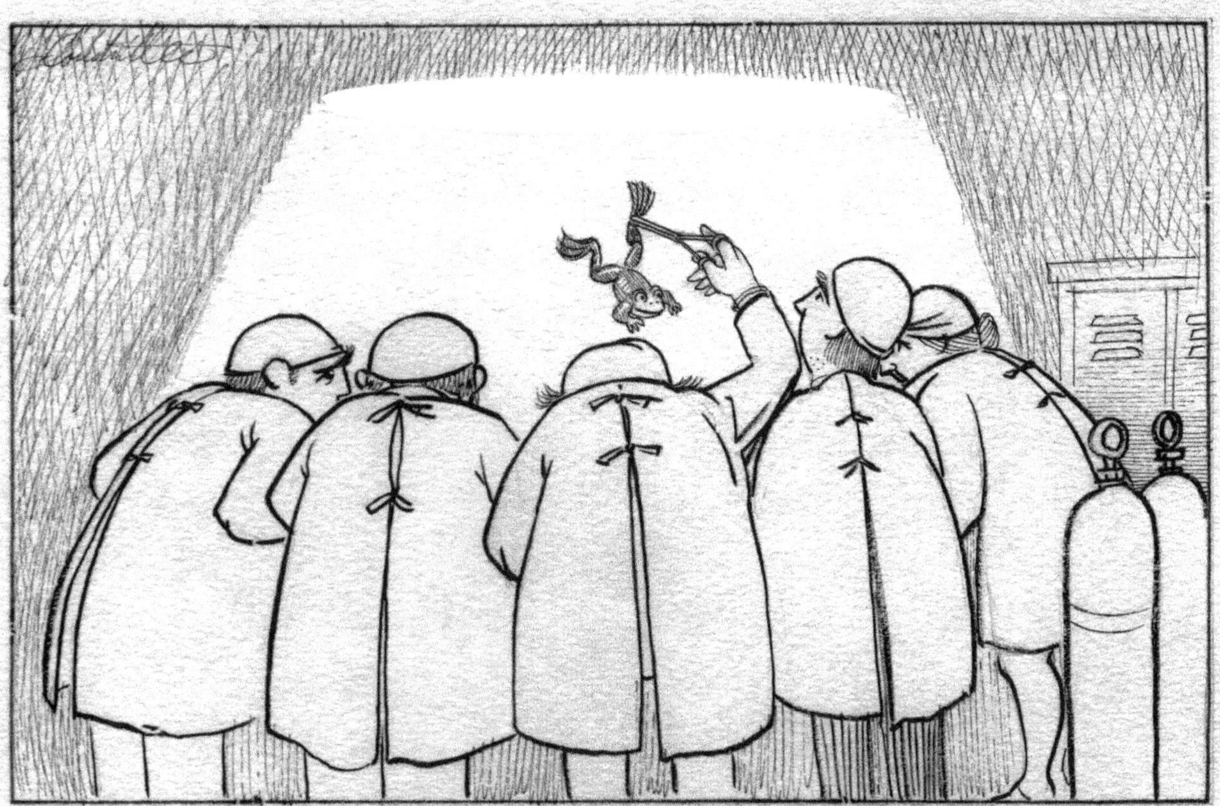

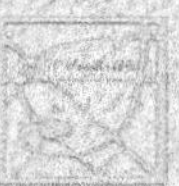

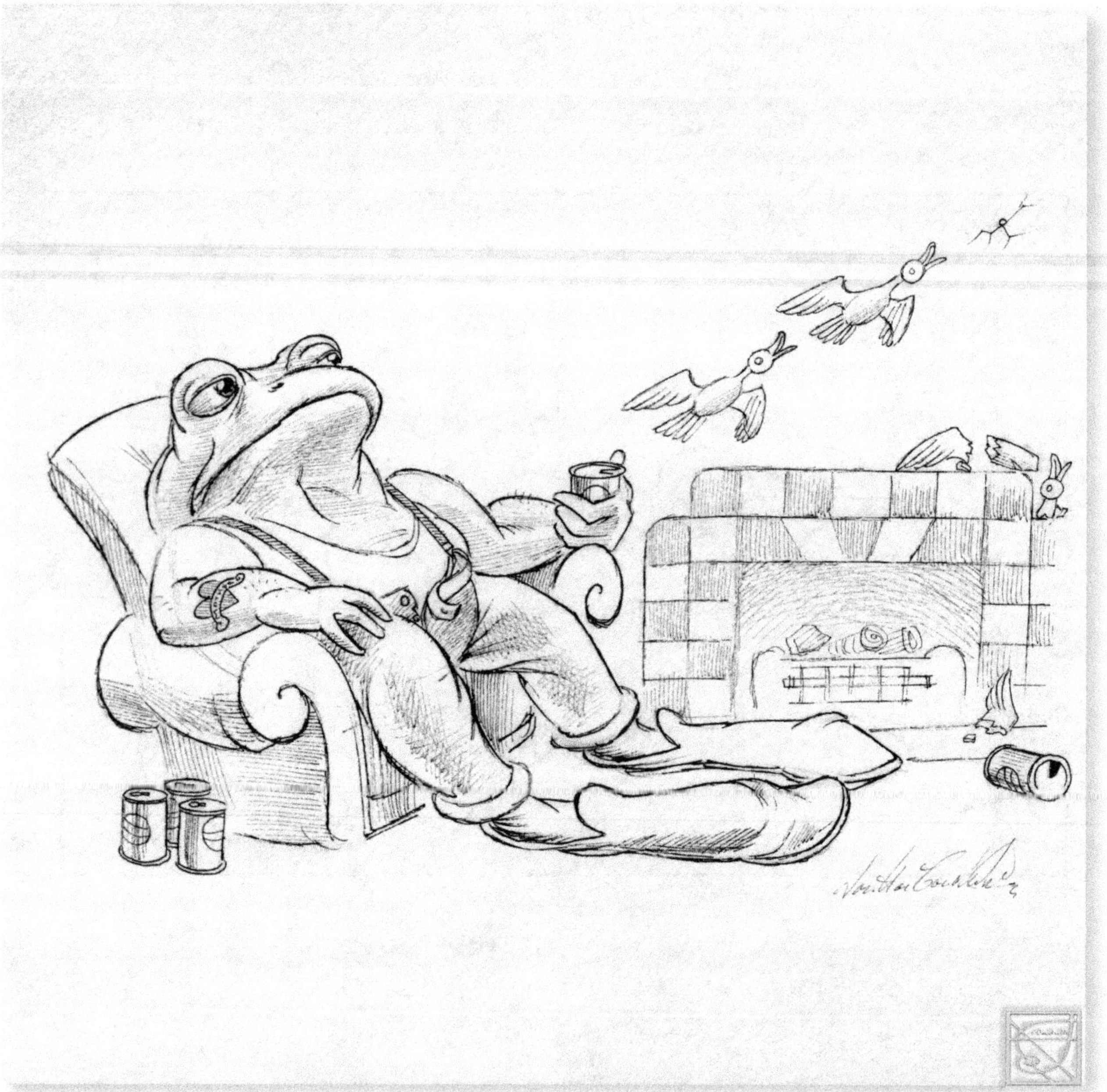

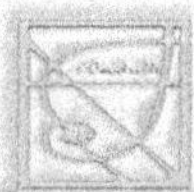

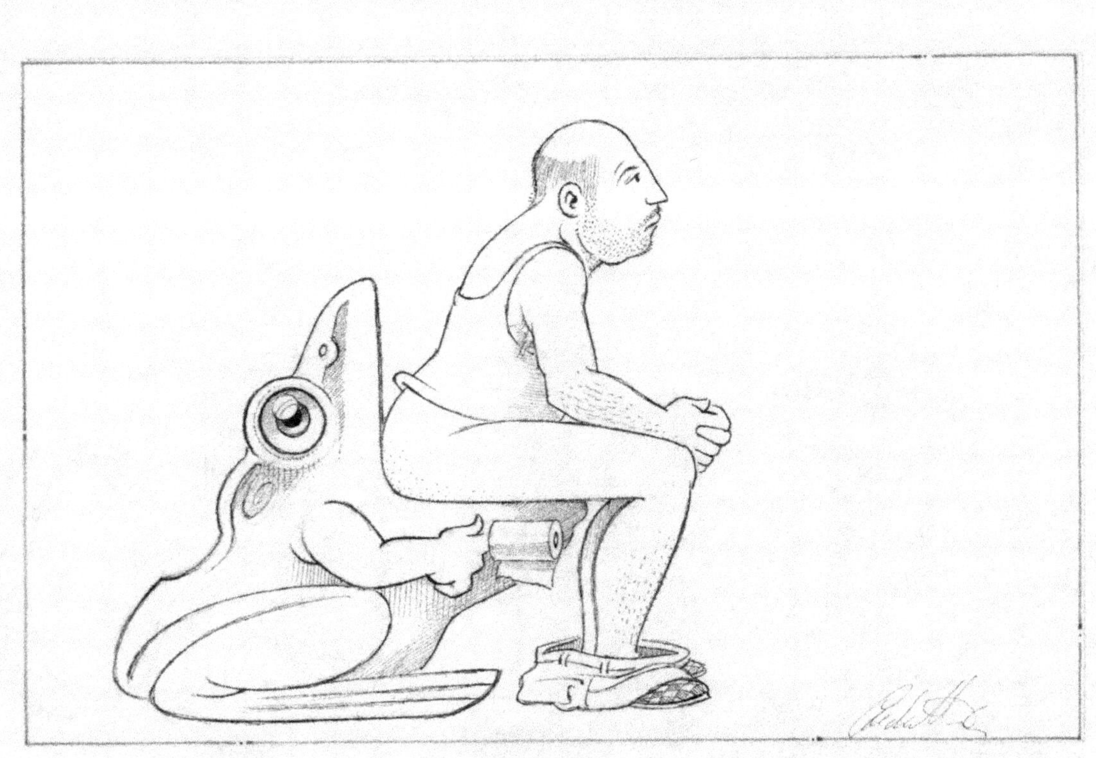

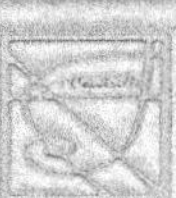

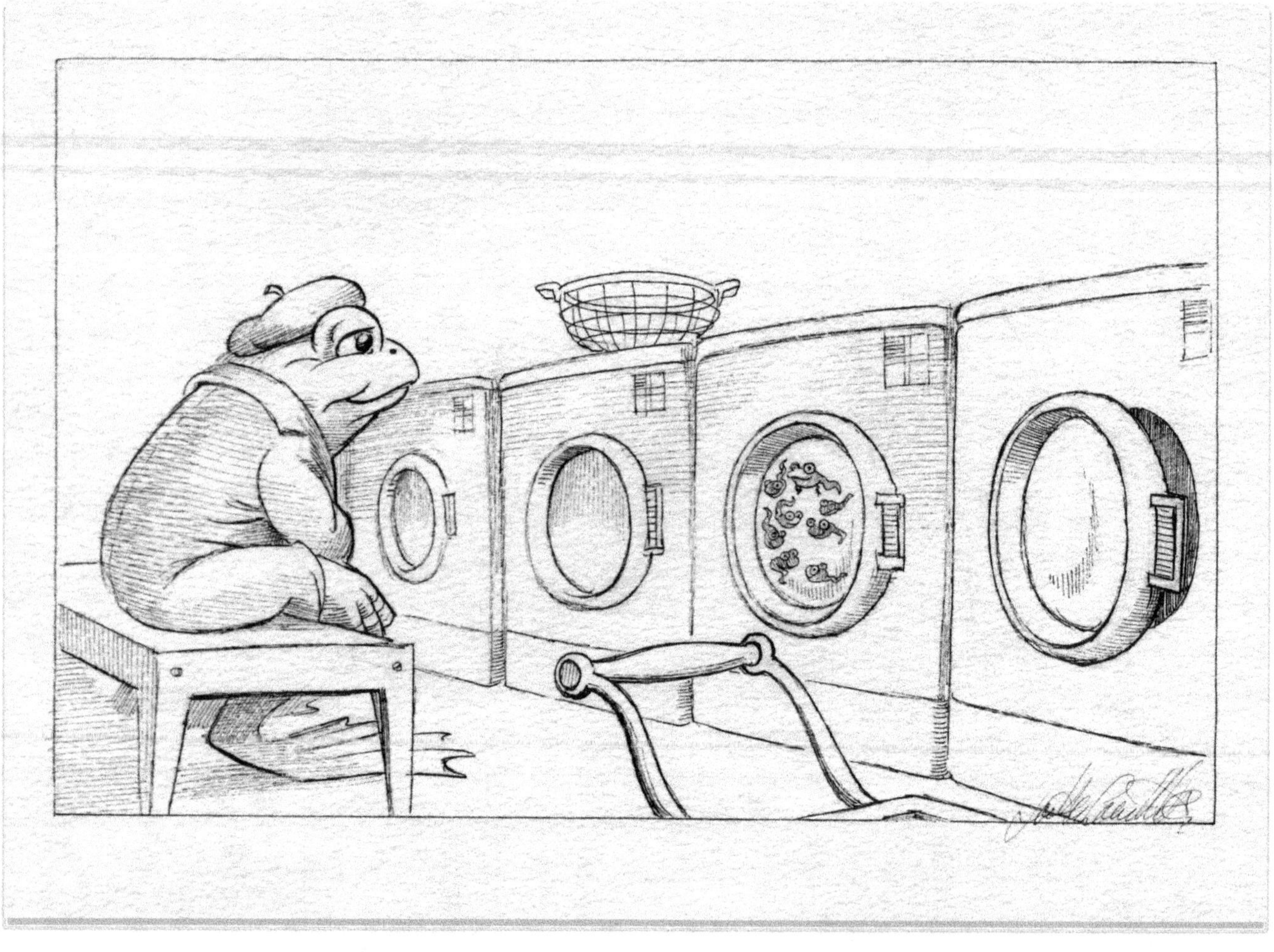

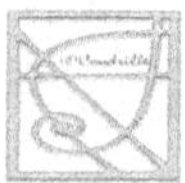

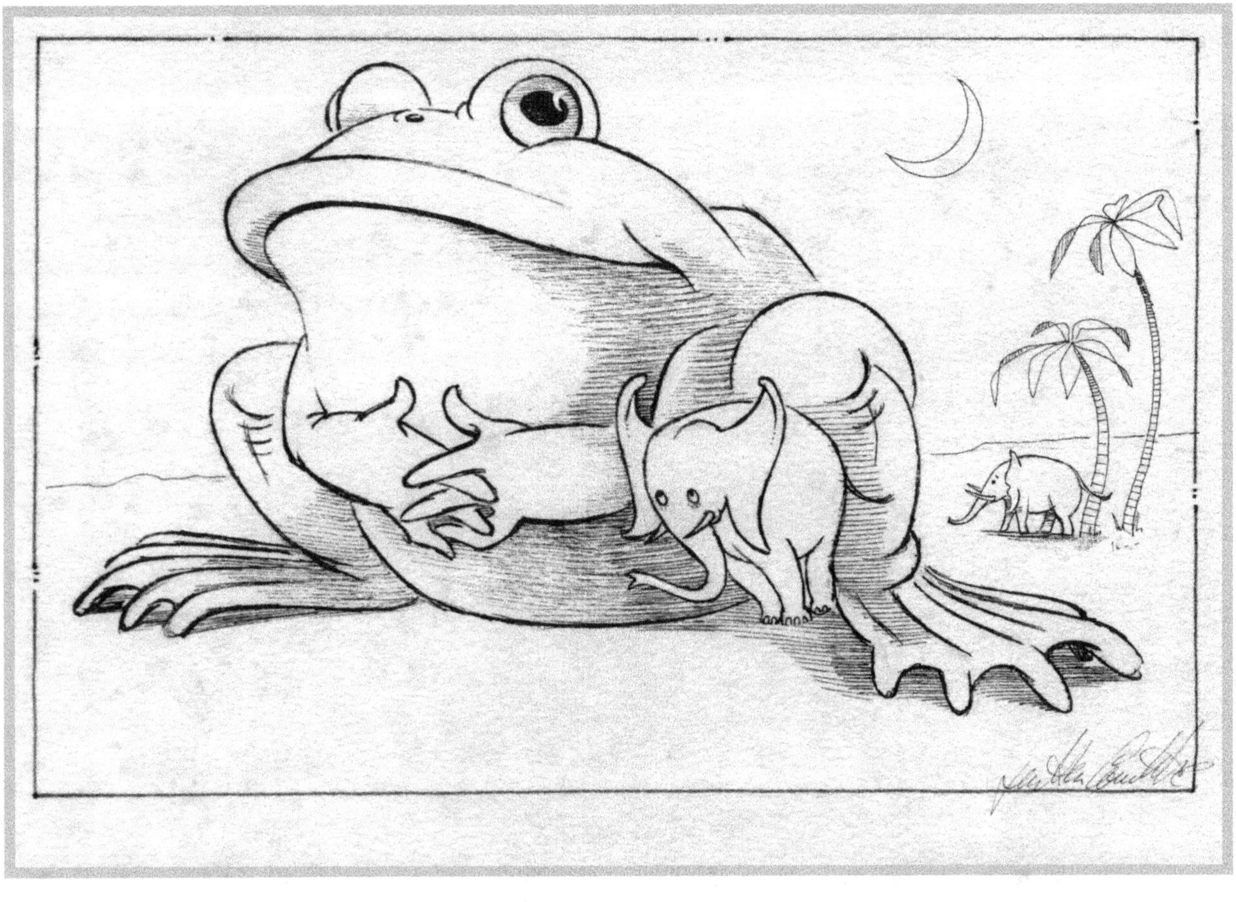

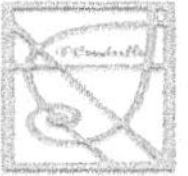

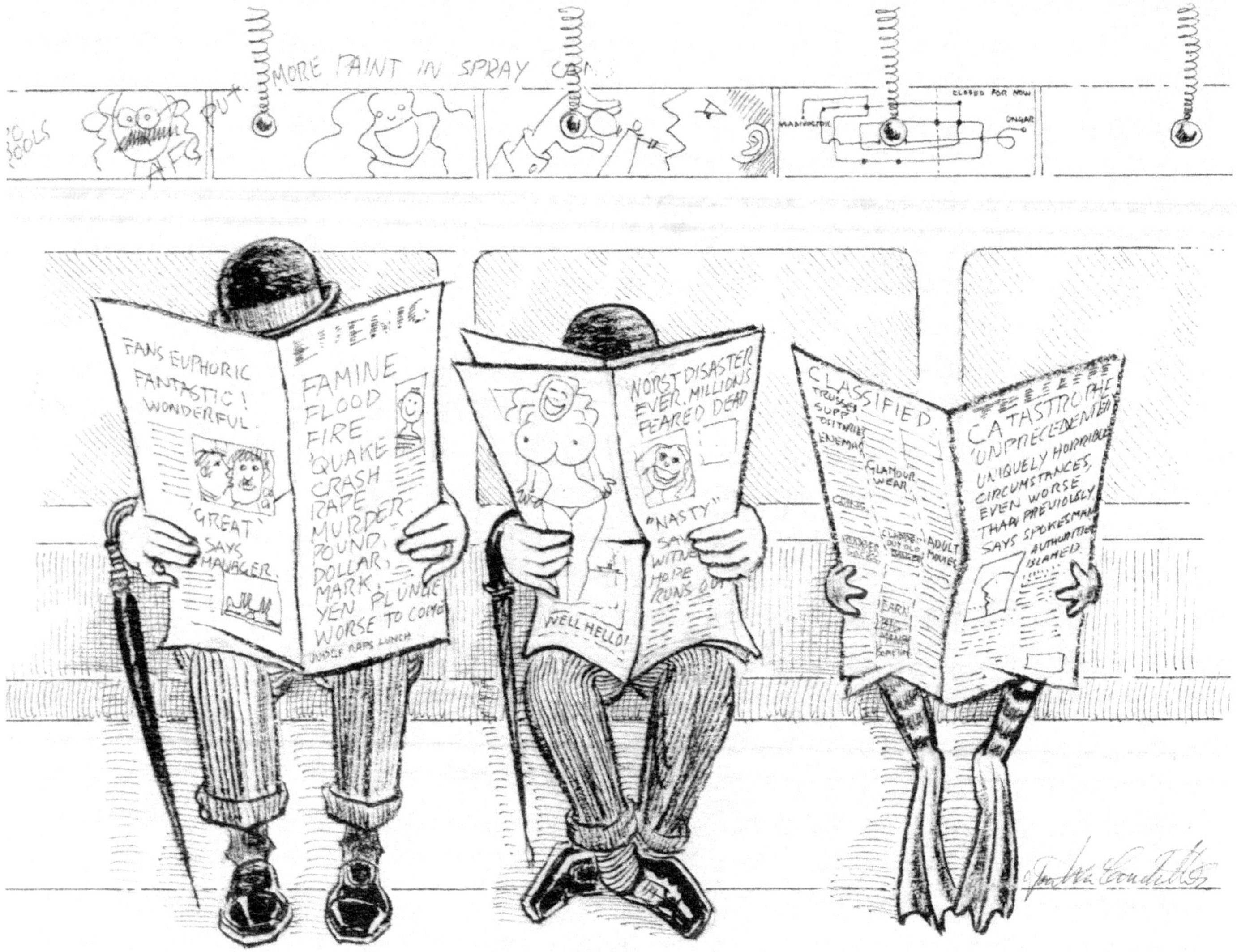

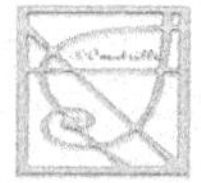

MORE PAINT IN SPRAY CAN
BOOLS
PUT
CLOSED FOR NOW
DANGER
FANS EUPHORIC
FANTASTIC!
WONDERFUL.
"GREAT"
SAYS MANAGER.
EPIDEMIC
FAMINE
FLOOD
FIRE
QUAKE
CRASH
RAPE
MURDER
POUND,
DOLLAR,
MARK,
YEN PLUNGE
WORSE TO COME
JUDGE RAPS LUNCH
WORST DISASTER
EVER, MILLIONS
FEARED DEAD
"NASTY"
SAYS
WITNESS
HOPE
RUNS OUT
WELL HELLO!
CLASSIFIED
TRUSSES
SUPP-
OSITRIES
ENEMAS
GLAMOUR
WEAR.
ADULT
MOVIES
EARN
CATASTROPHE
'UNPRECEDENTED'
UNIQUELY HORRIBLE
CIRCUMSTANCES,
EVEN WORSE
THAN PREVIOUSLY,
SAYS SPOKESMAN
AUTHORITIES
BLAMED

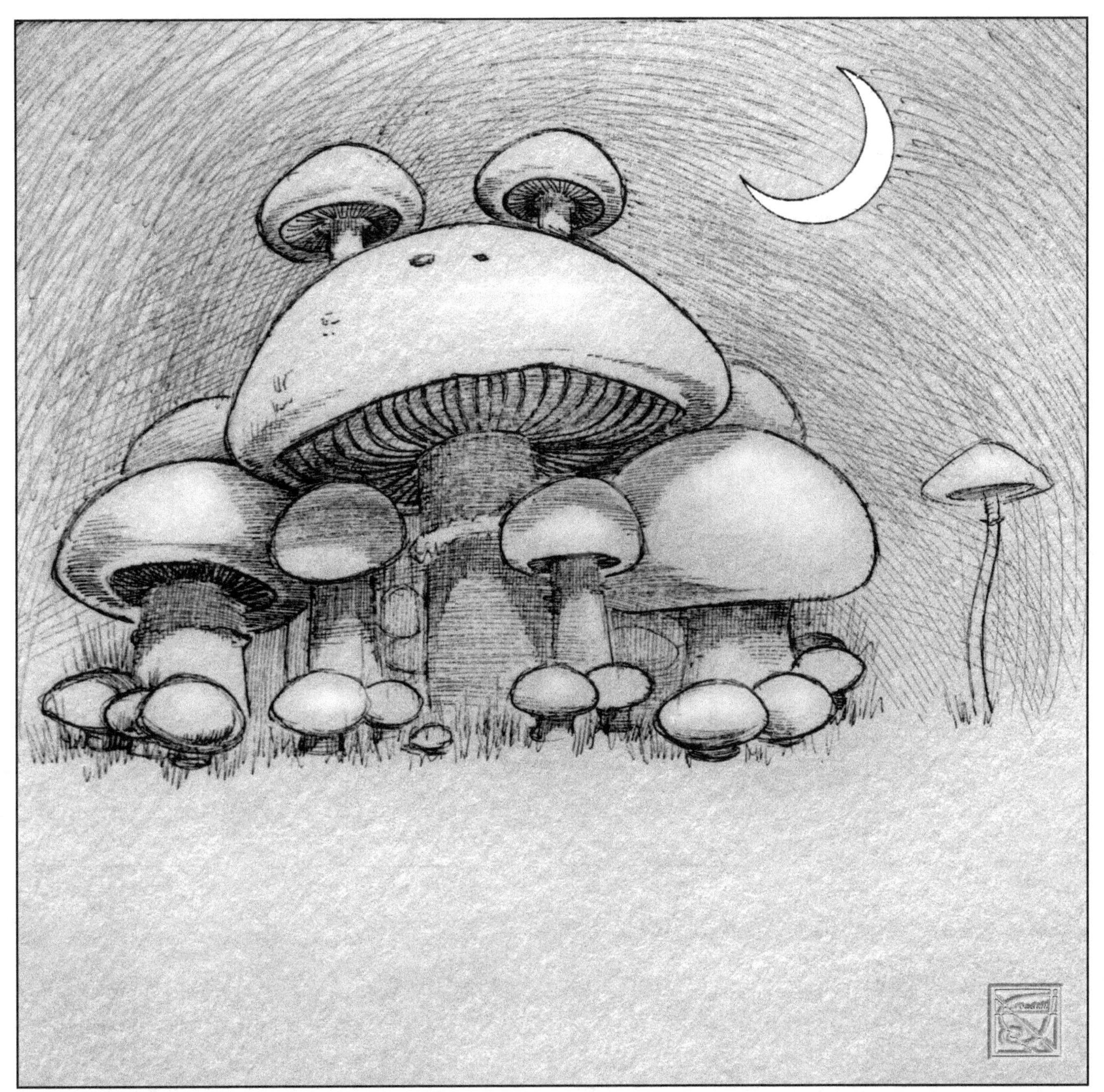

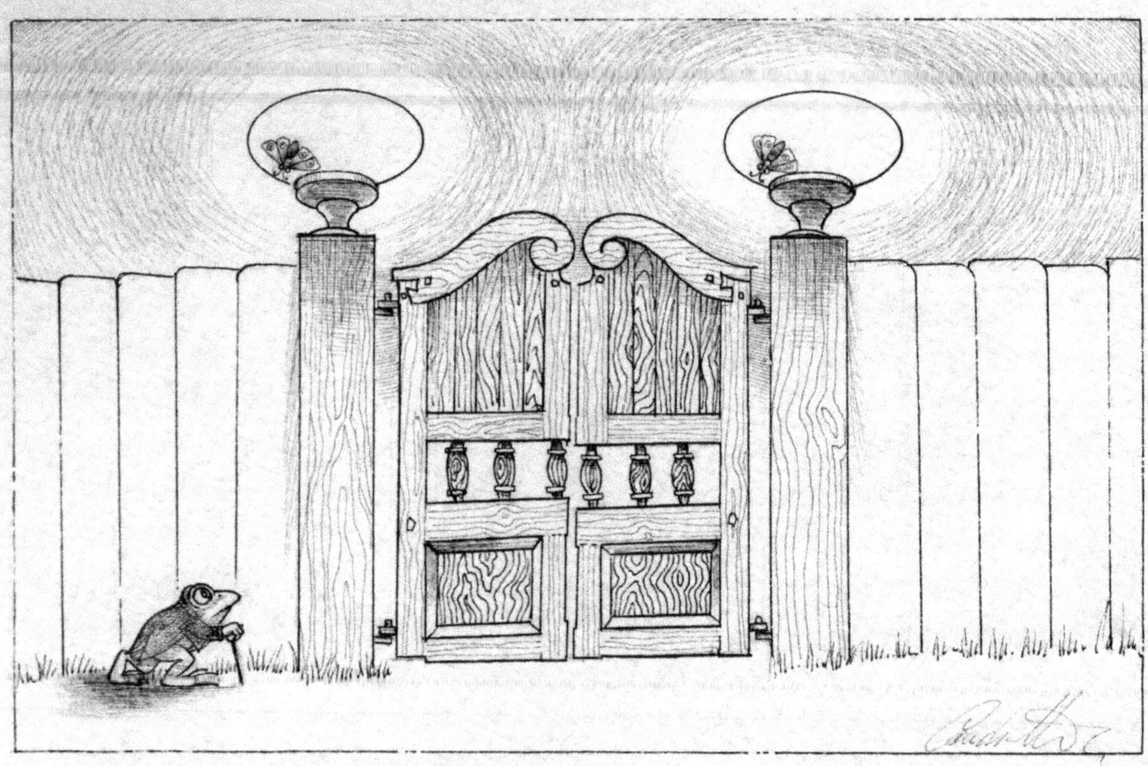

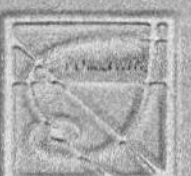

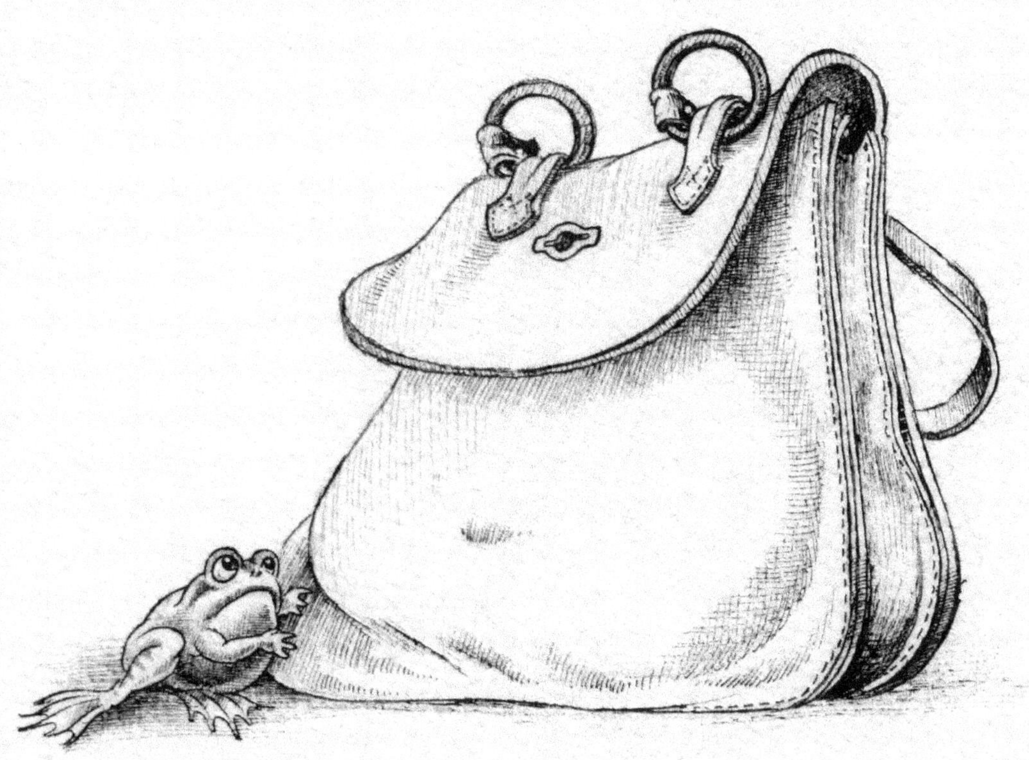
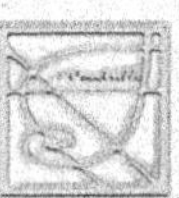

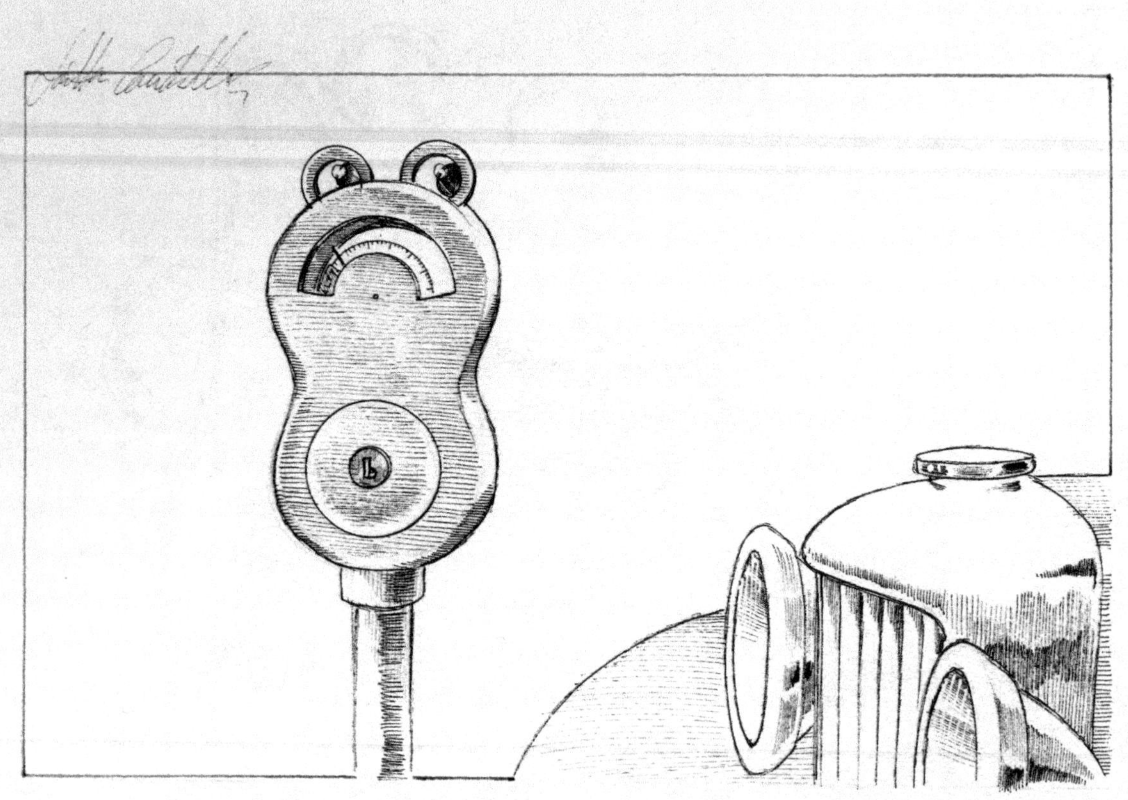
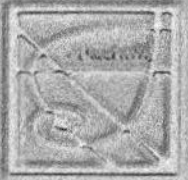

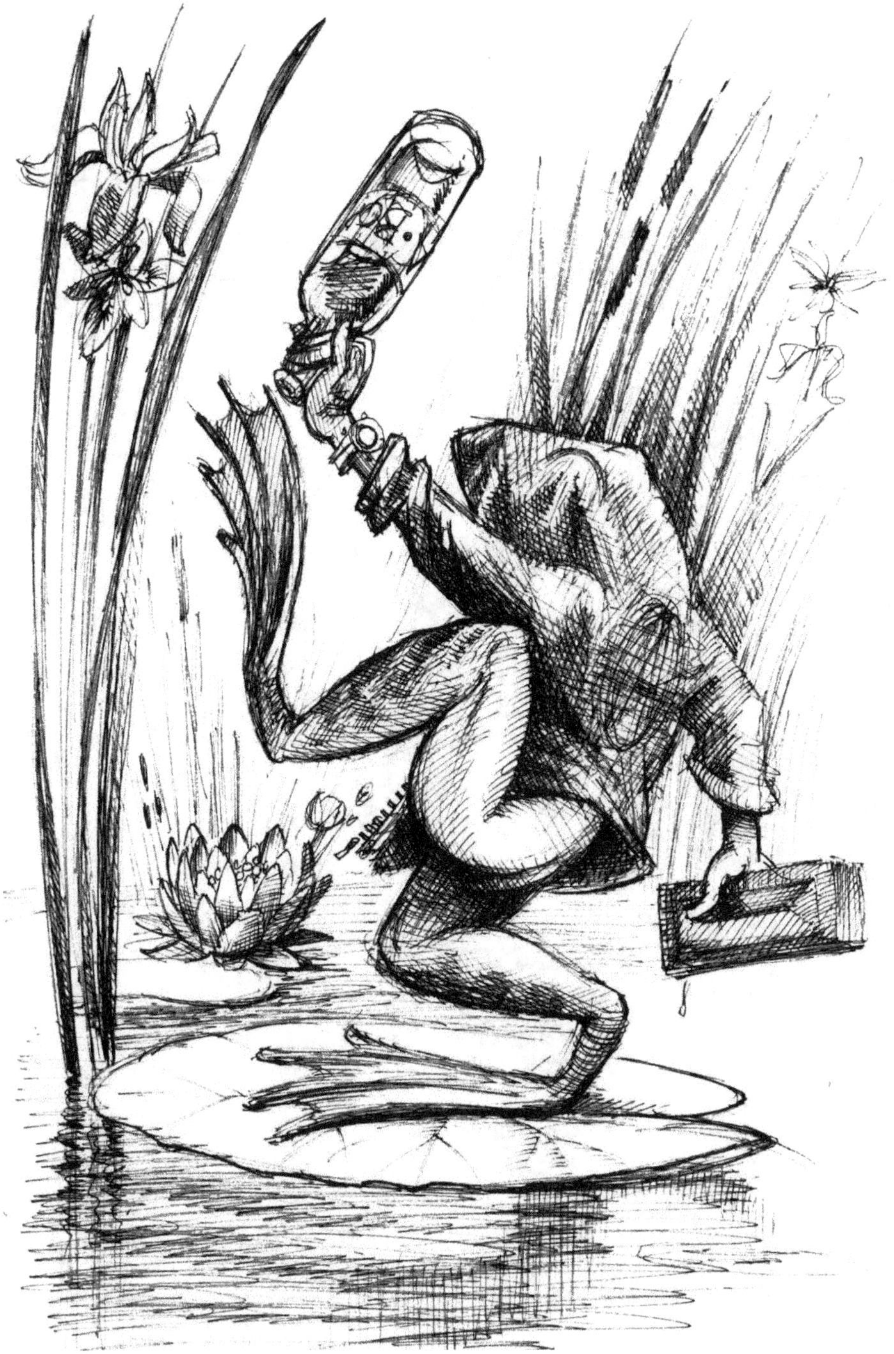

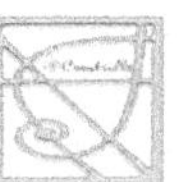

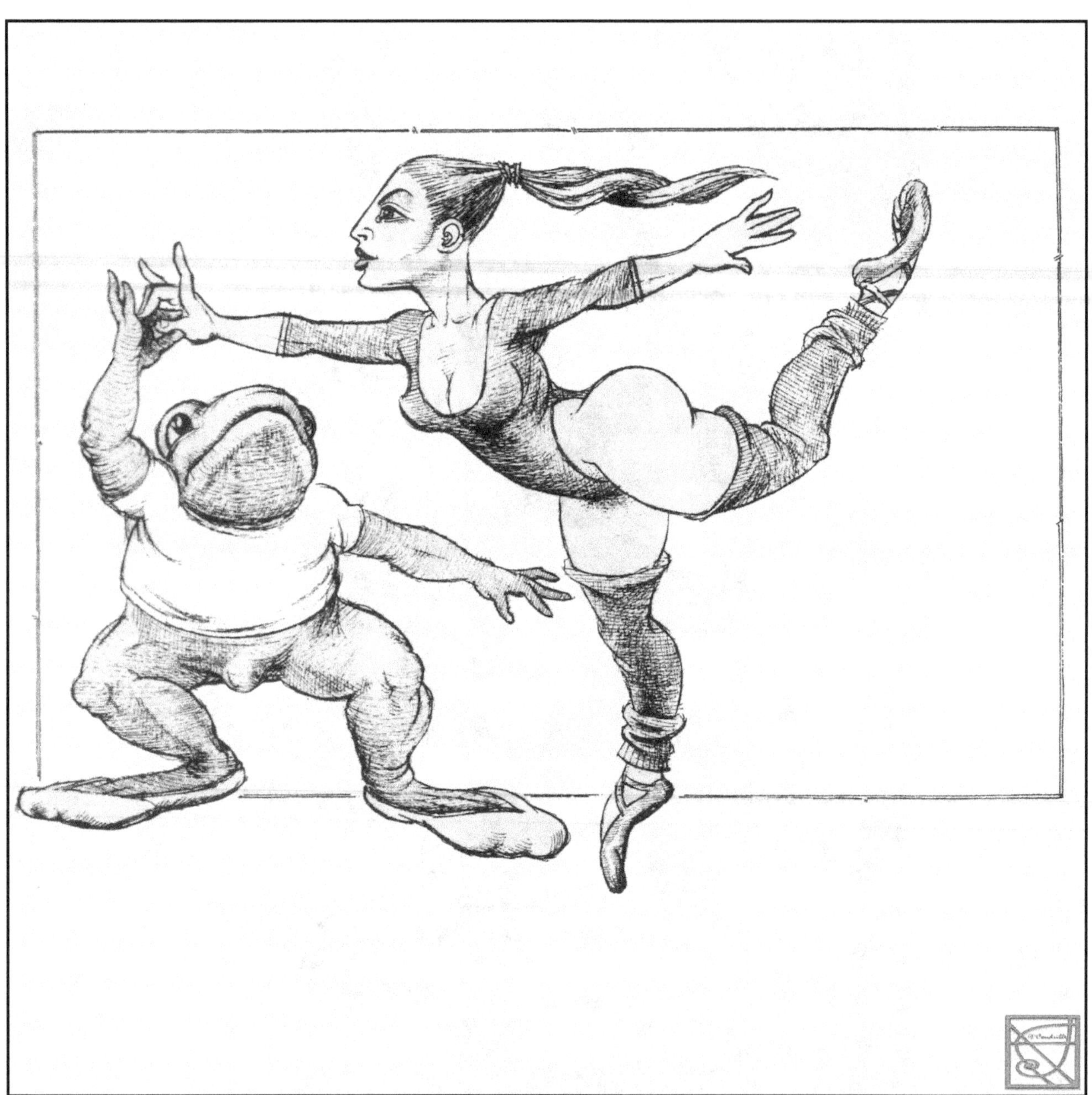

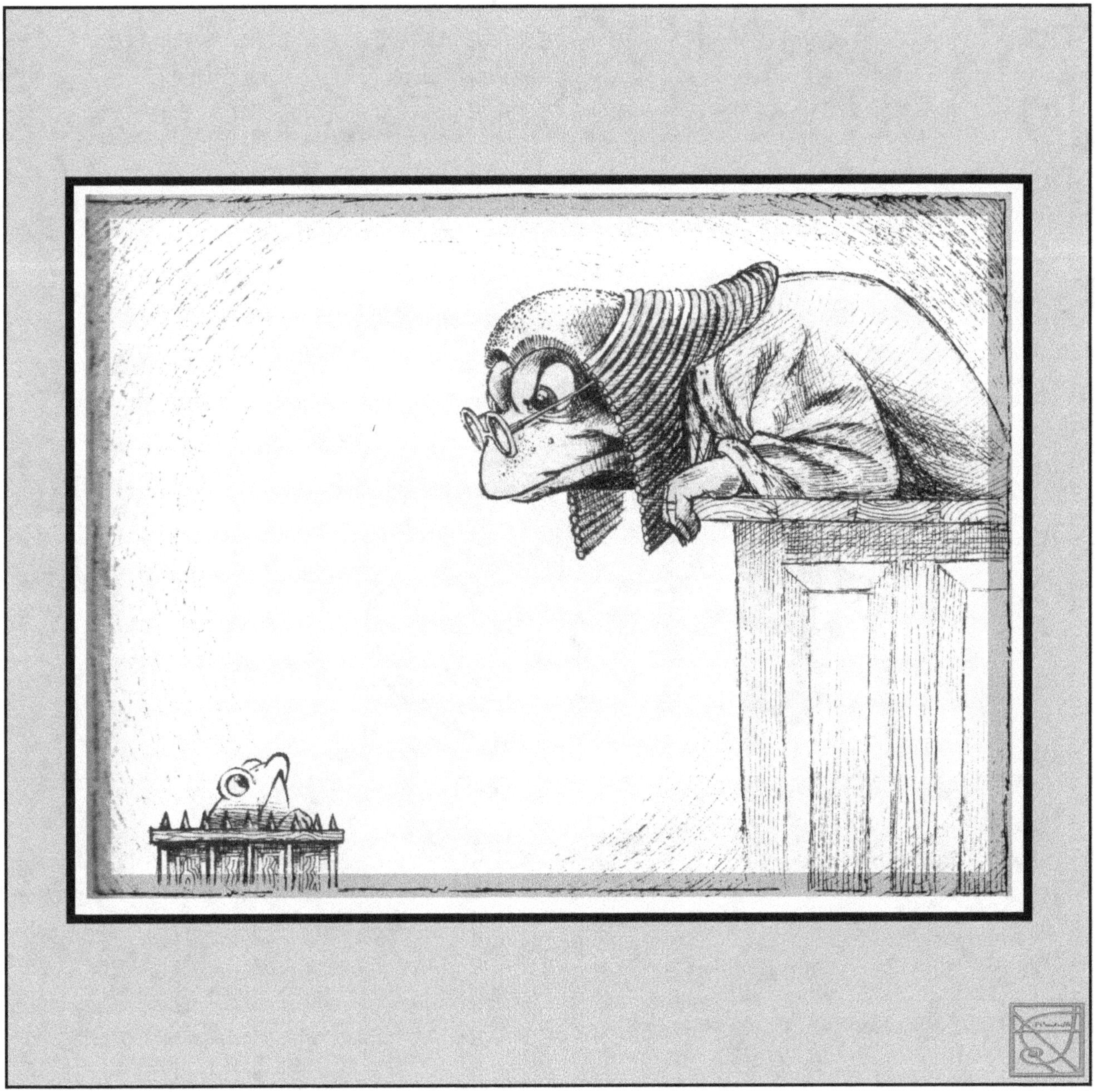

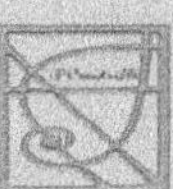

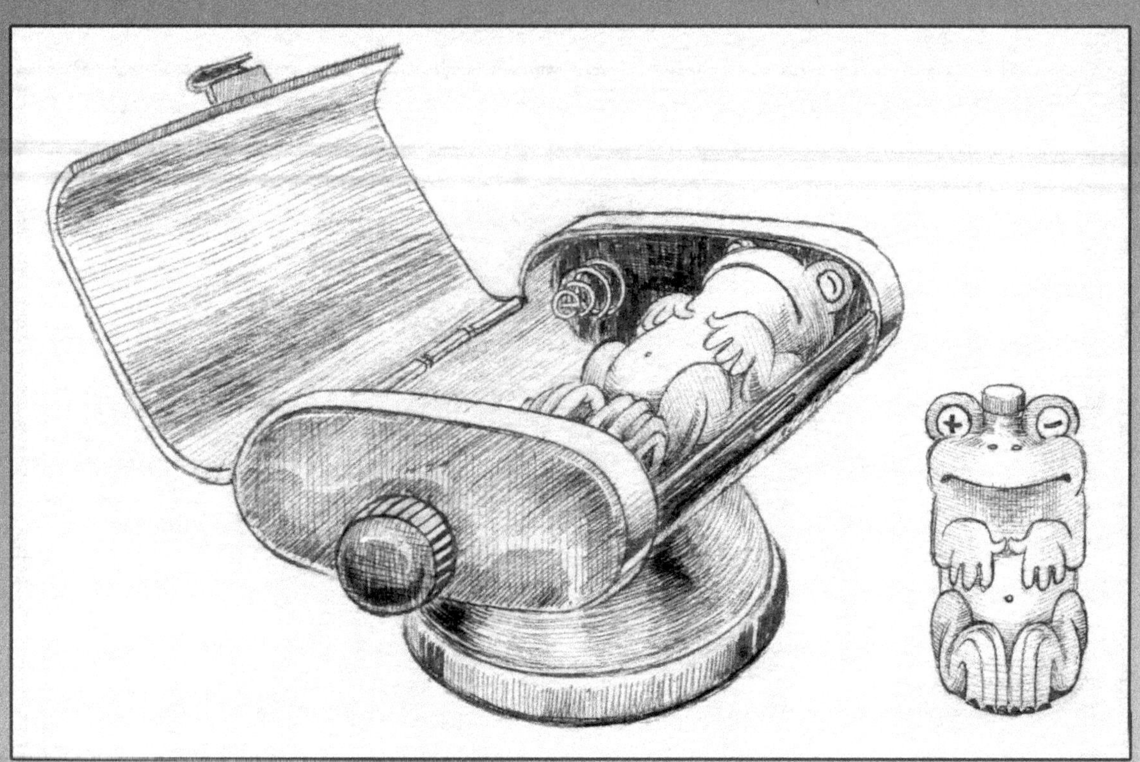
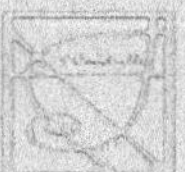

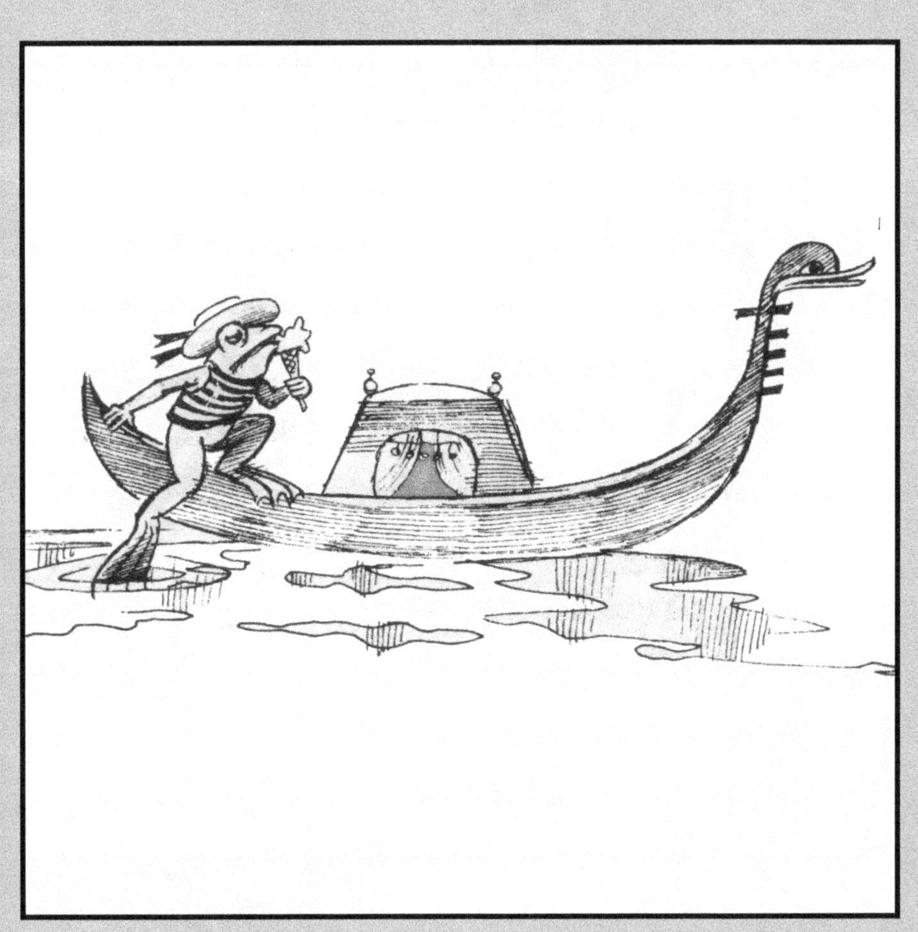
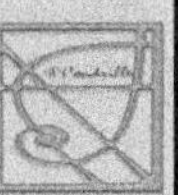

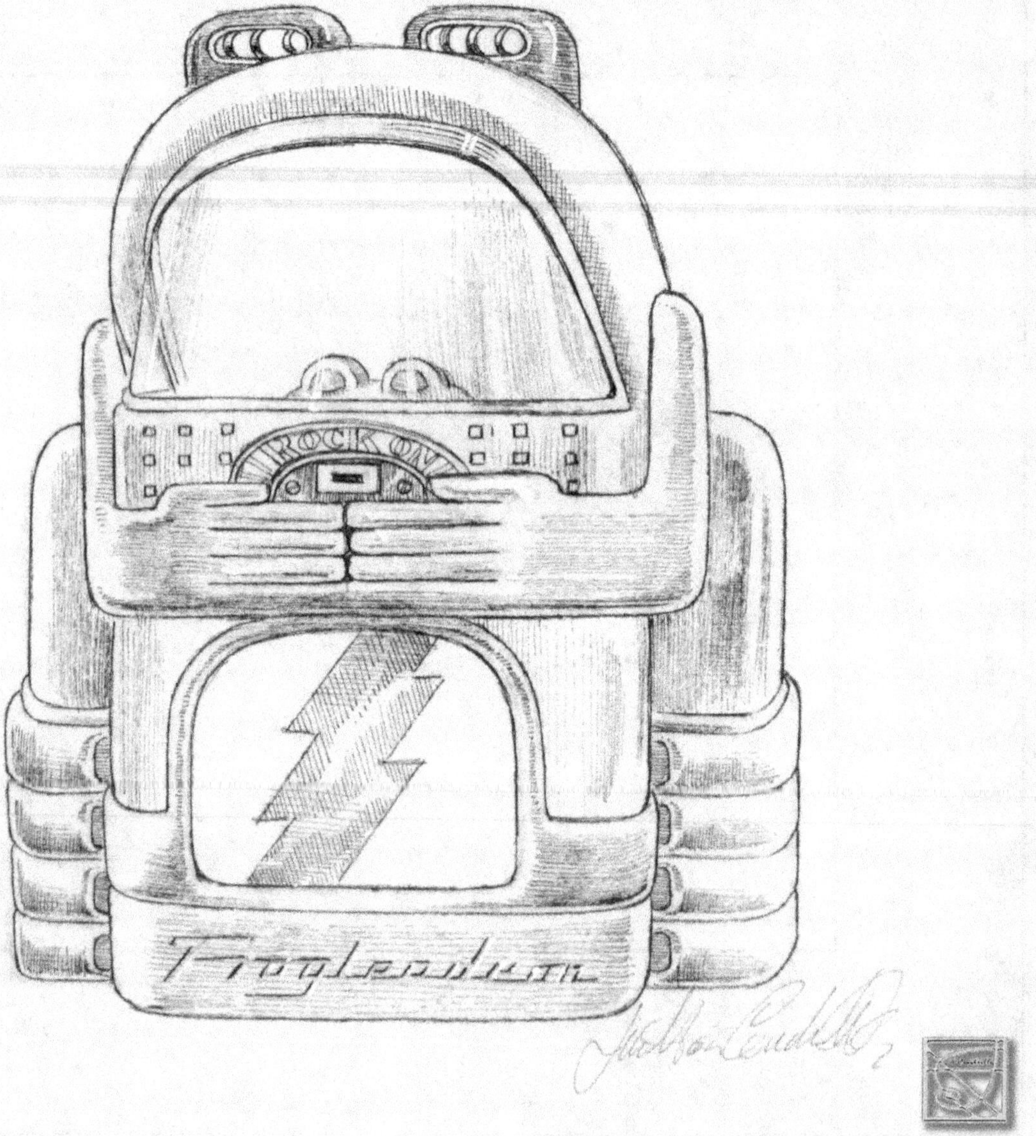

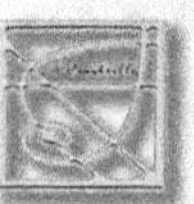

ROCK ON
Froglodeum

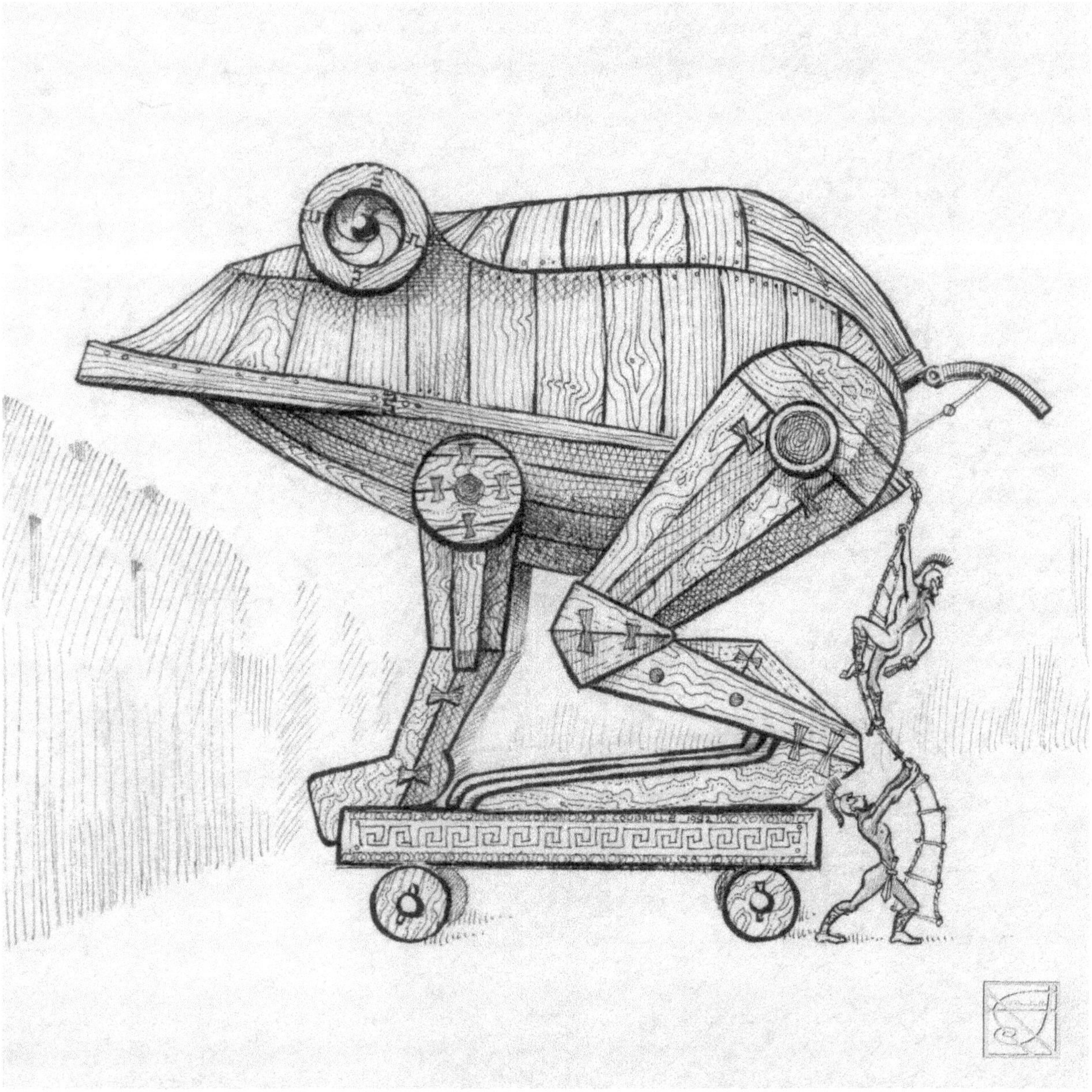

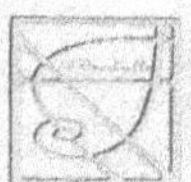

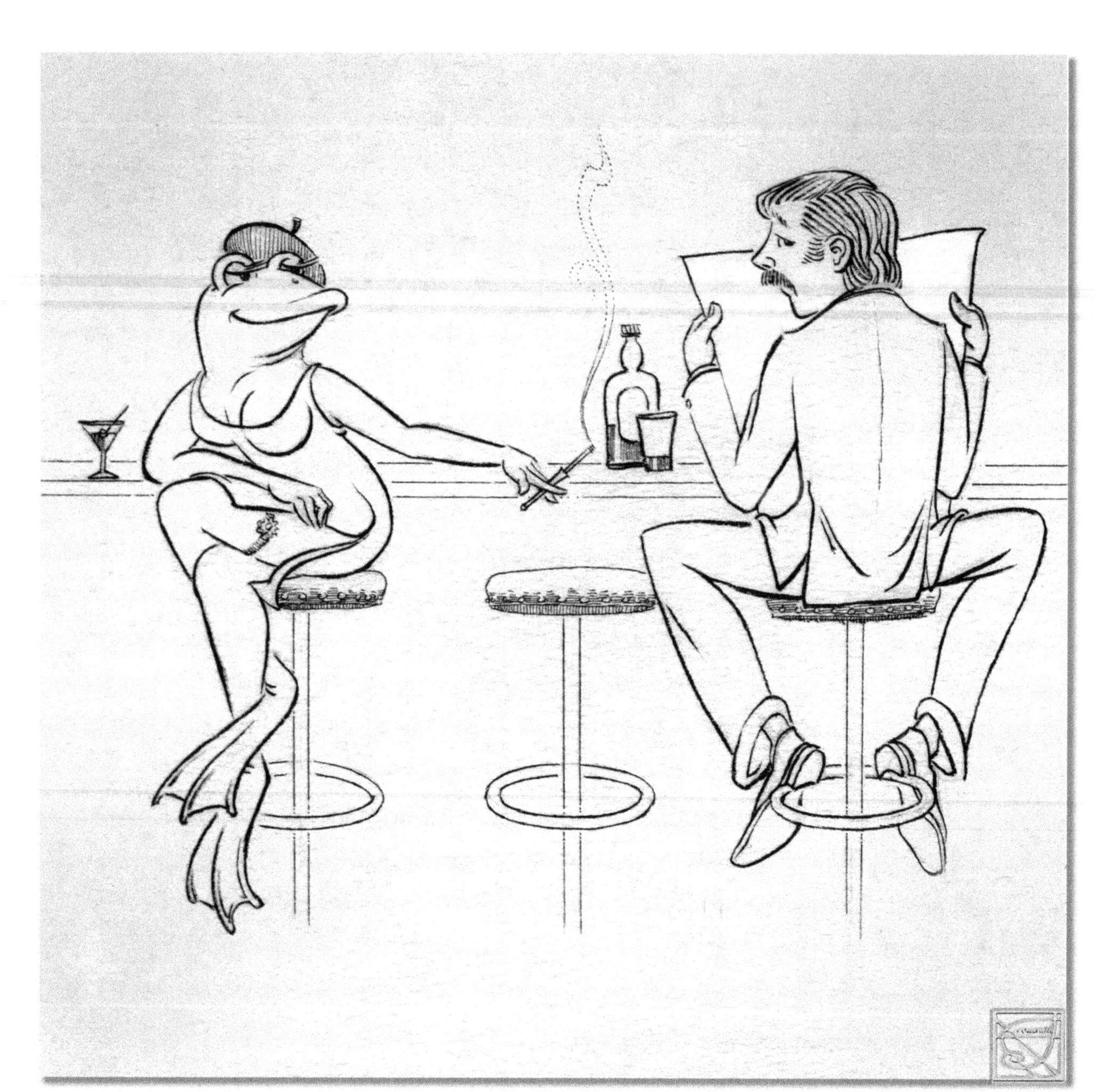

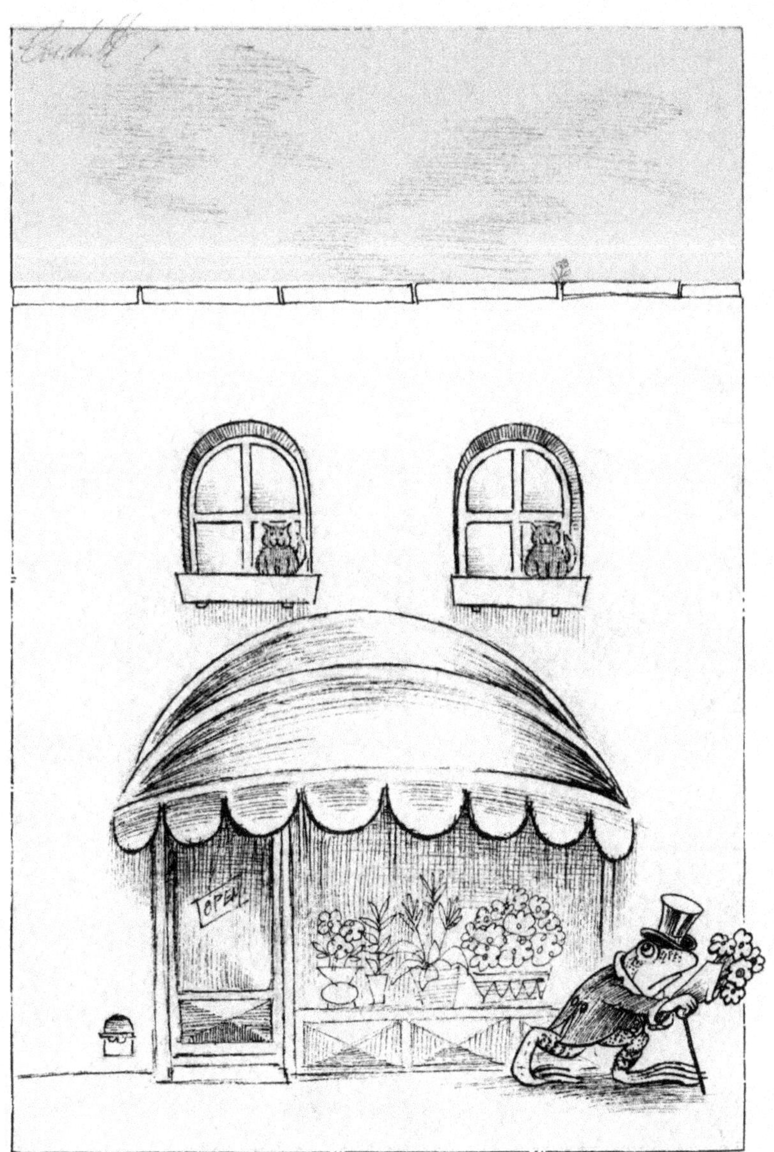

OPEN

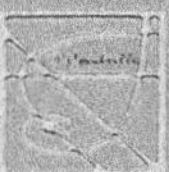

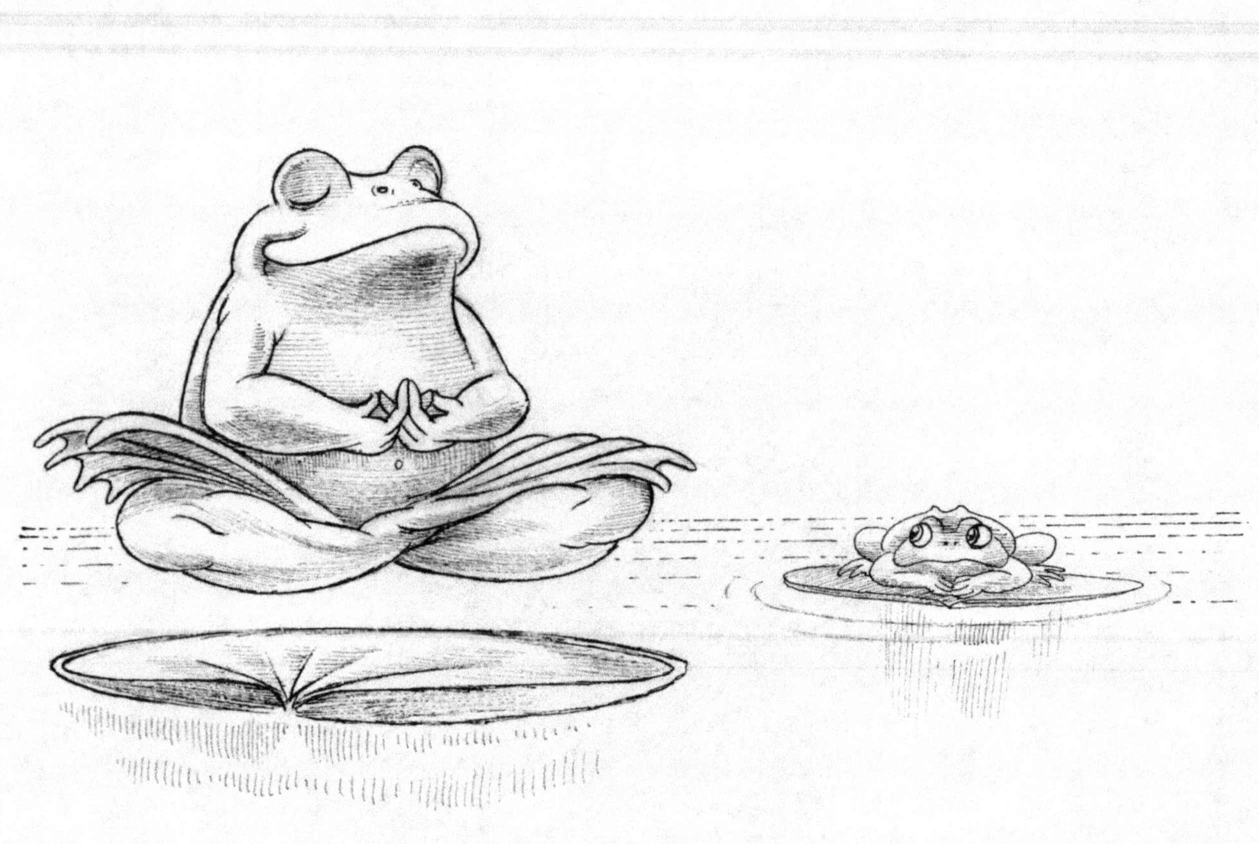

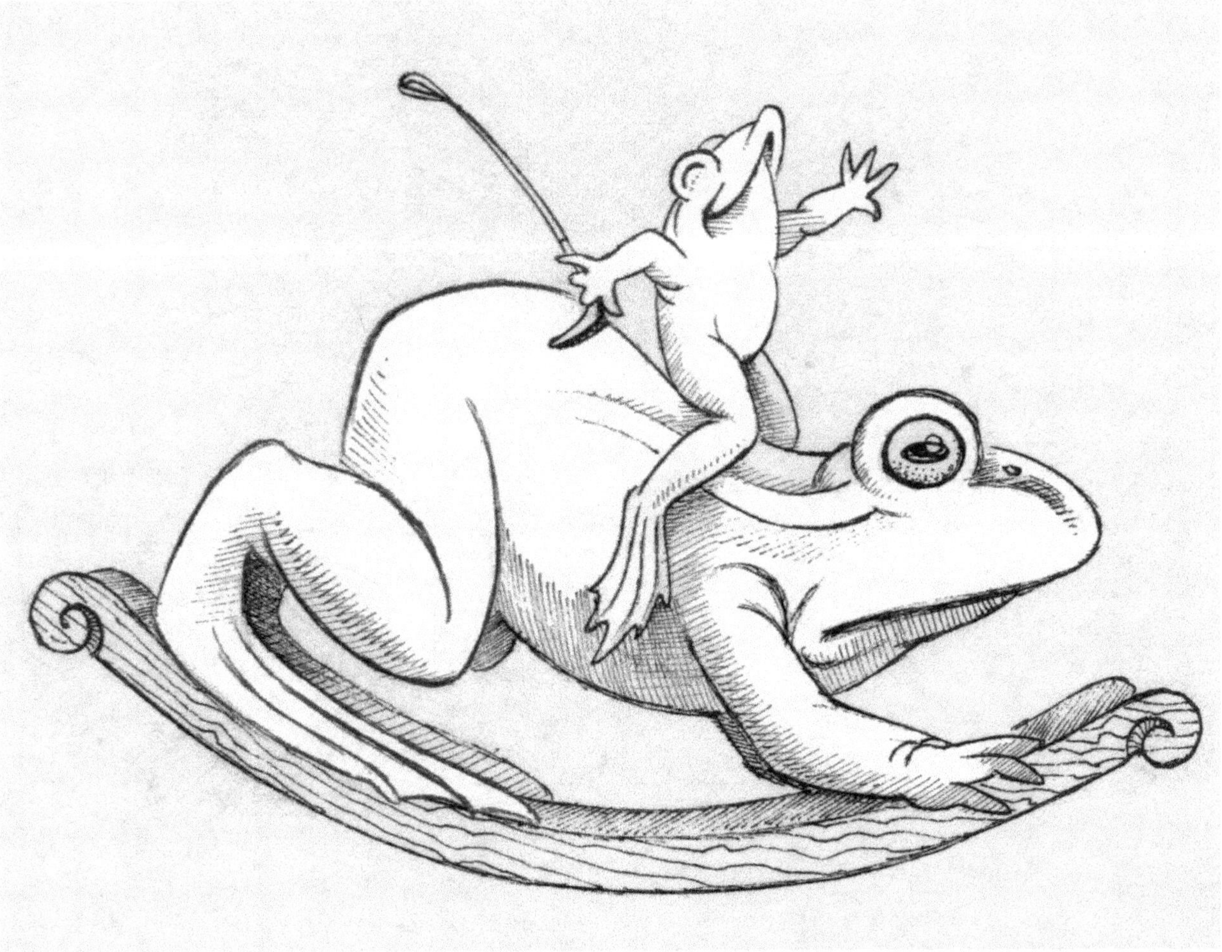

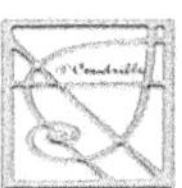

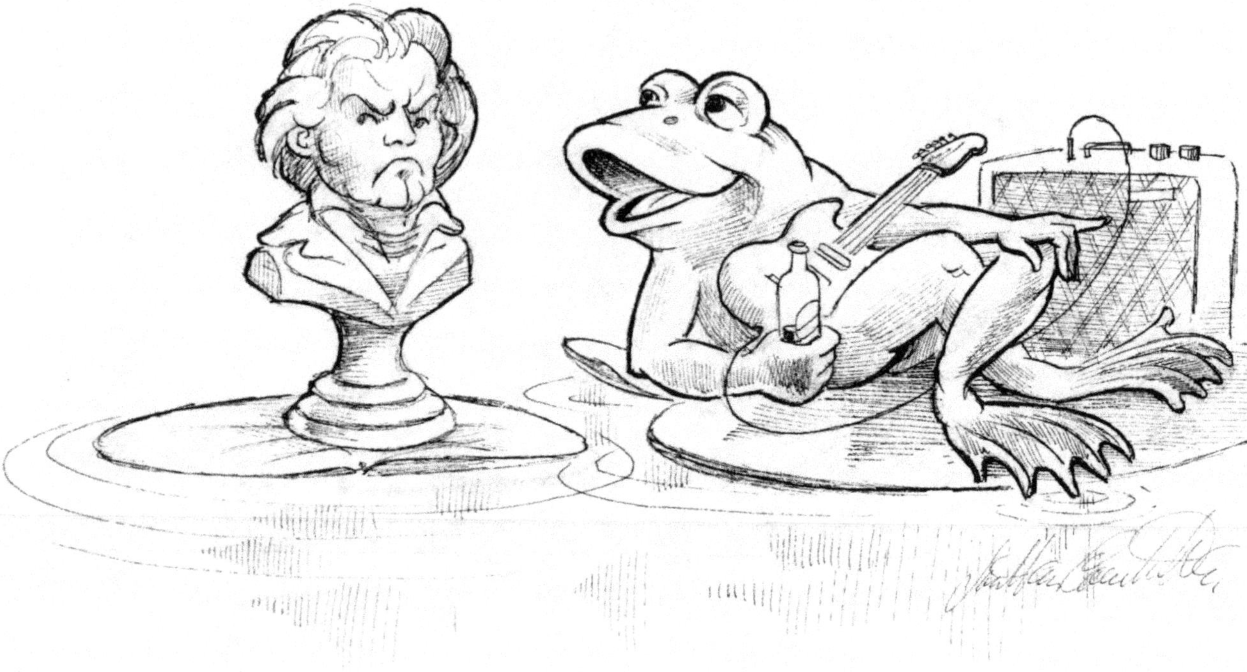

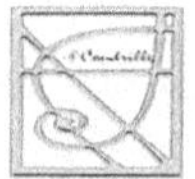

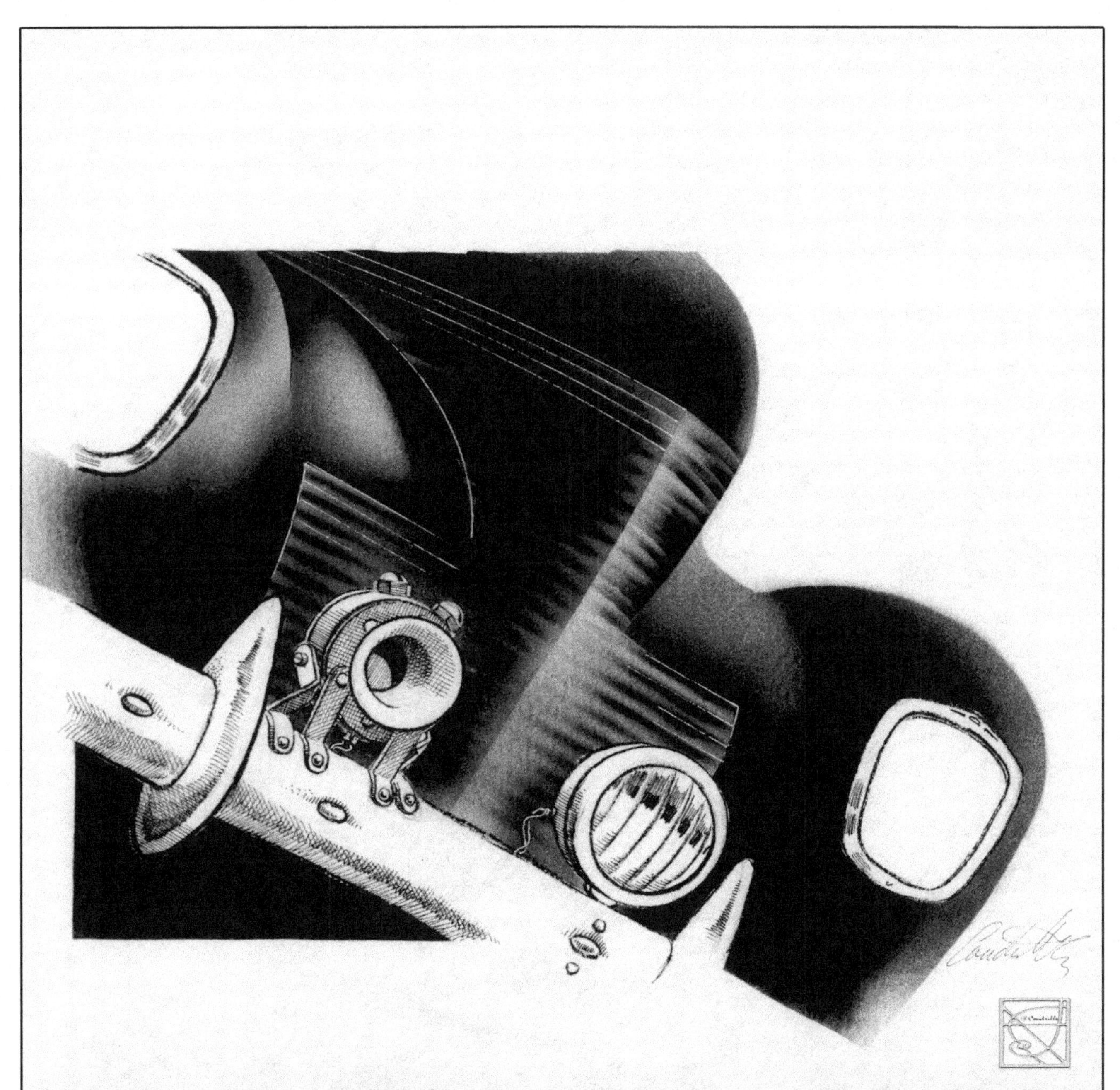

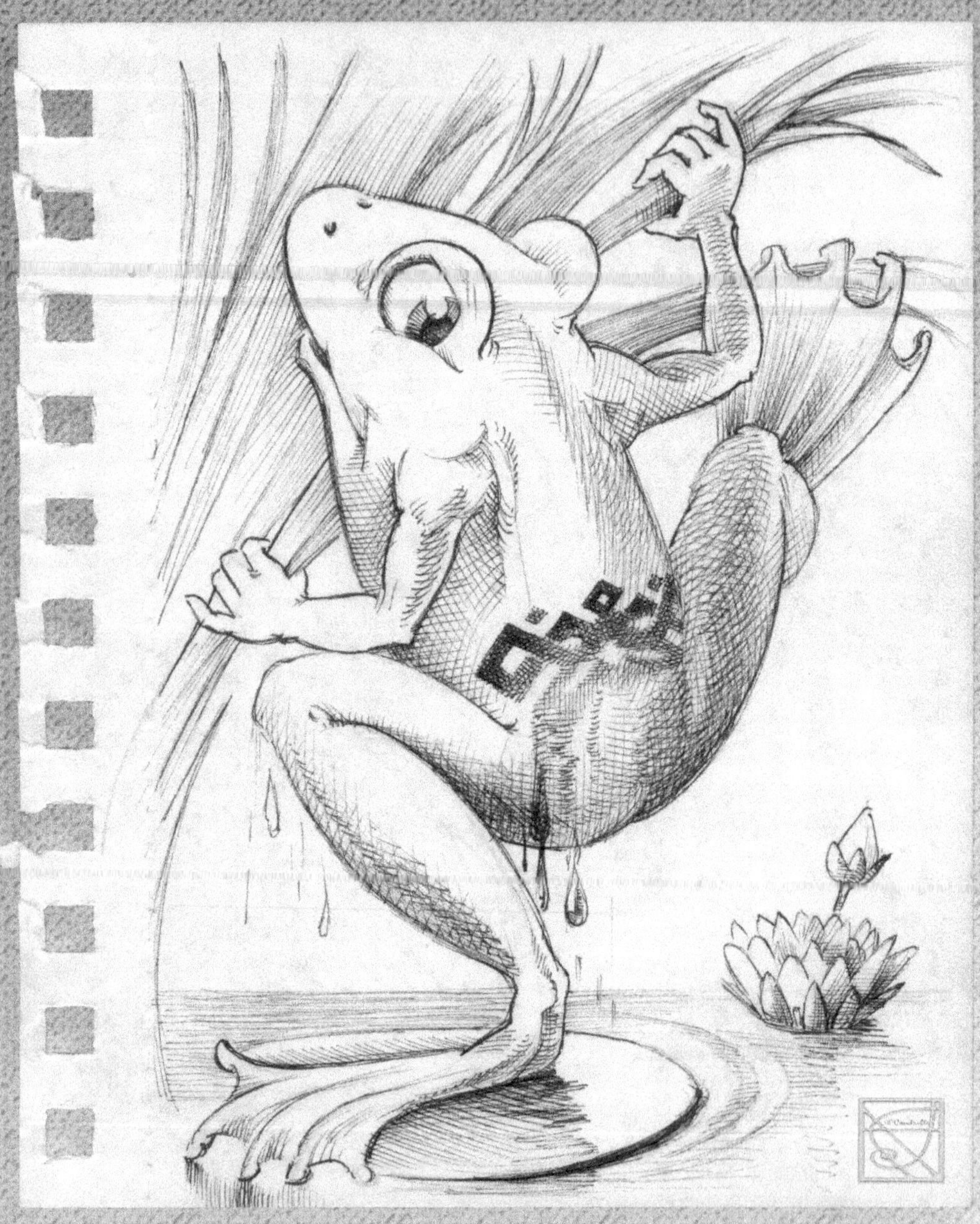

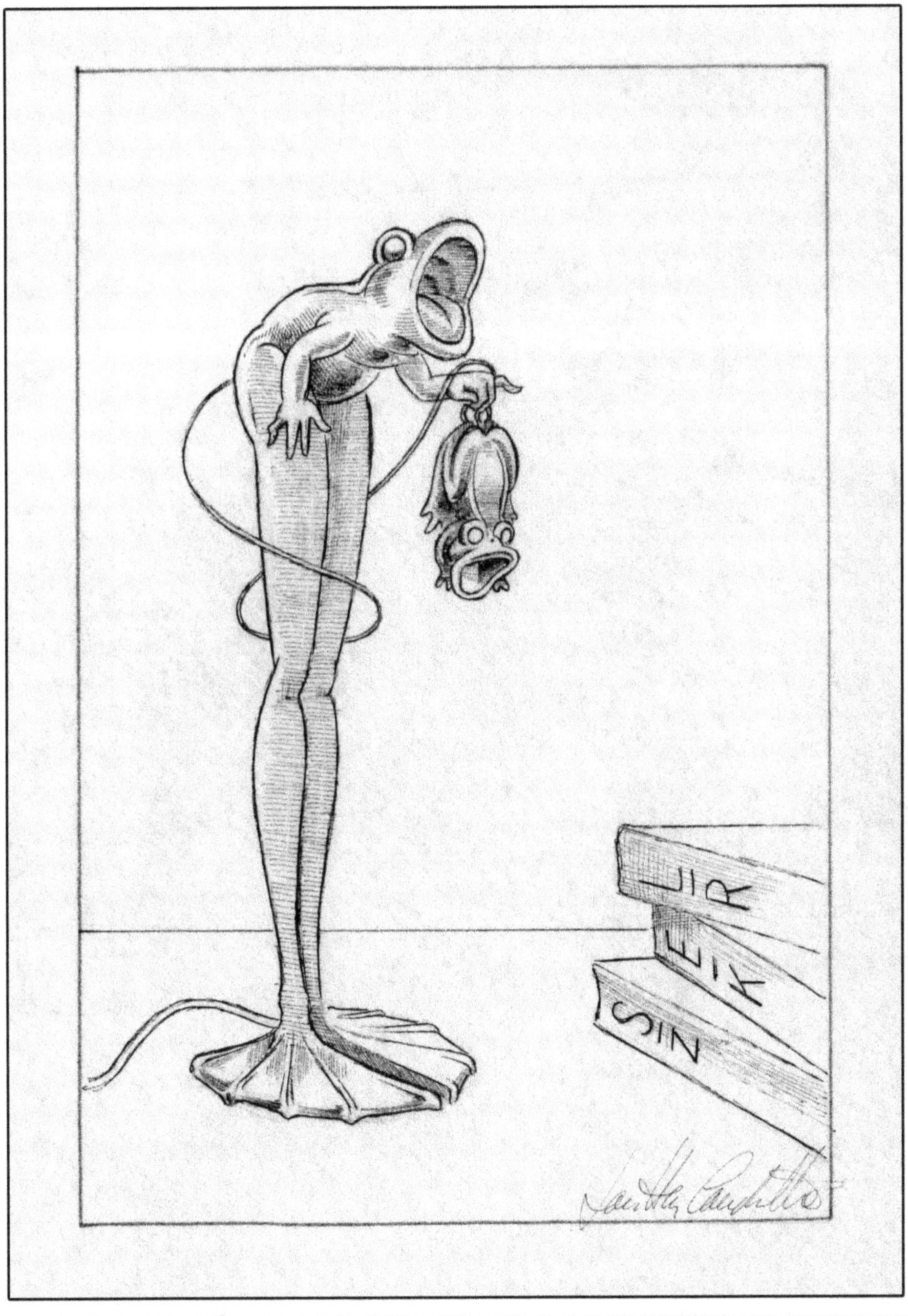

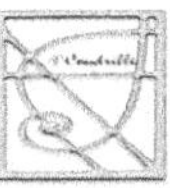
LIR
EIK
SIN

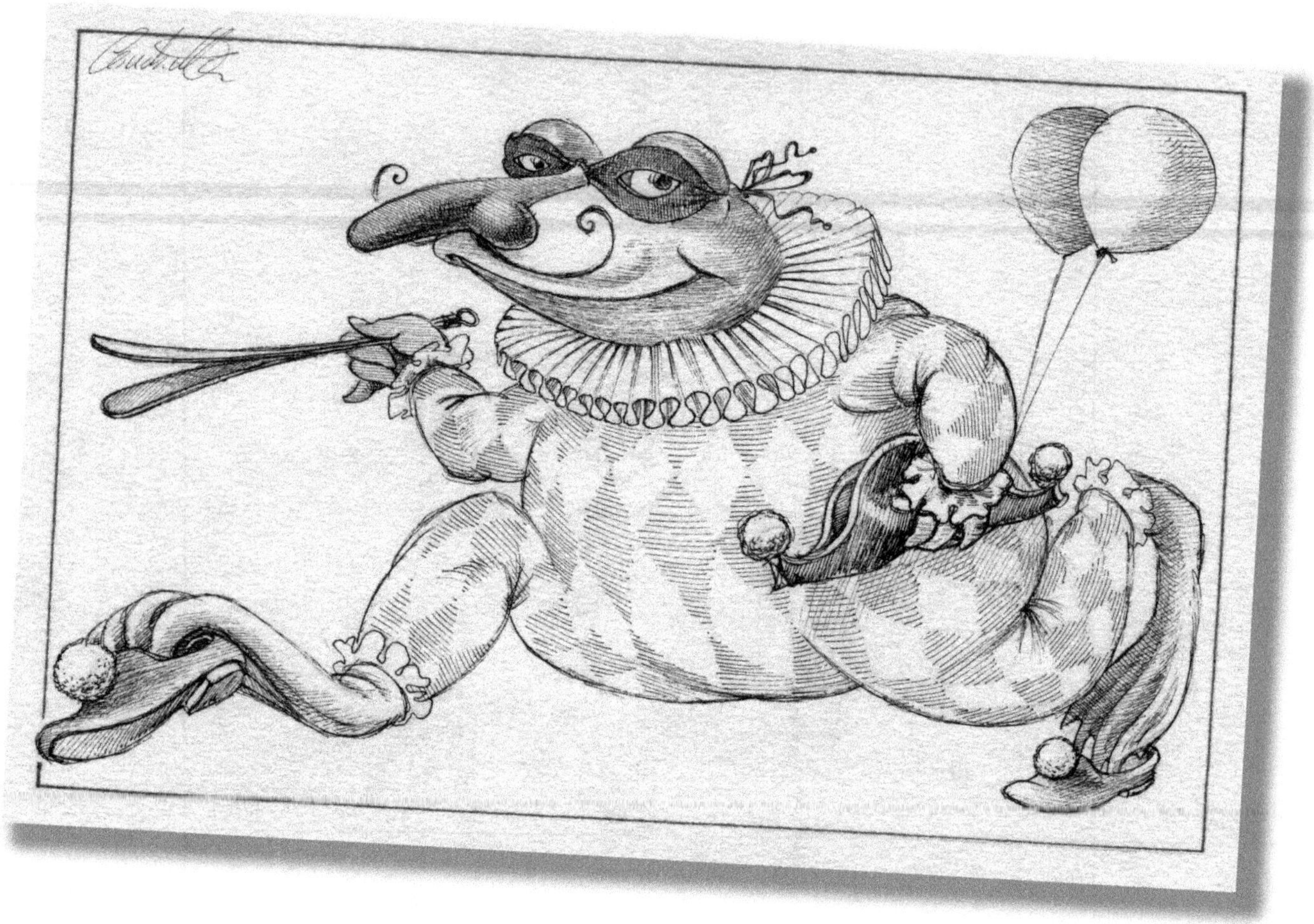

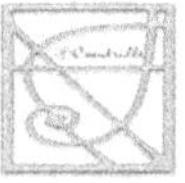

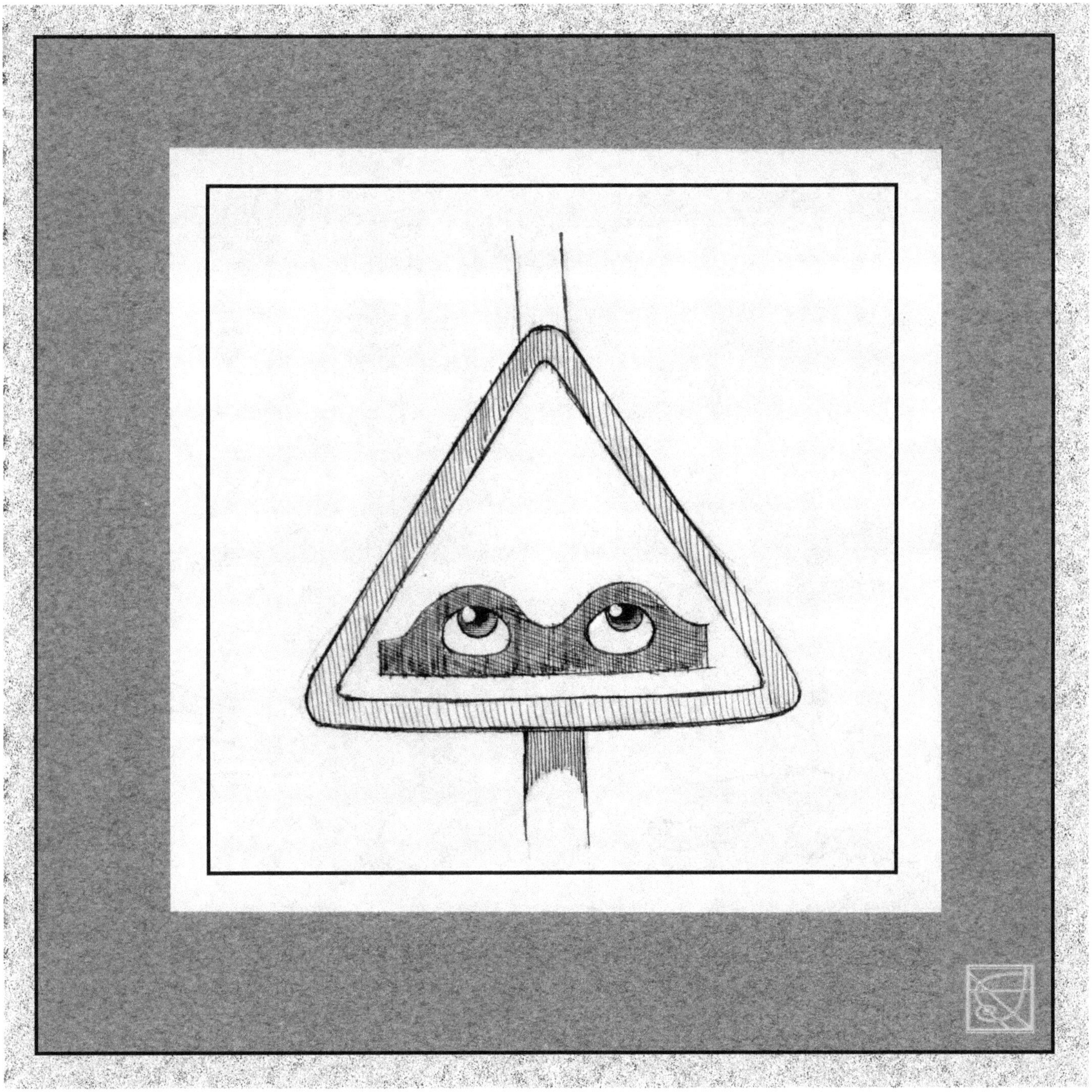

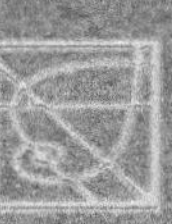

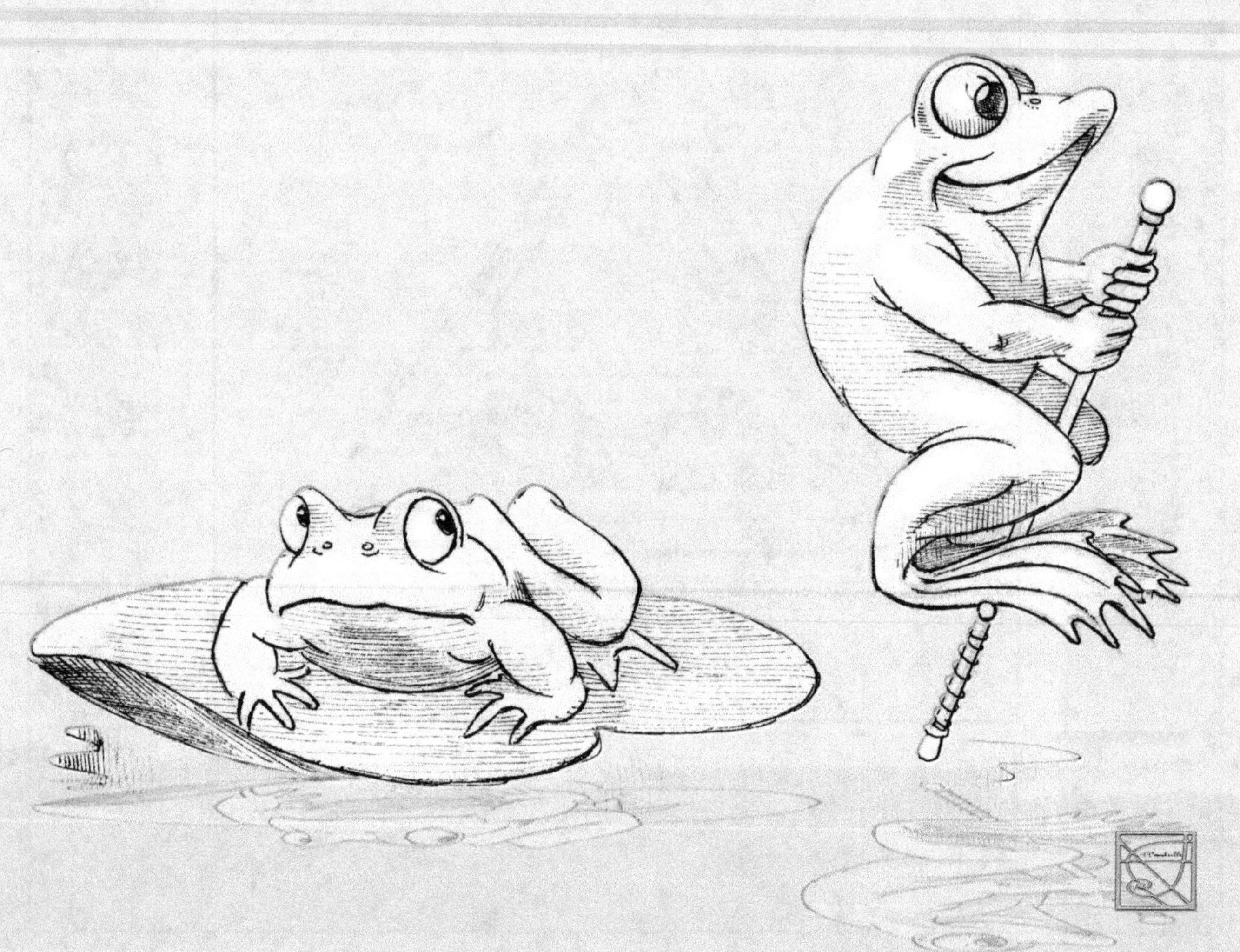

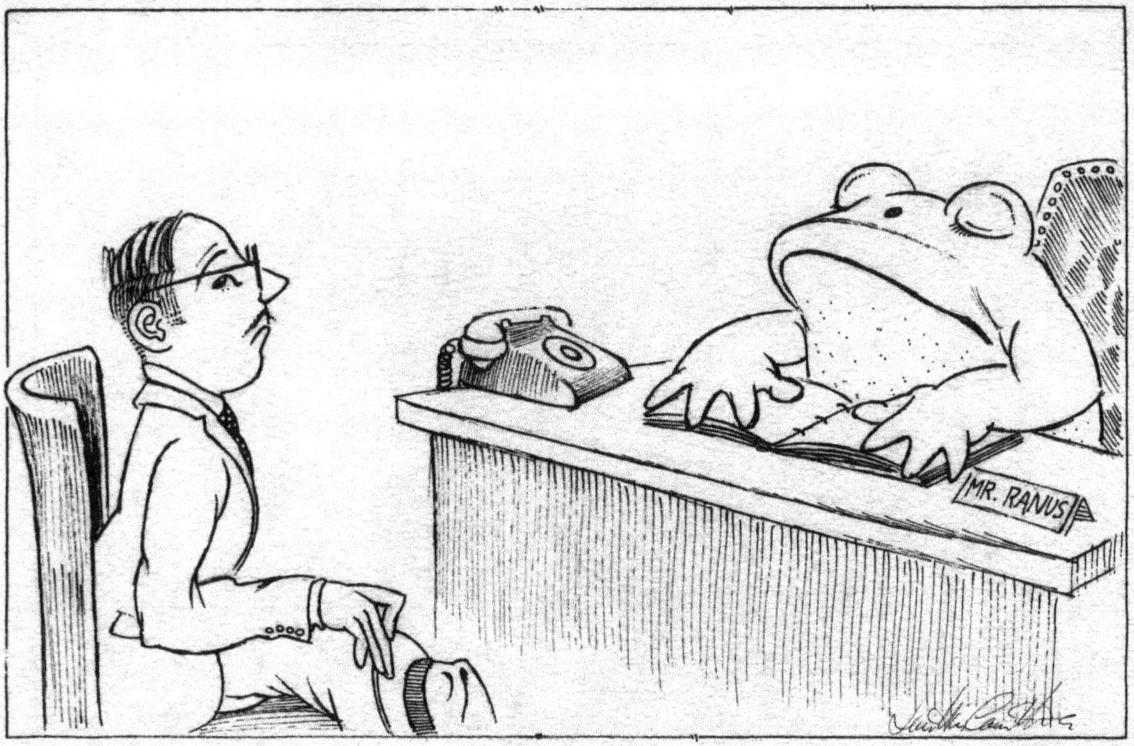

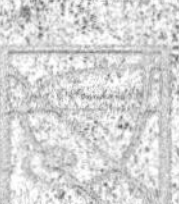

MR. RANUS

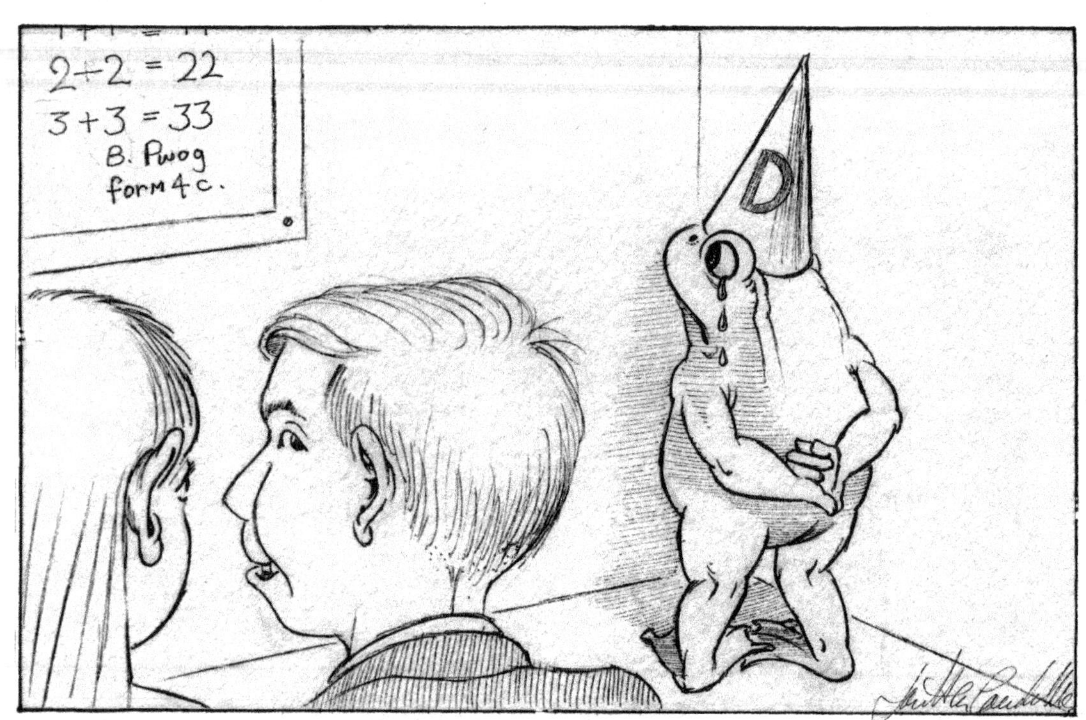

2+2 = 22
3+3 = 33
B. Pwog
form 4c.
D

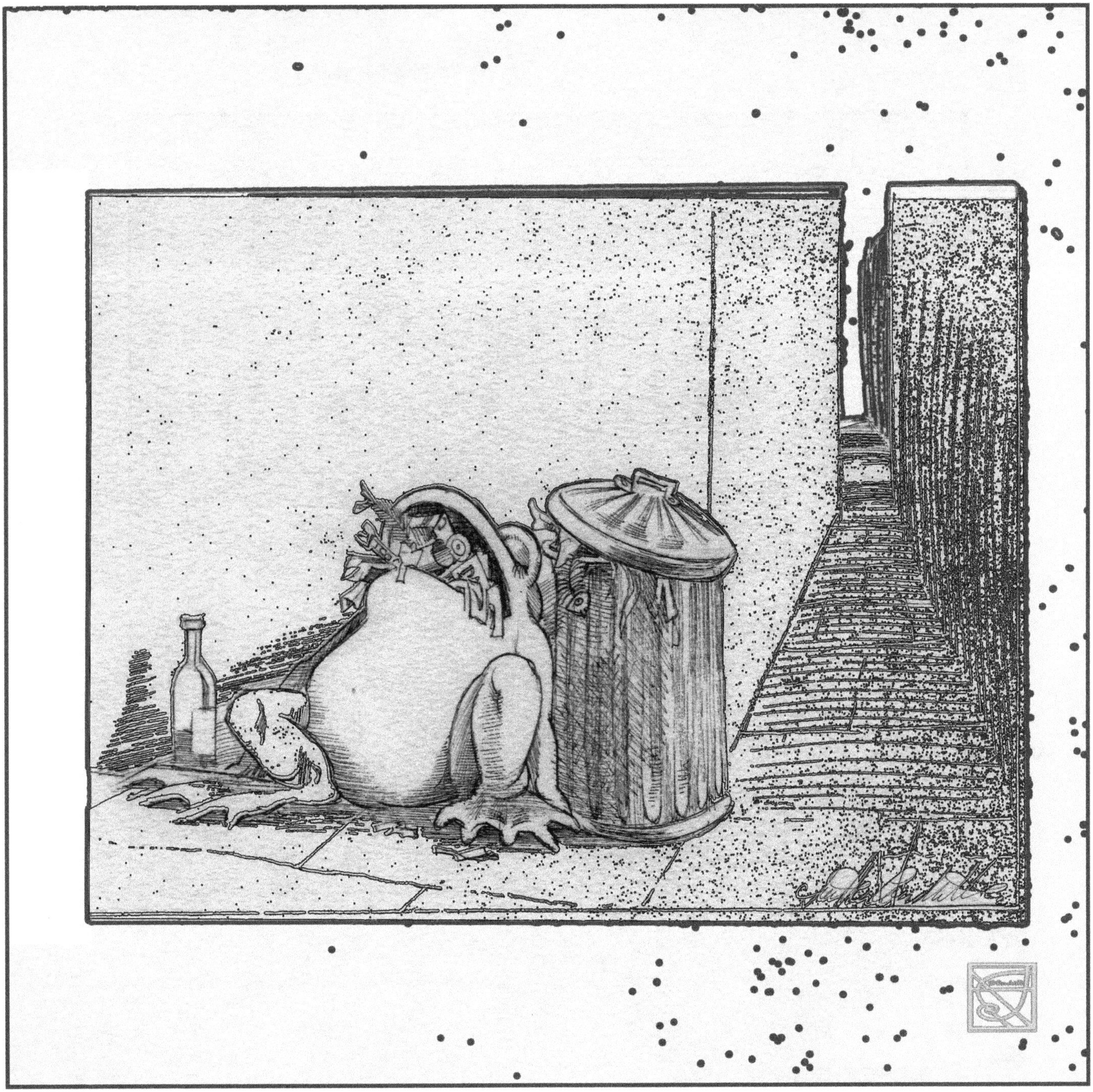

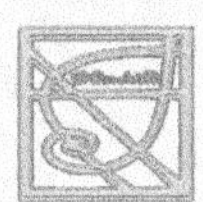

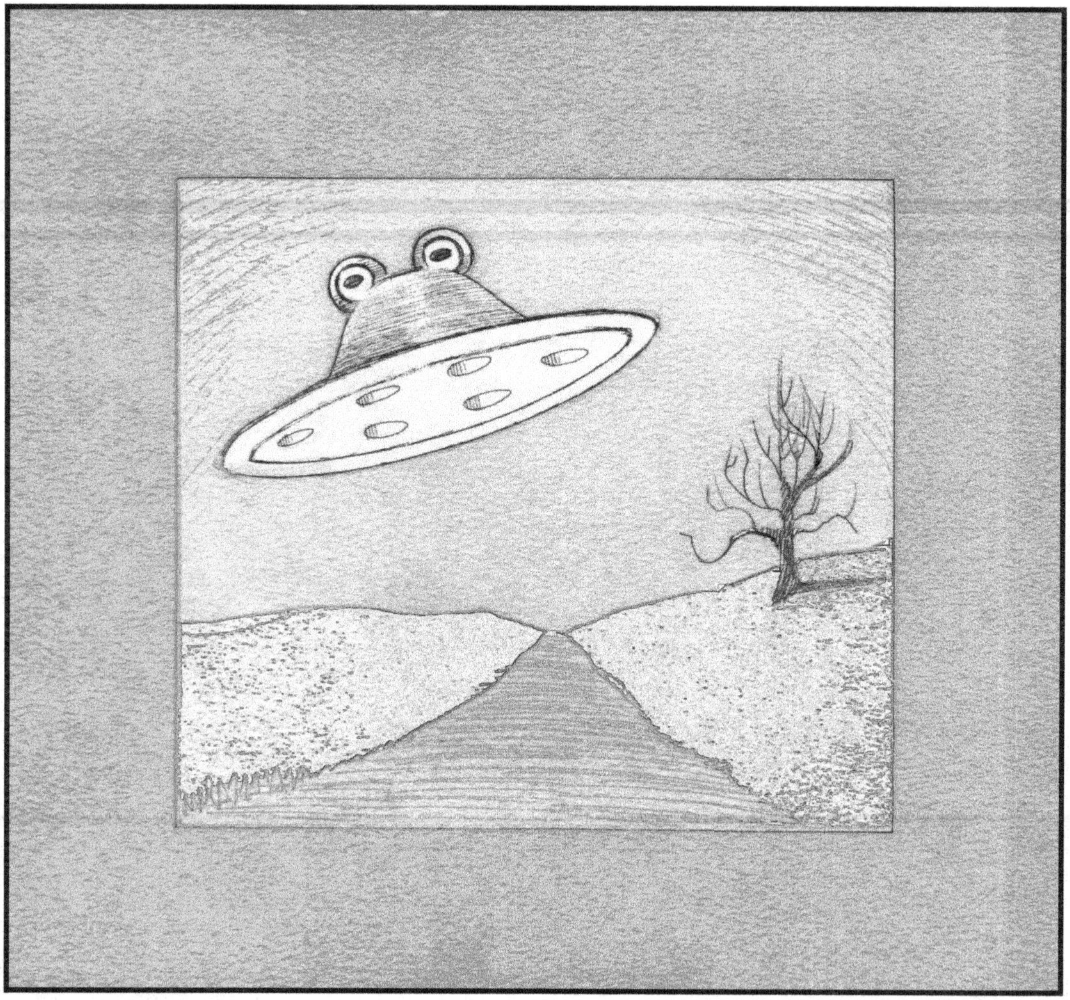

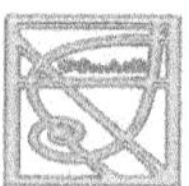

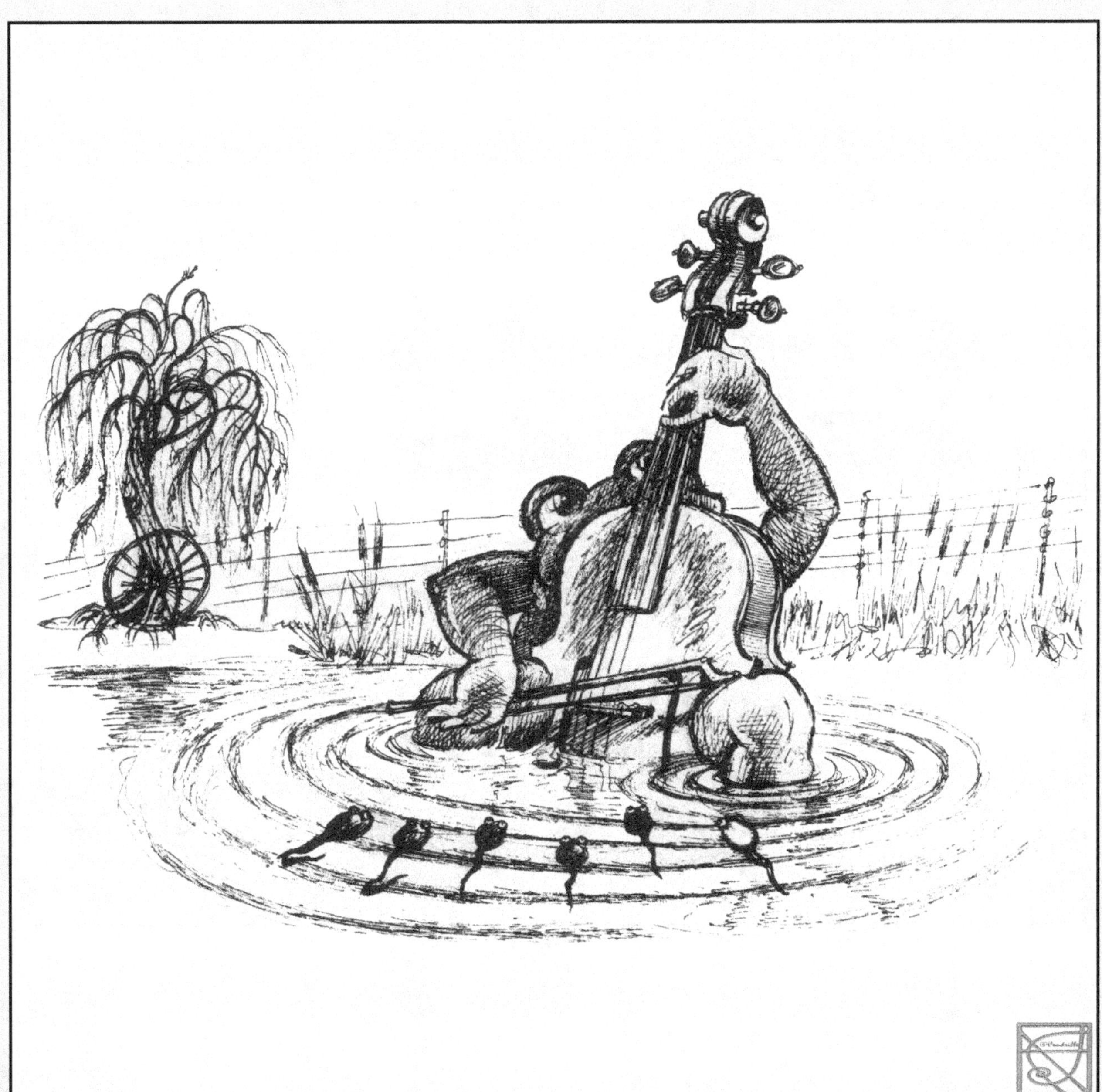

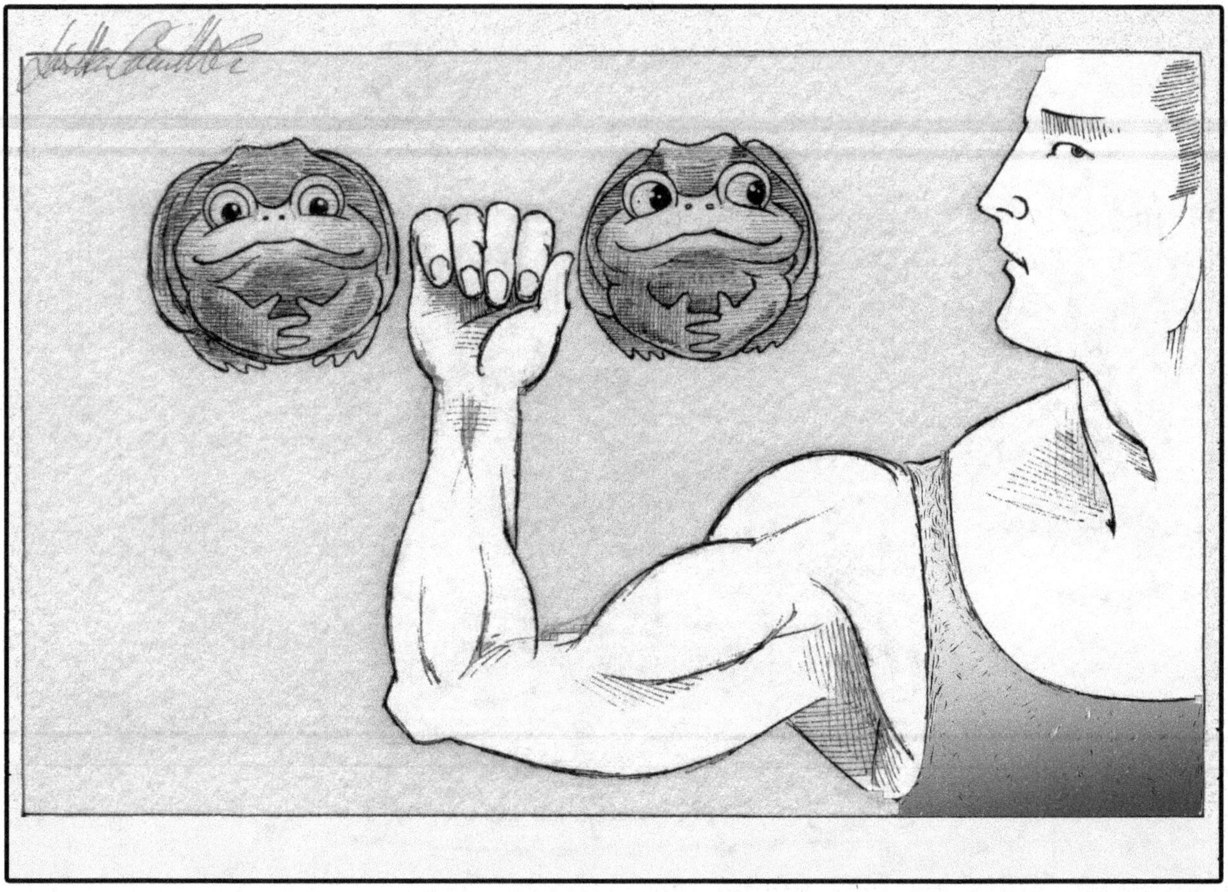

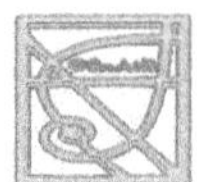

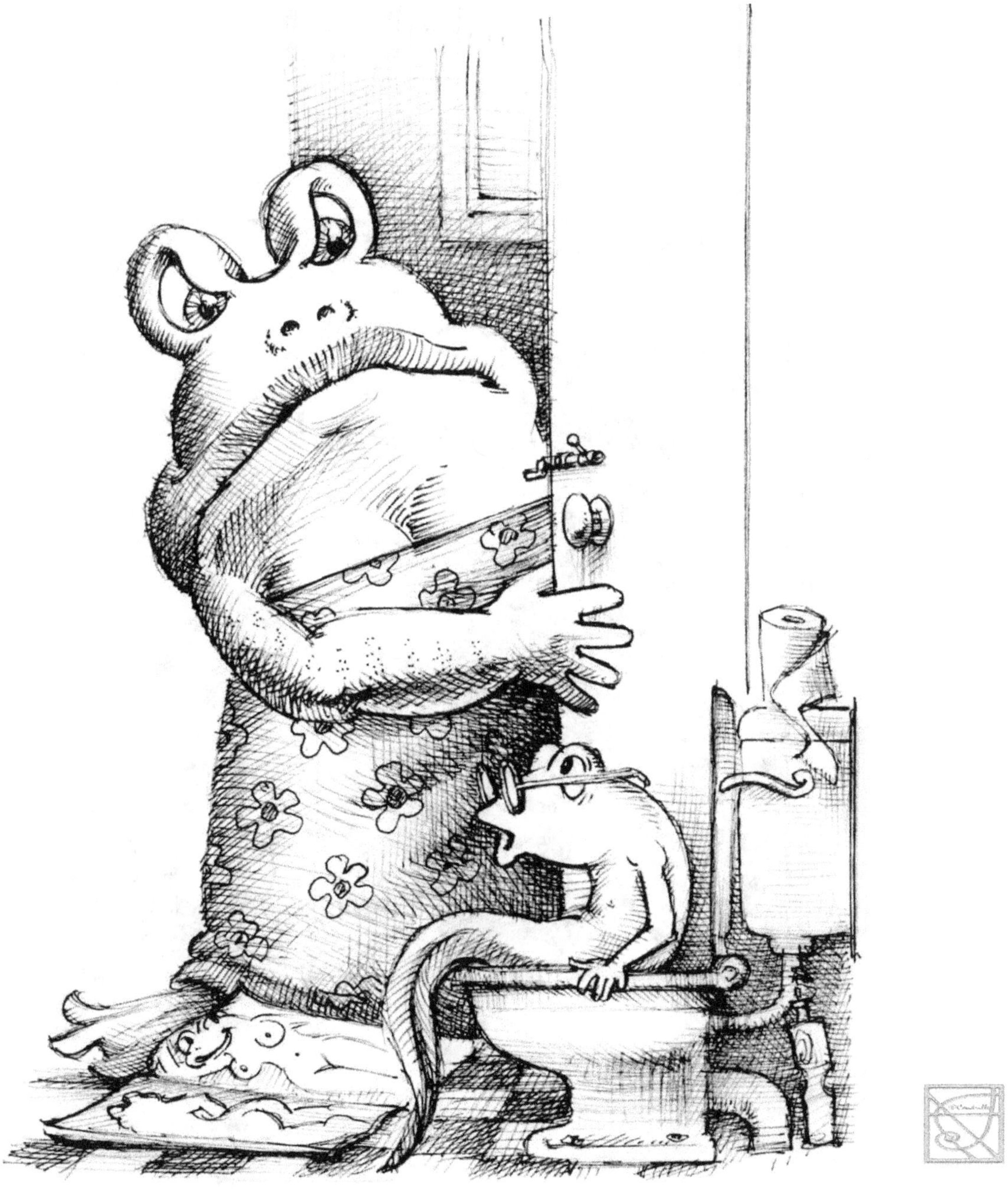

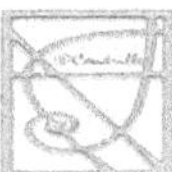

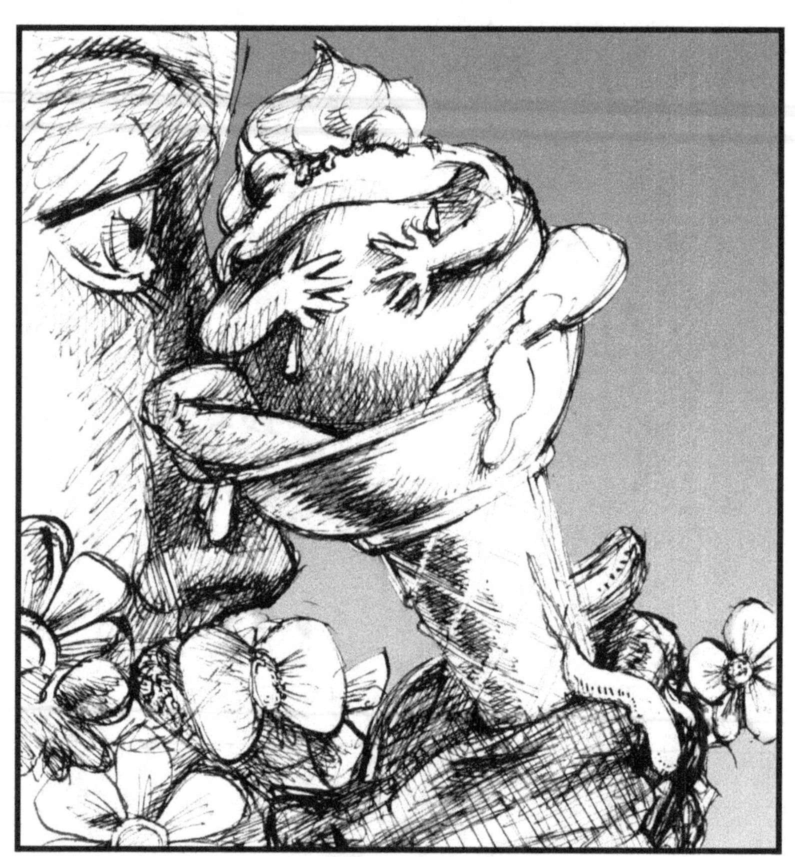

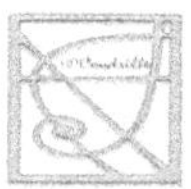

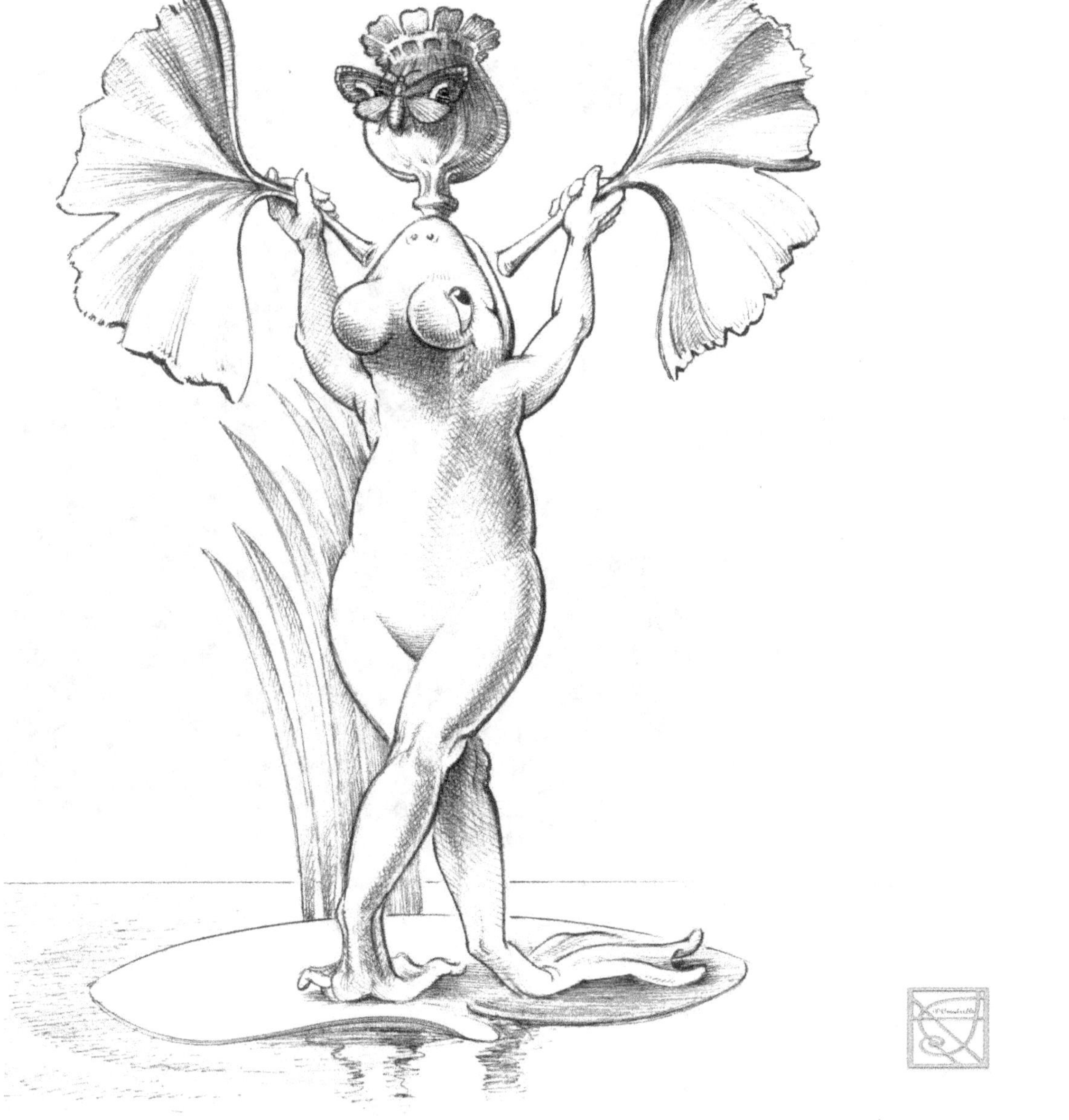

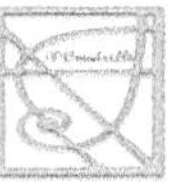

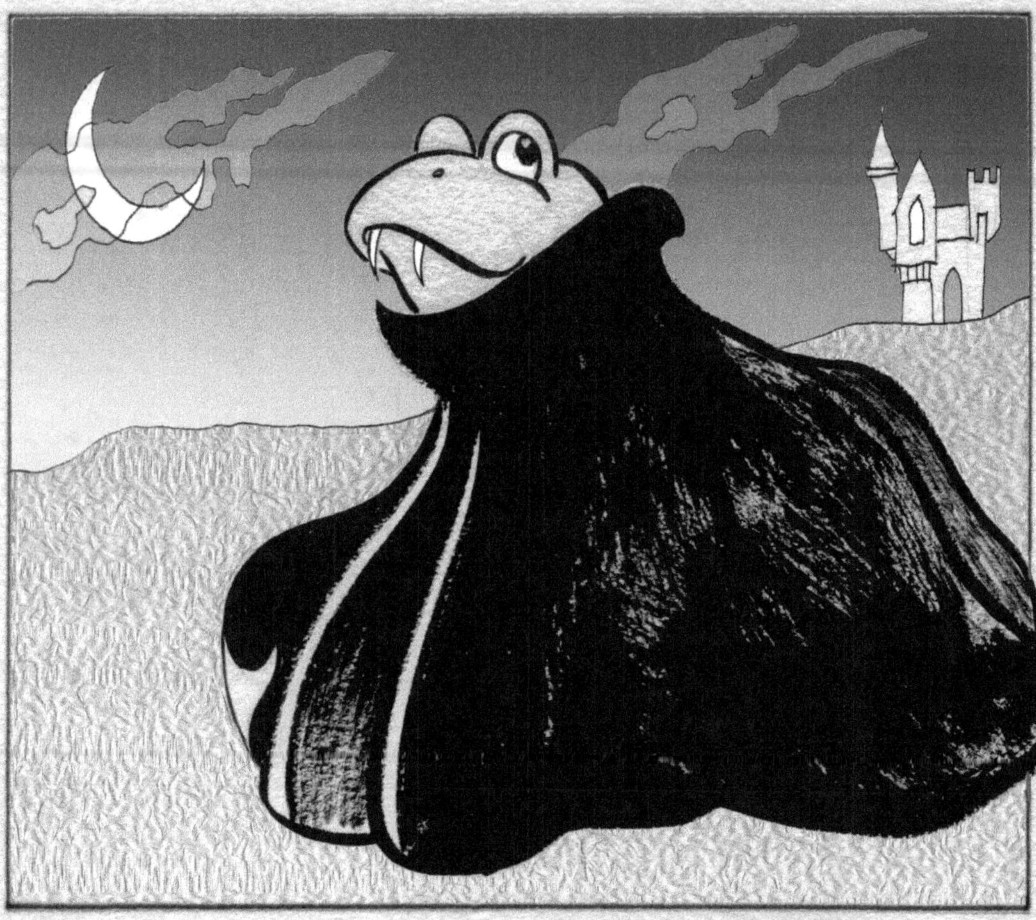

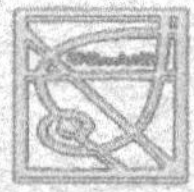

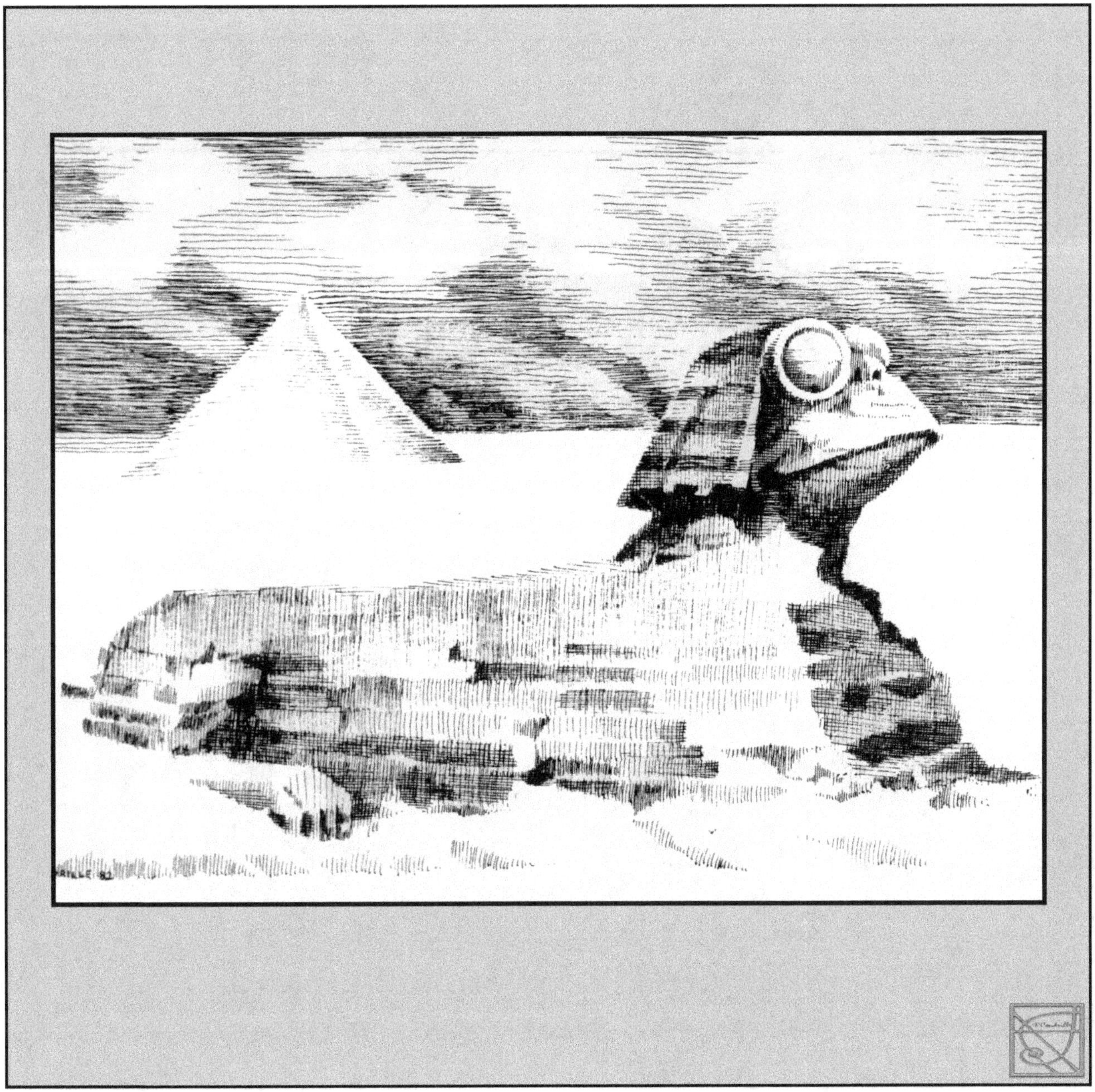

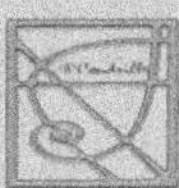

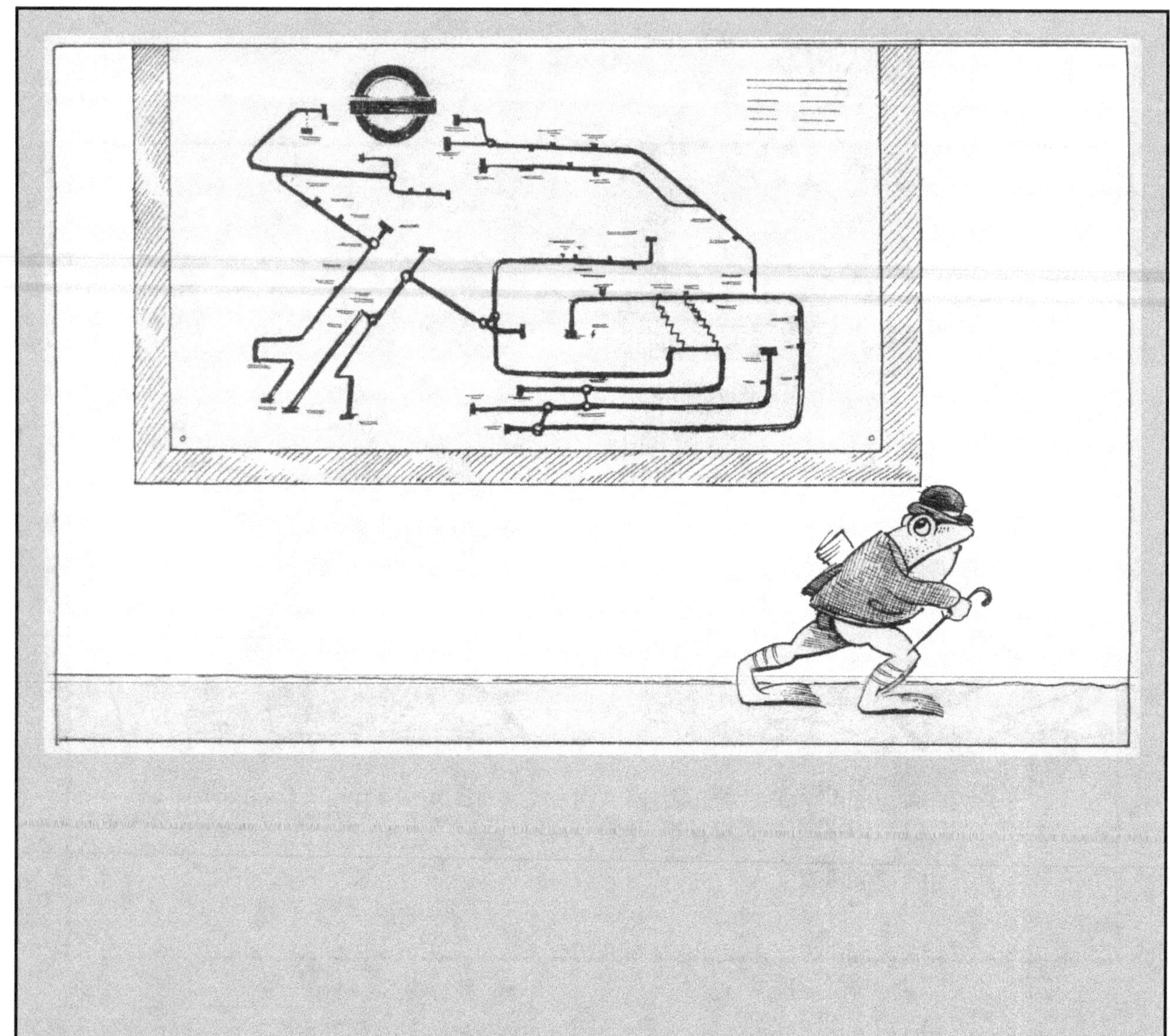

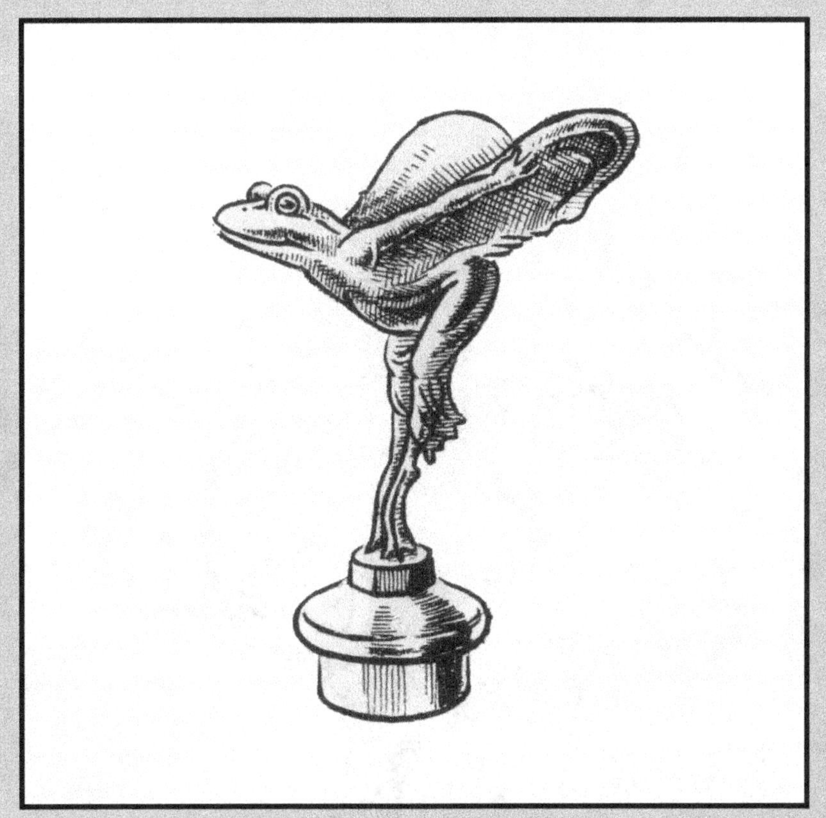

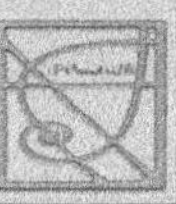

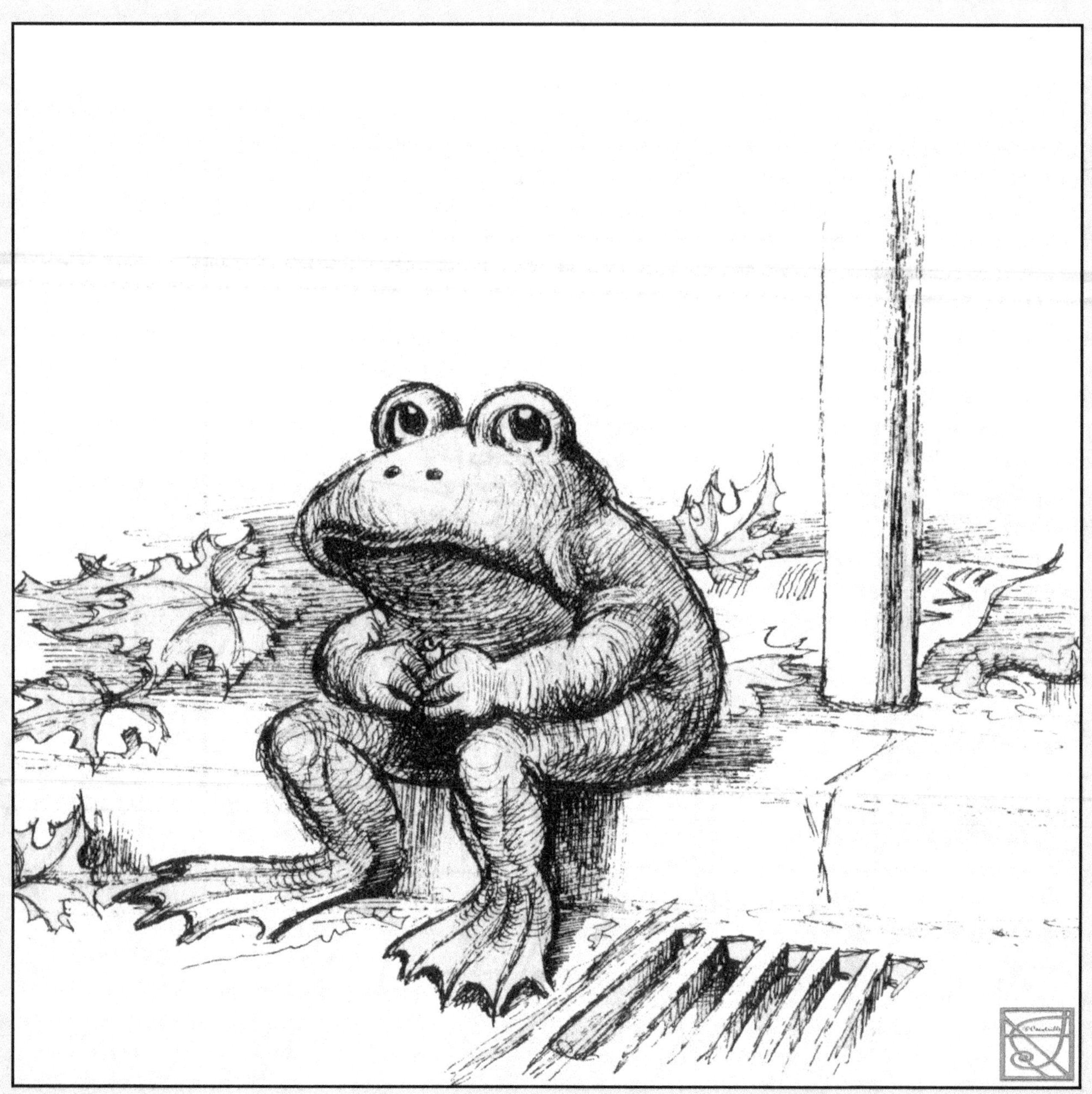

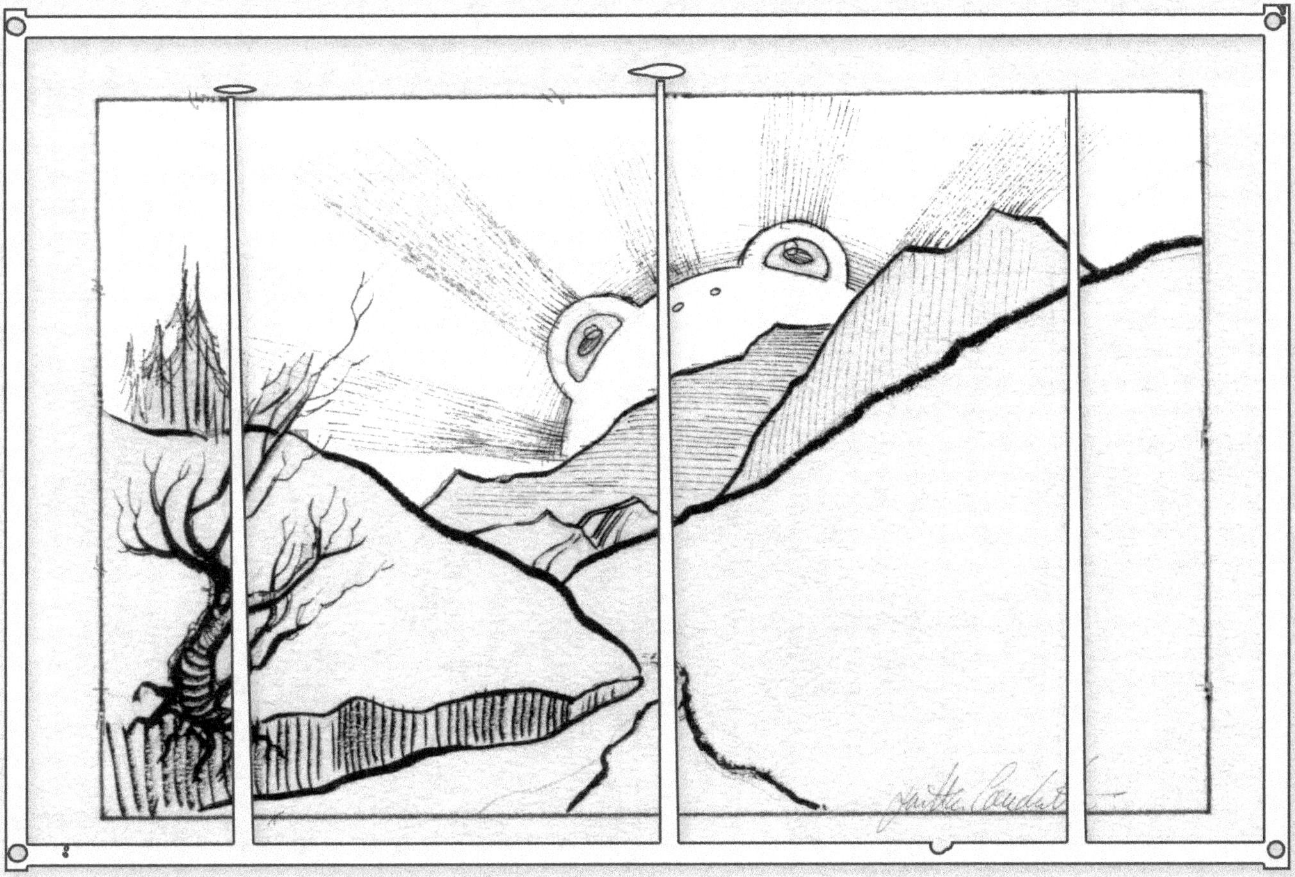

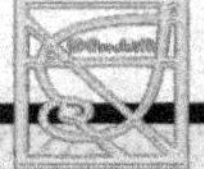

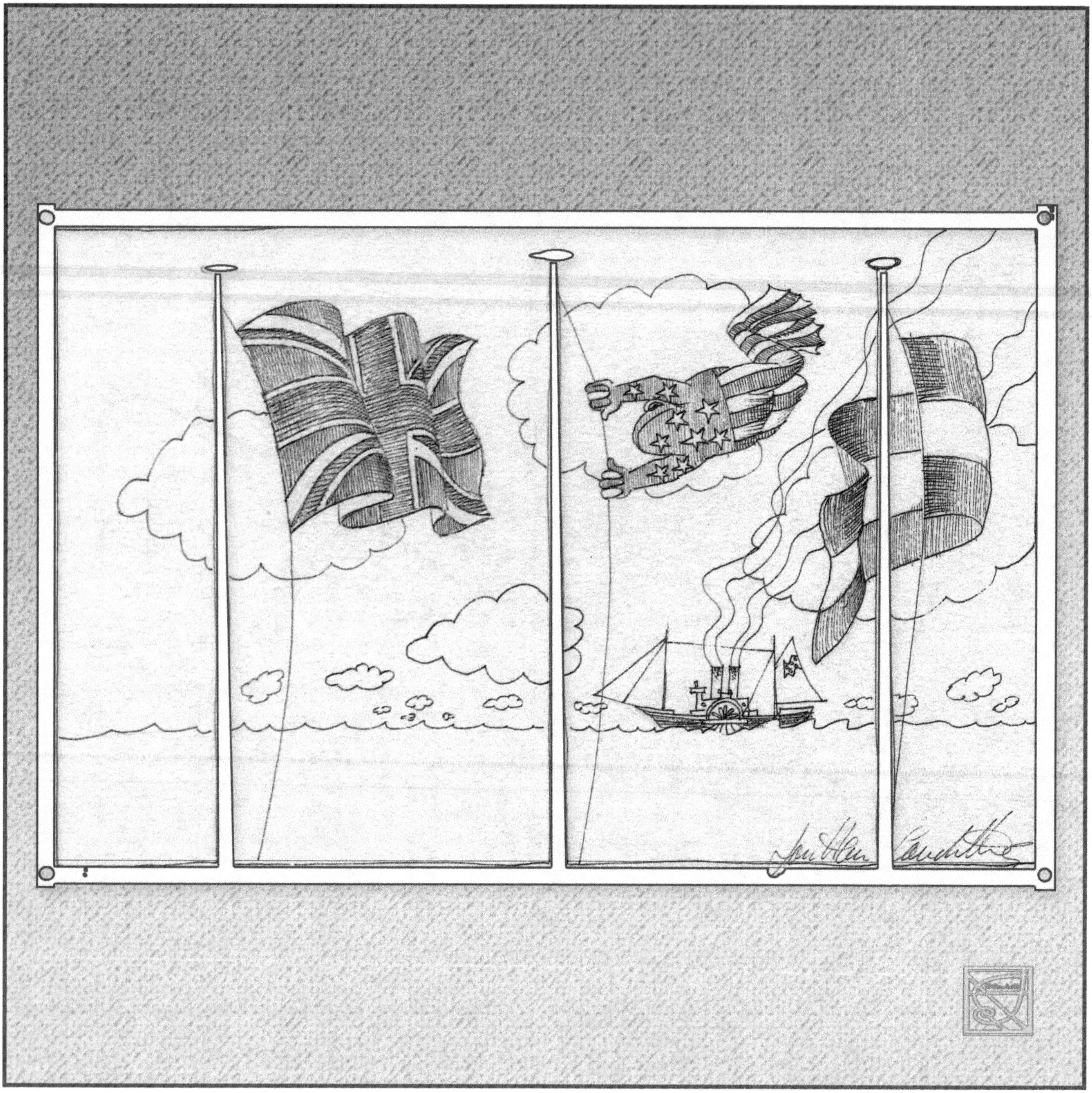

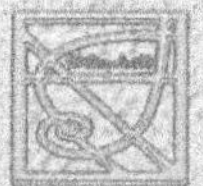

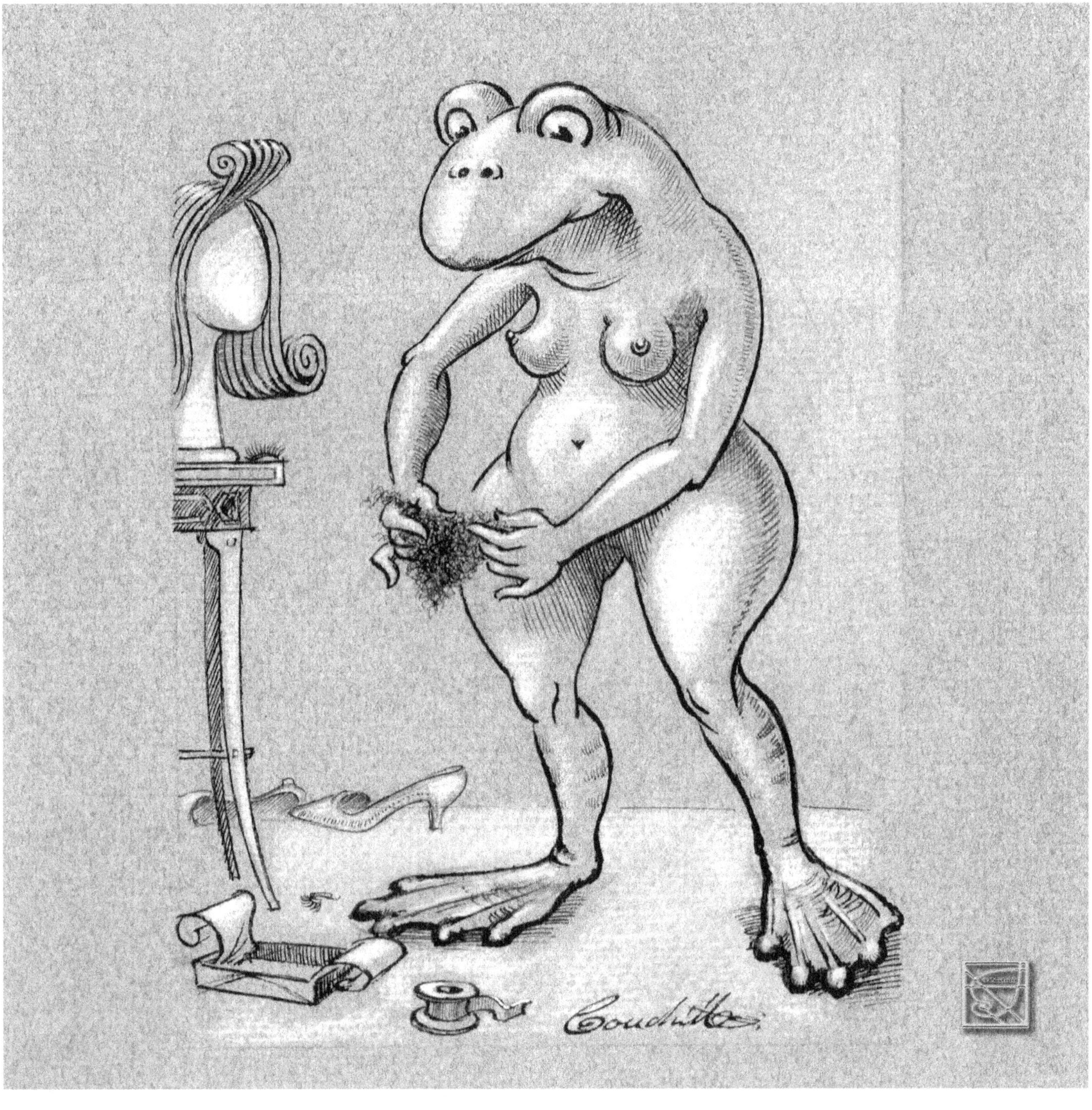

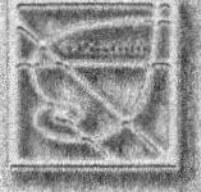

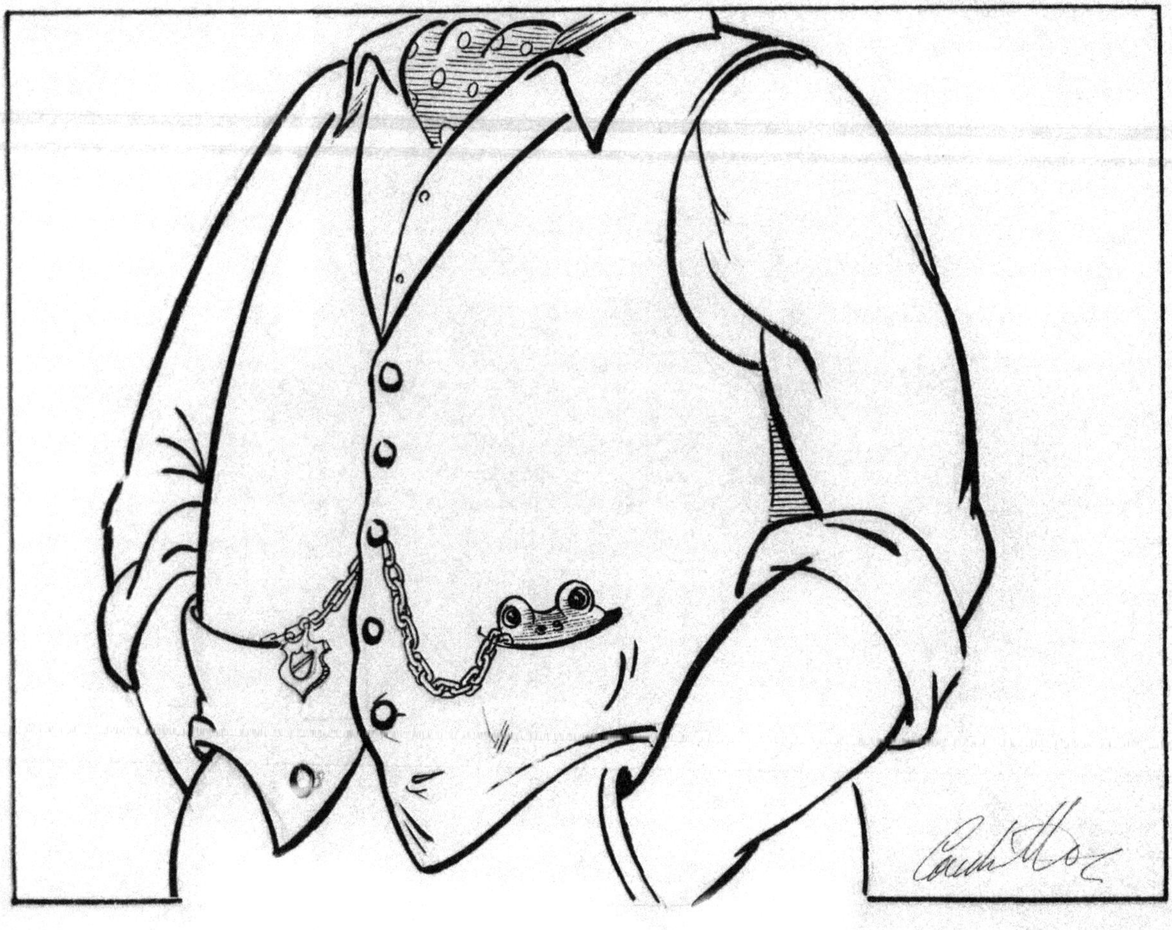

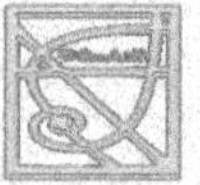

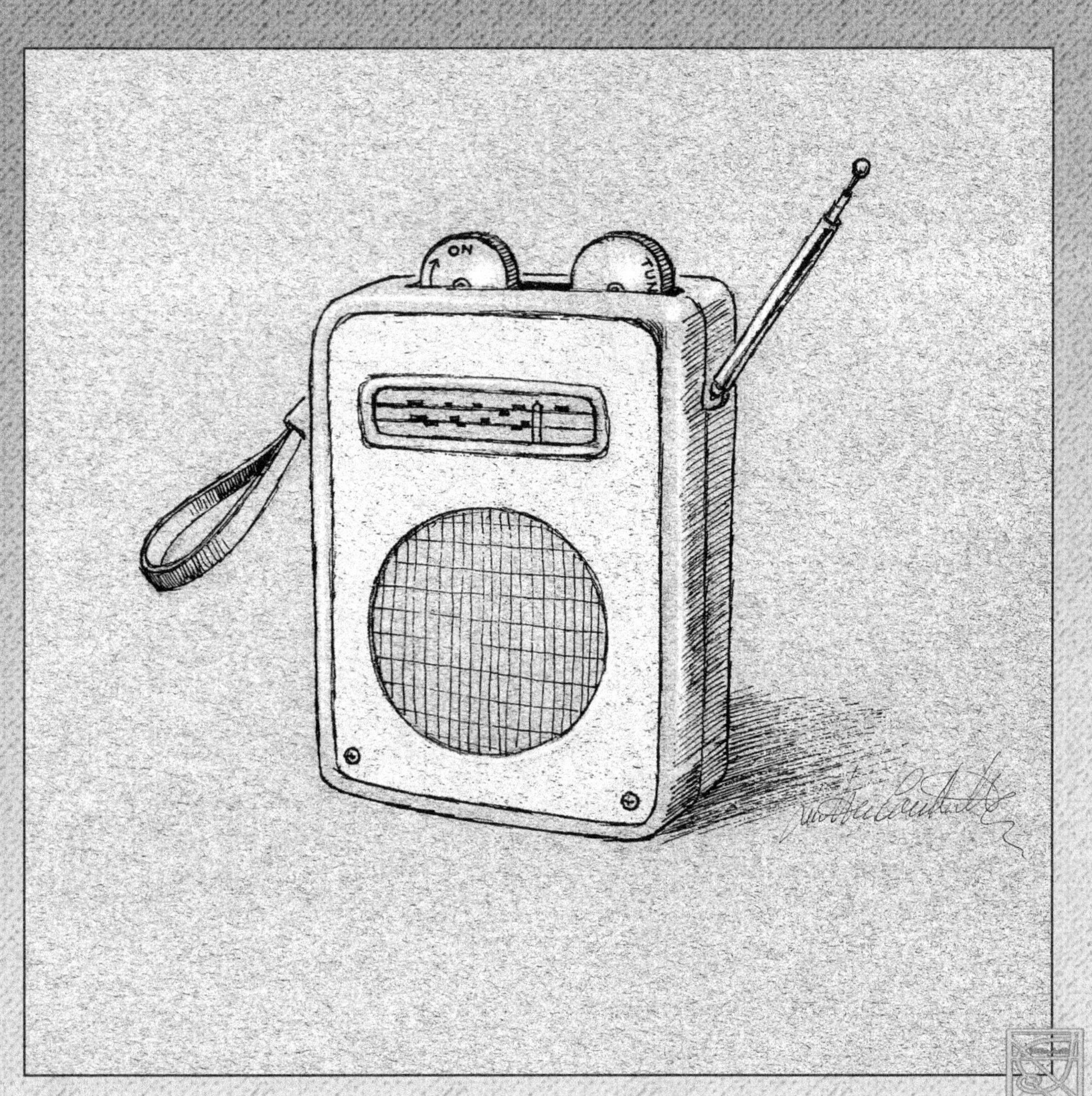

ON
TUN

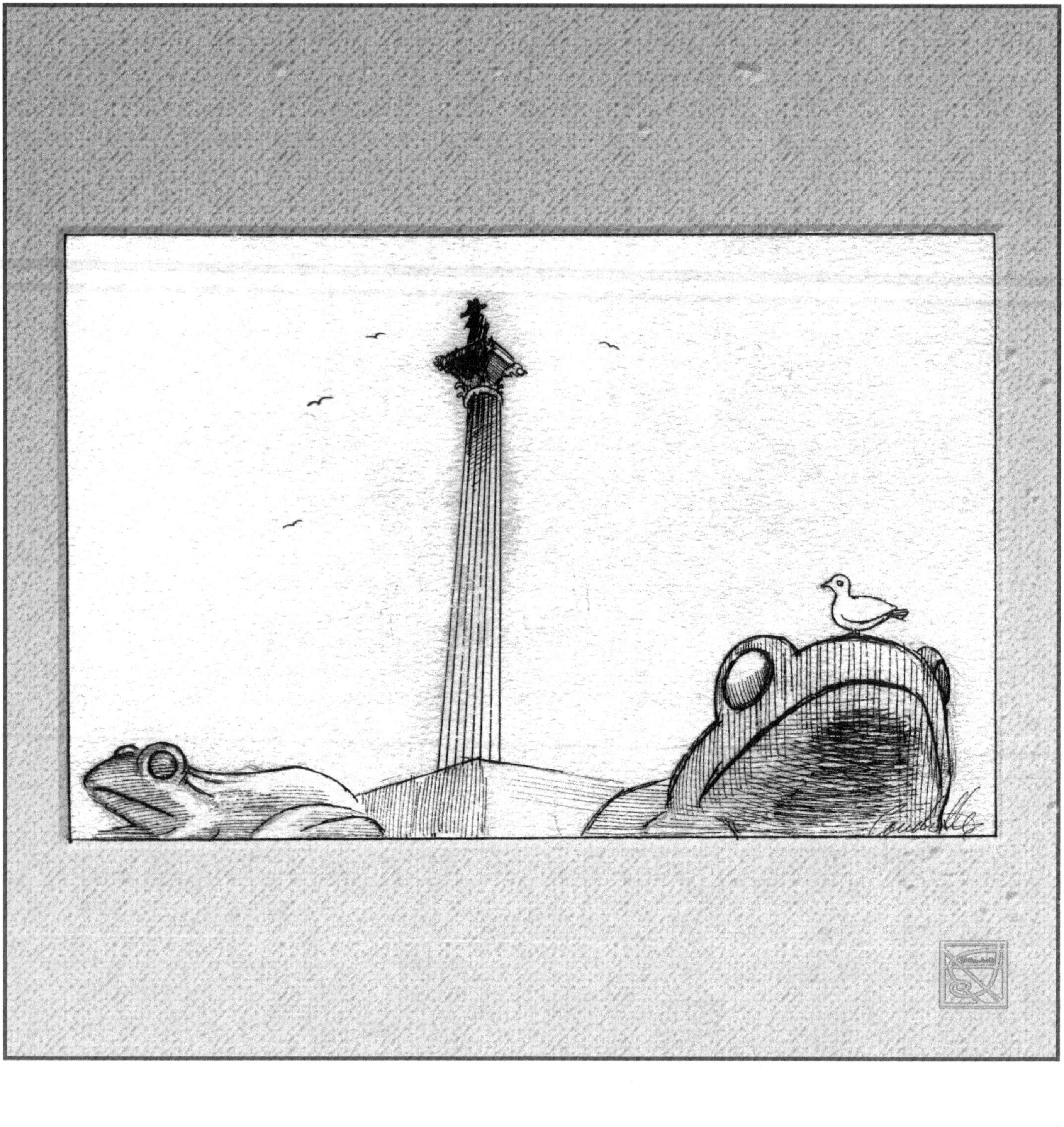

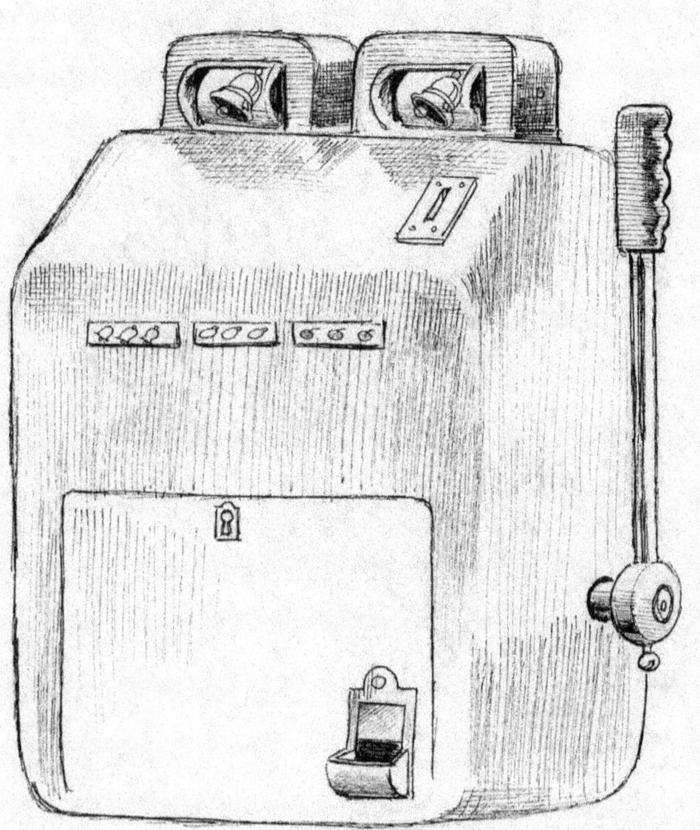
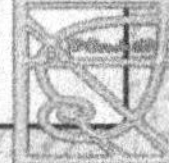

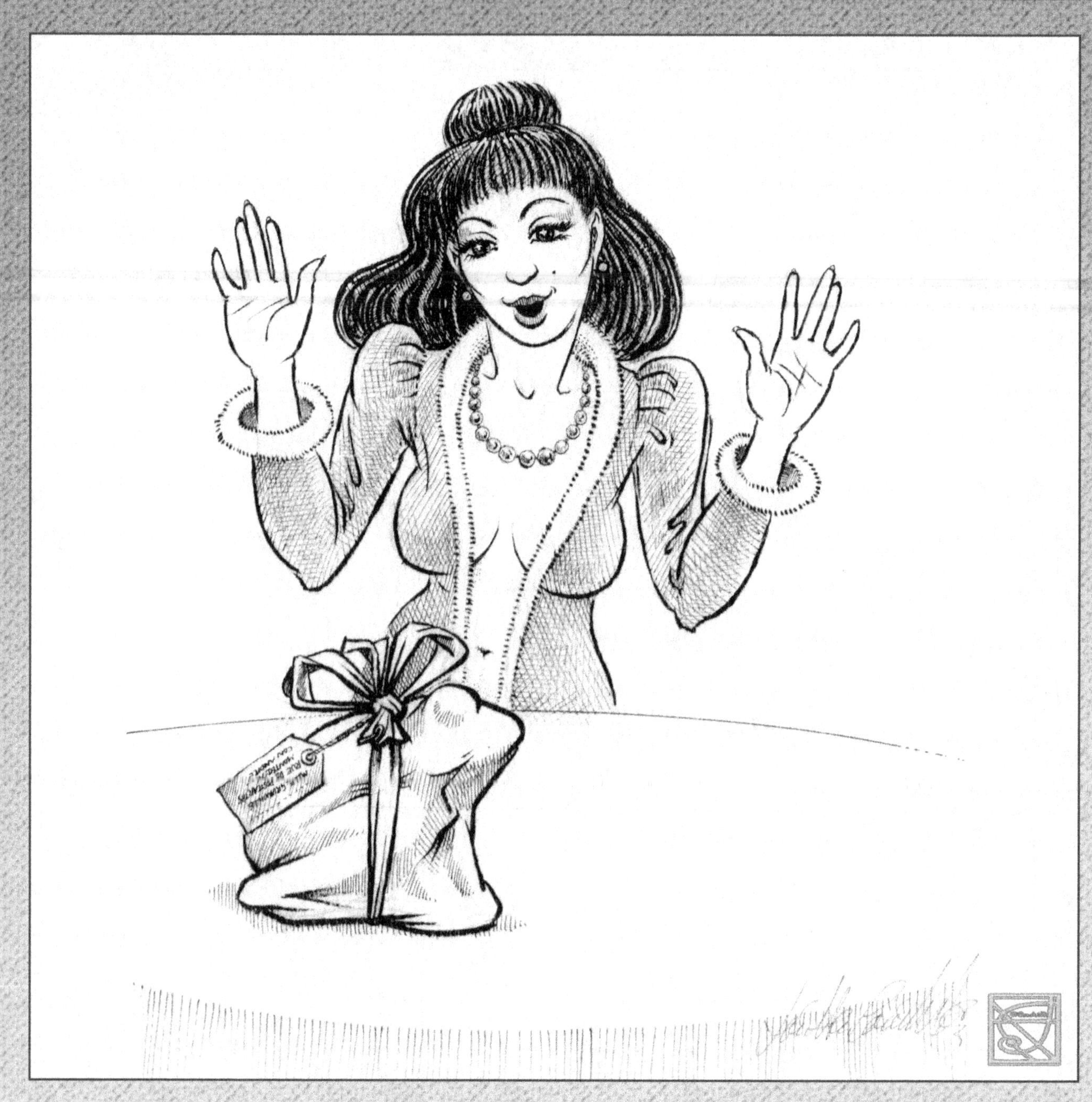

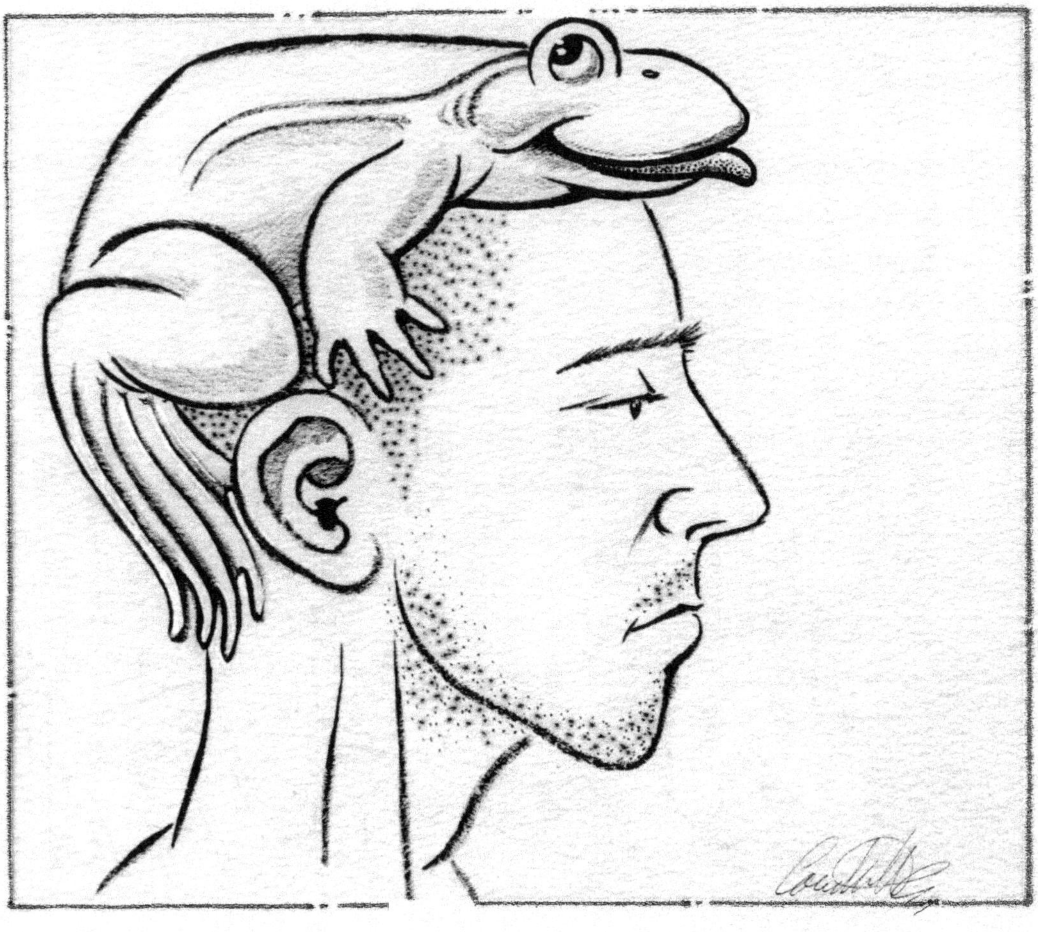

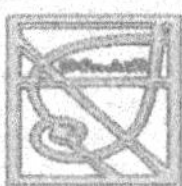

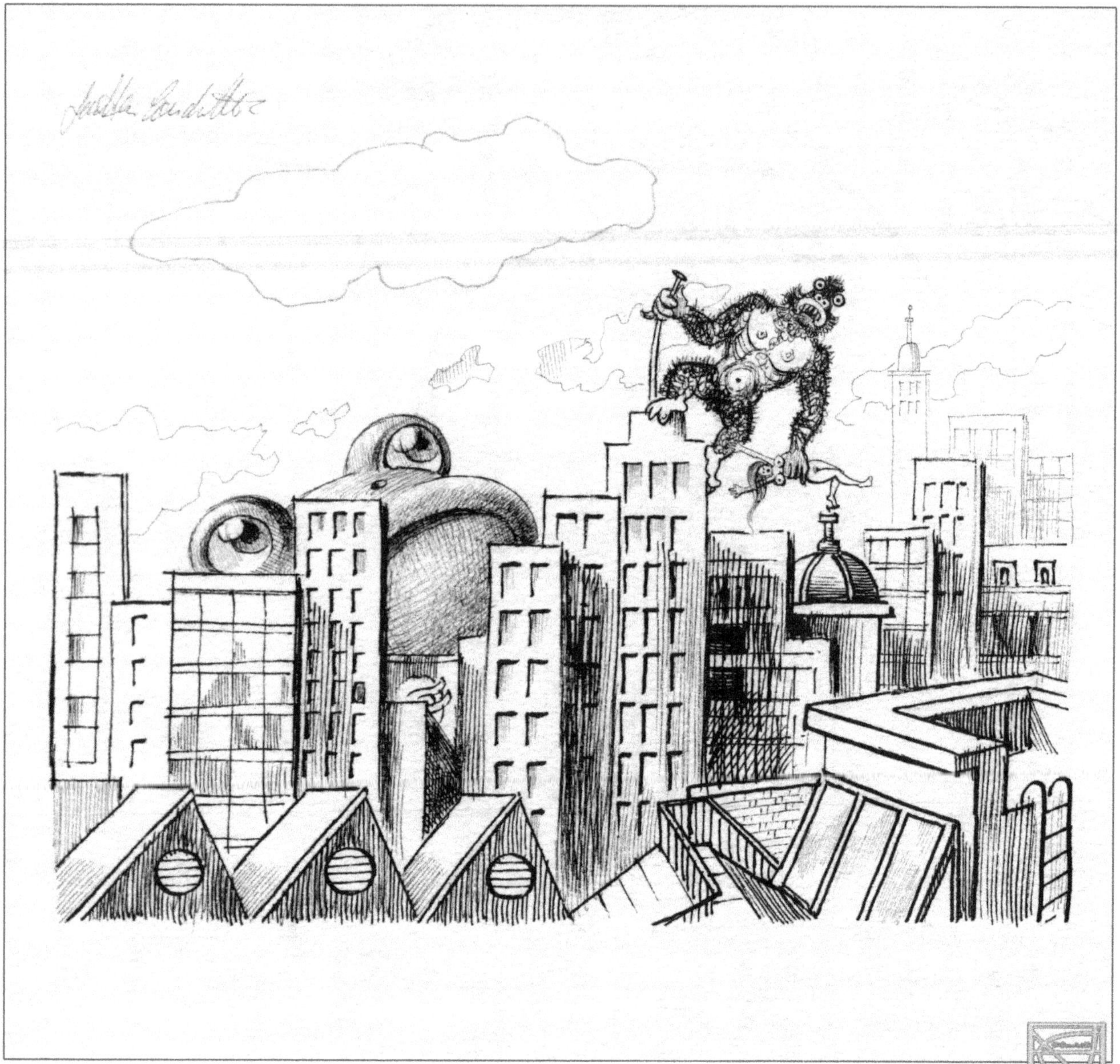

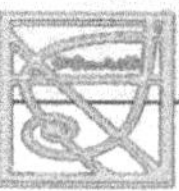

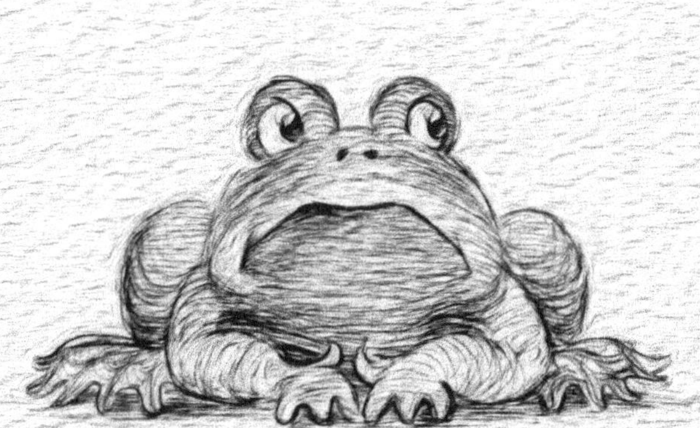
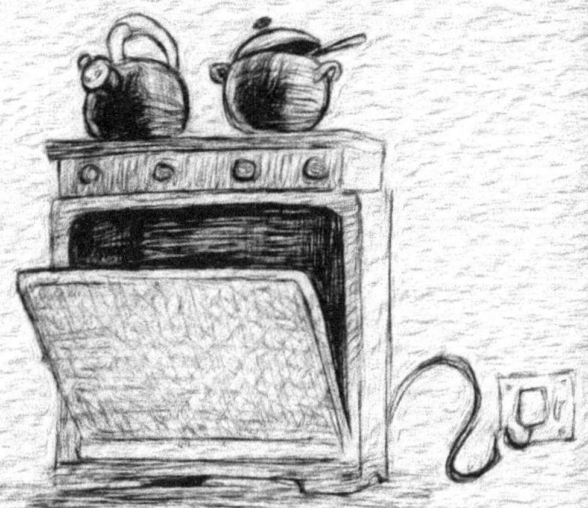
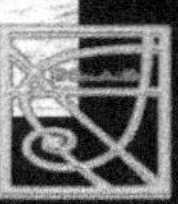

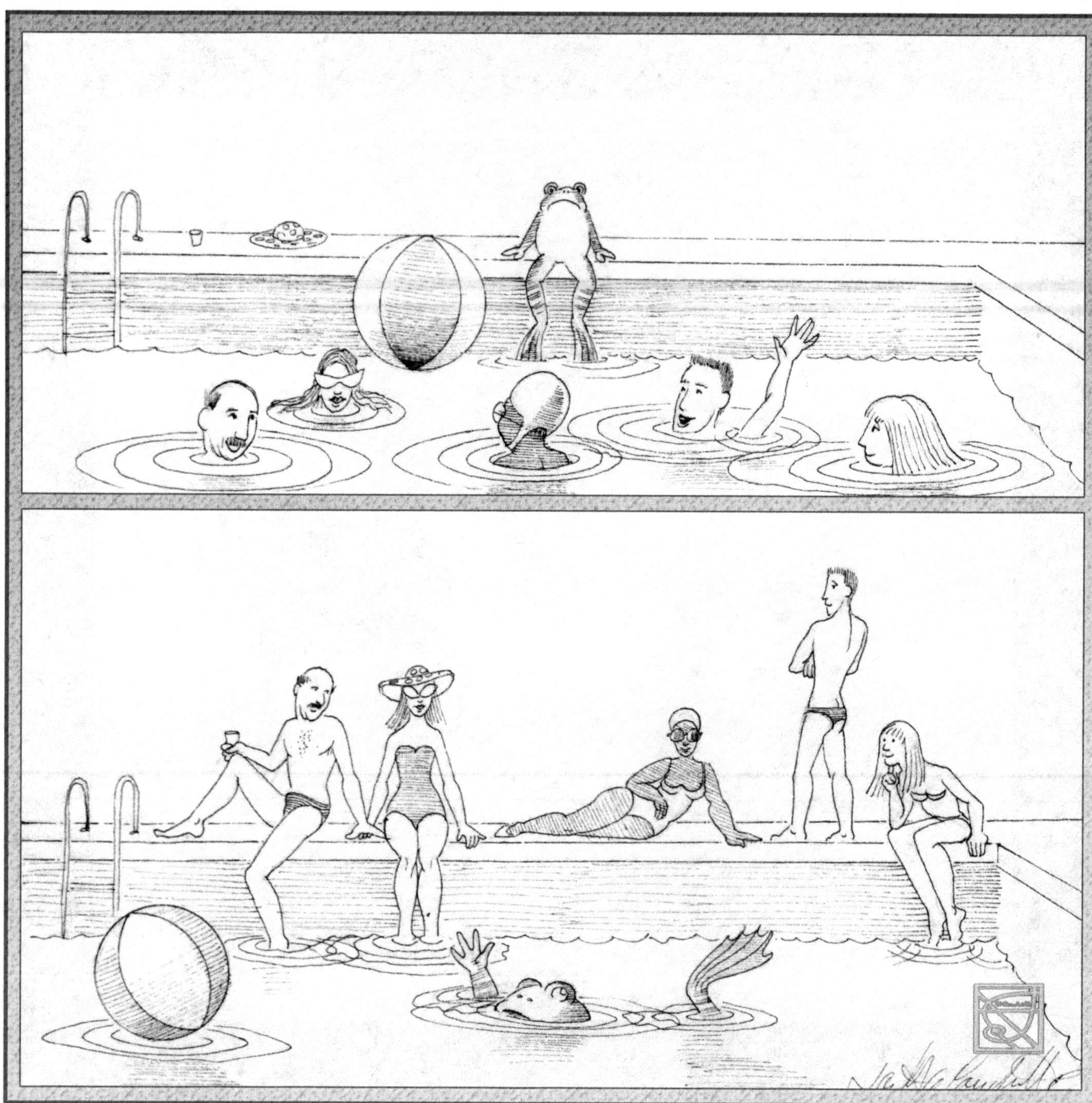

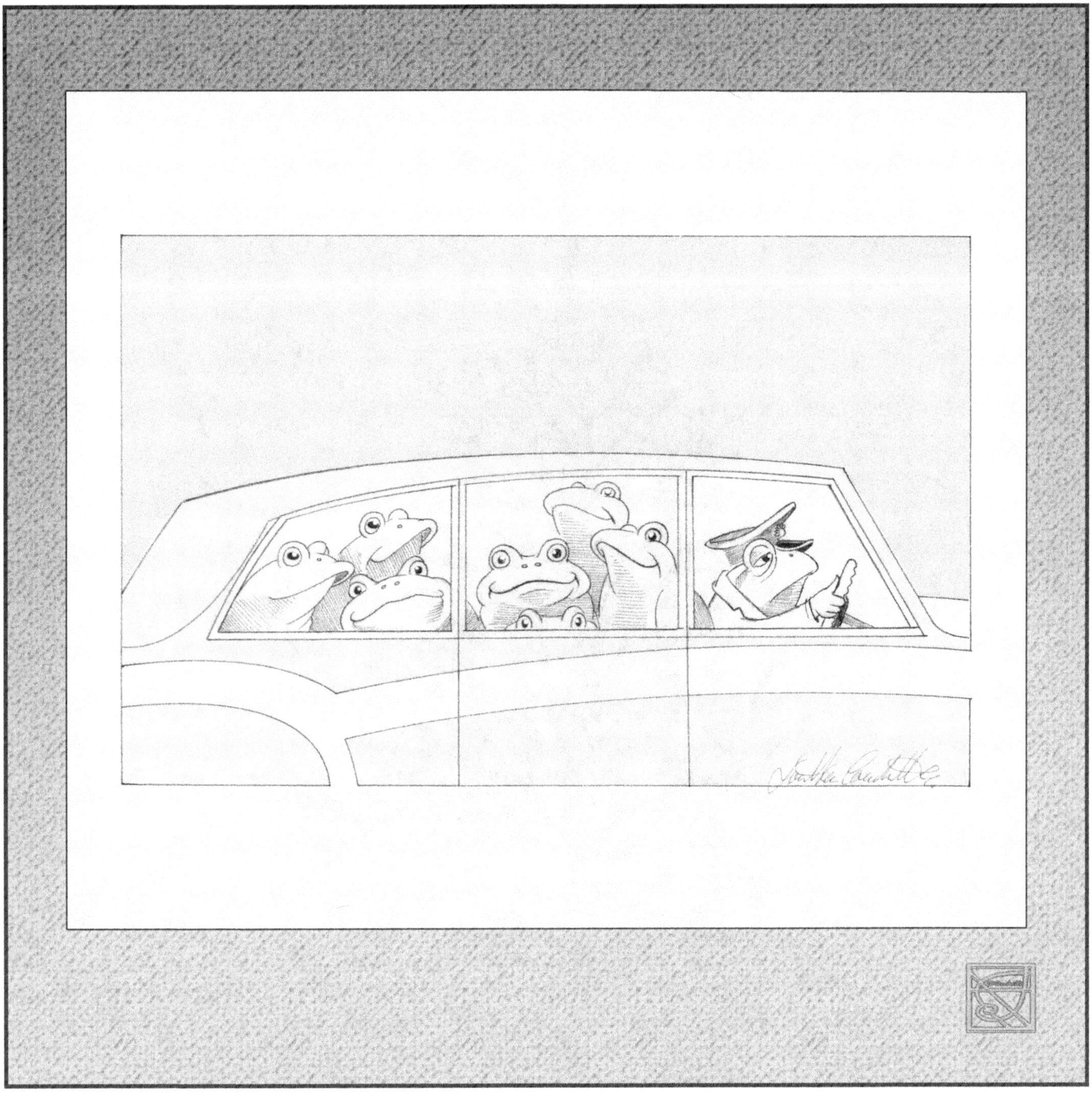

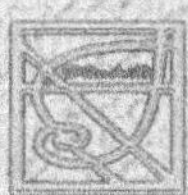

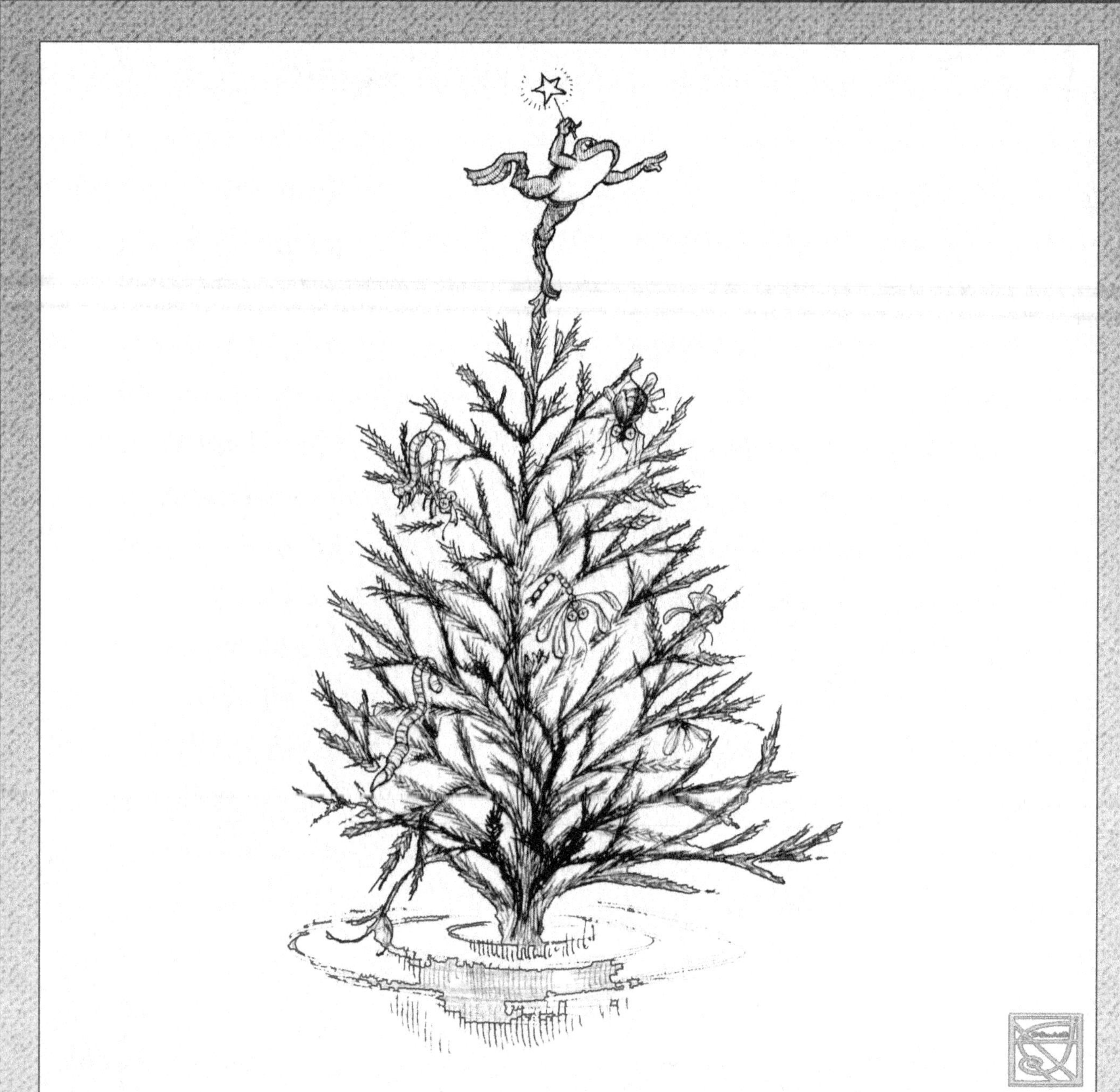

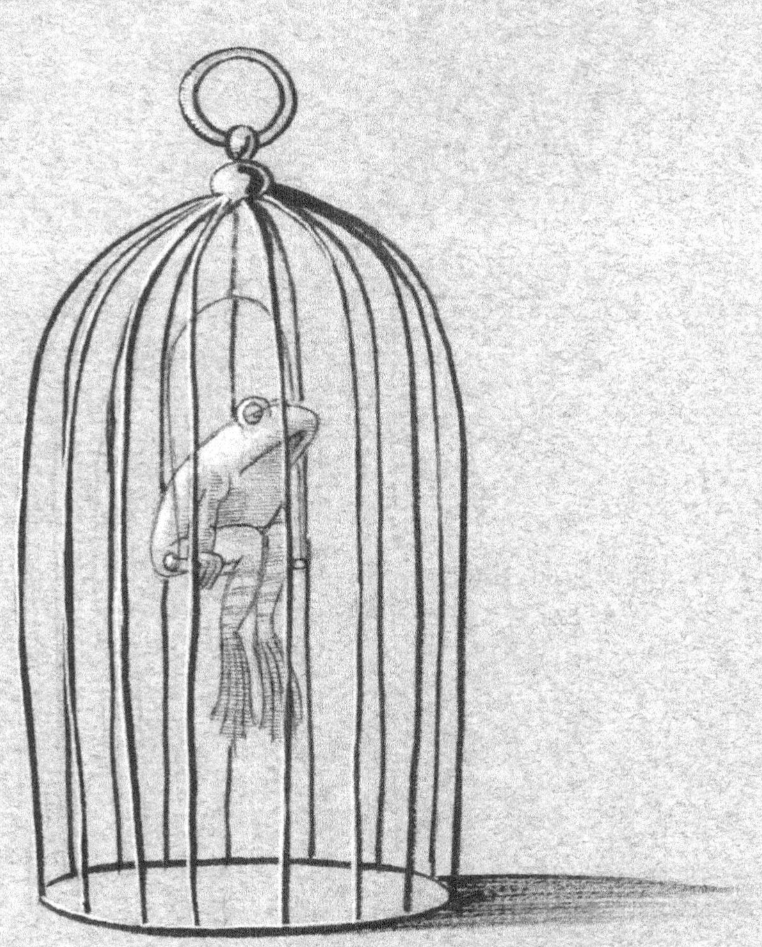
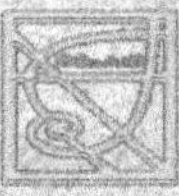

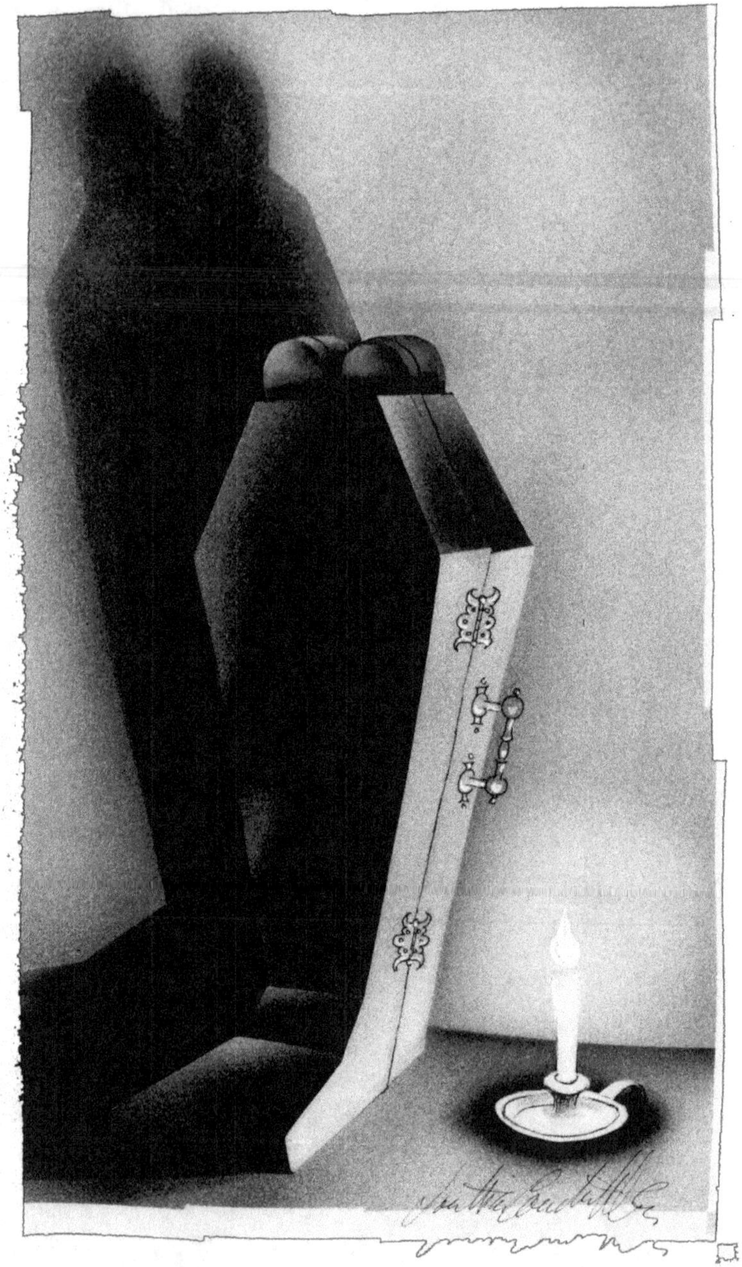

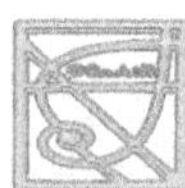

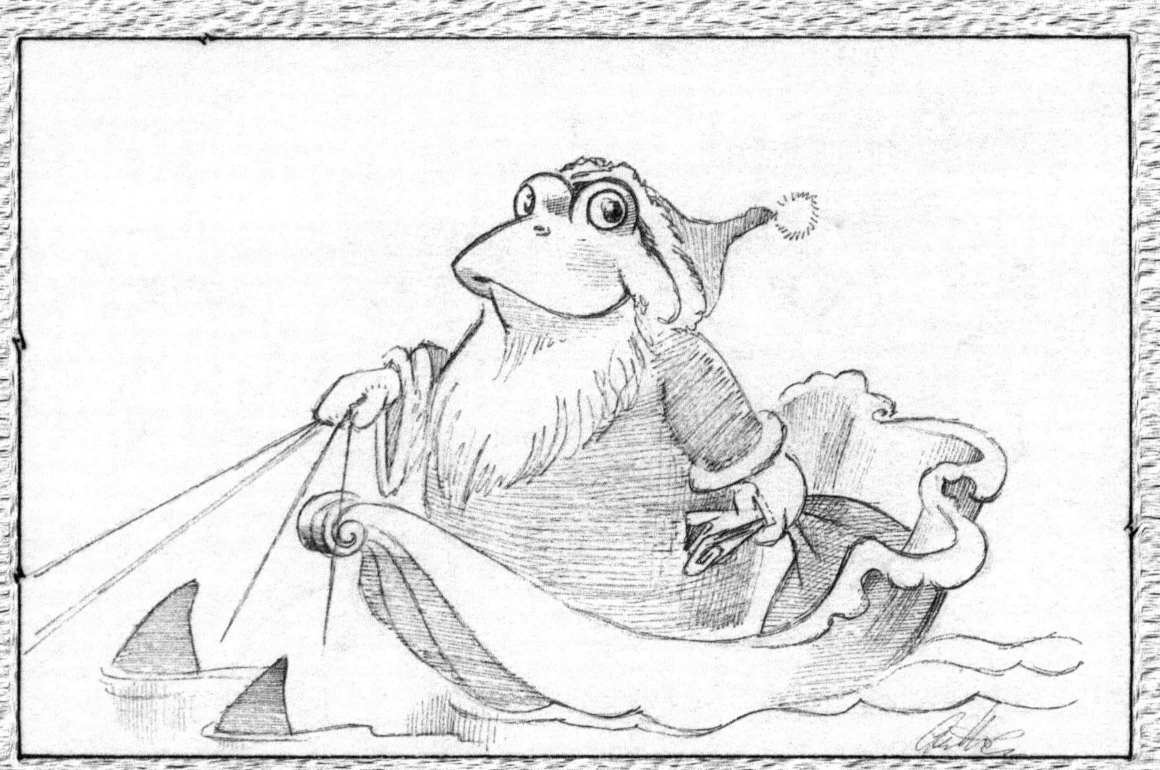
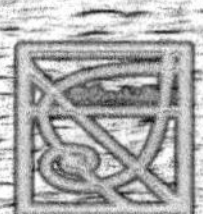

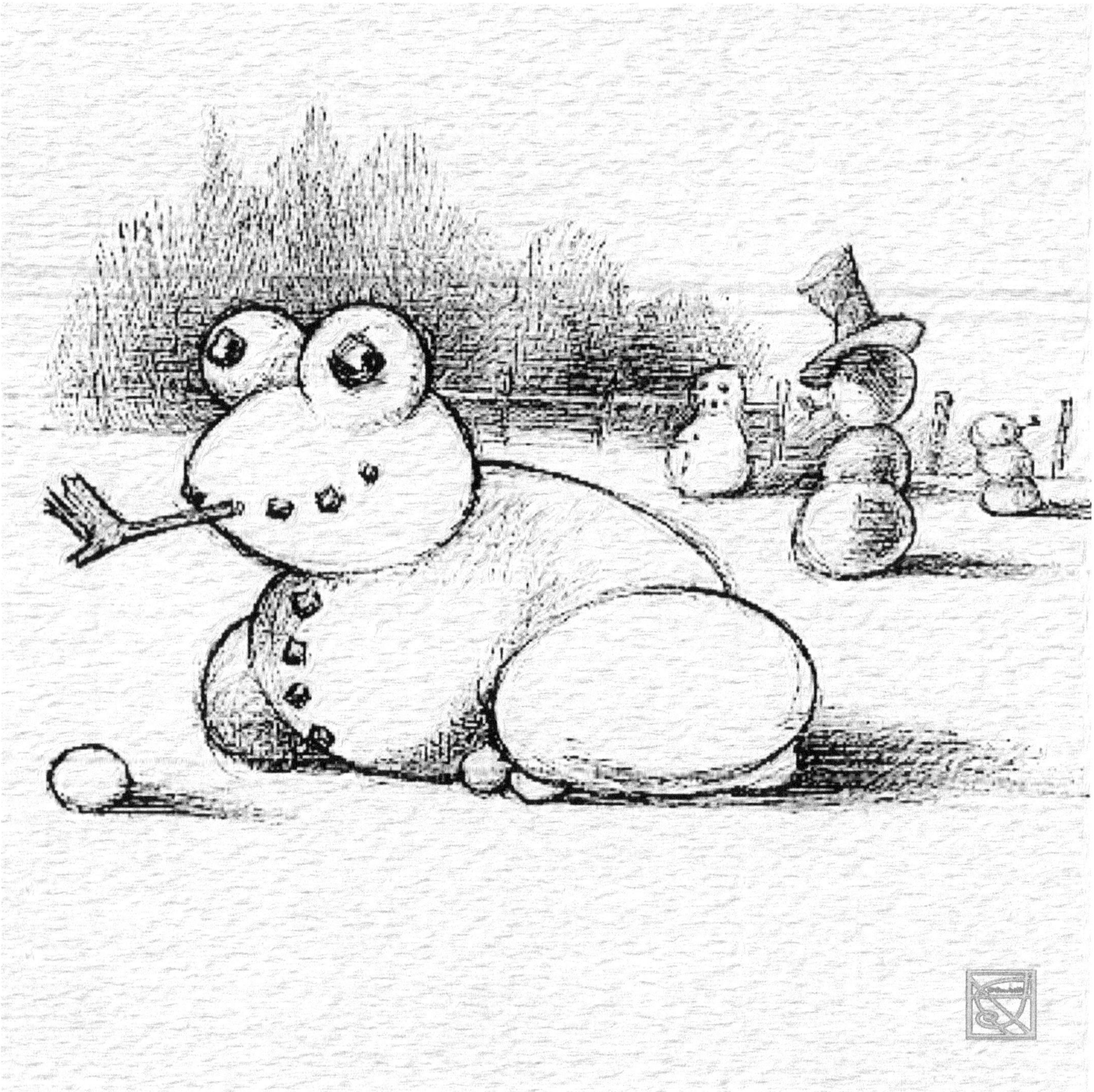

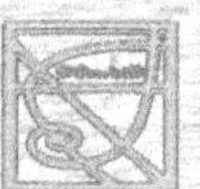

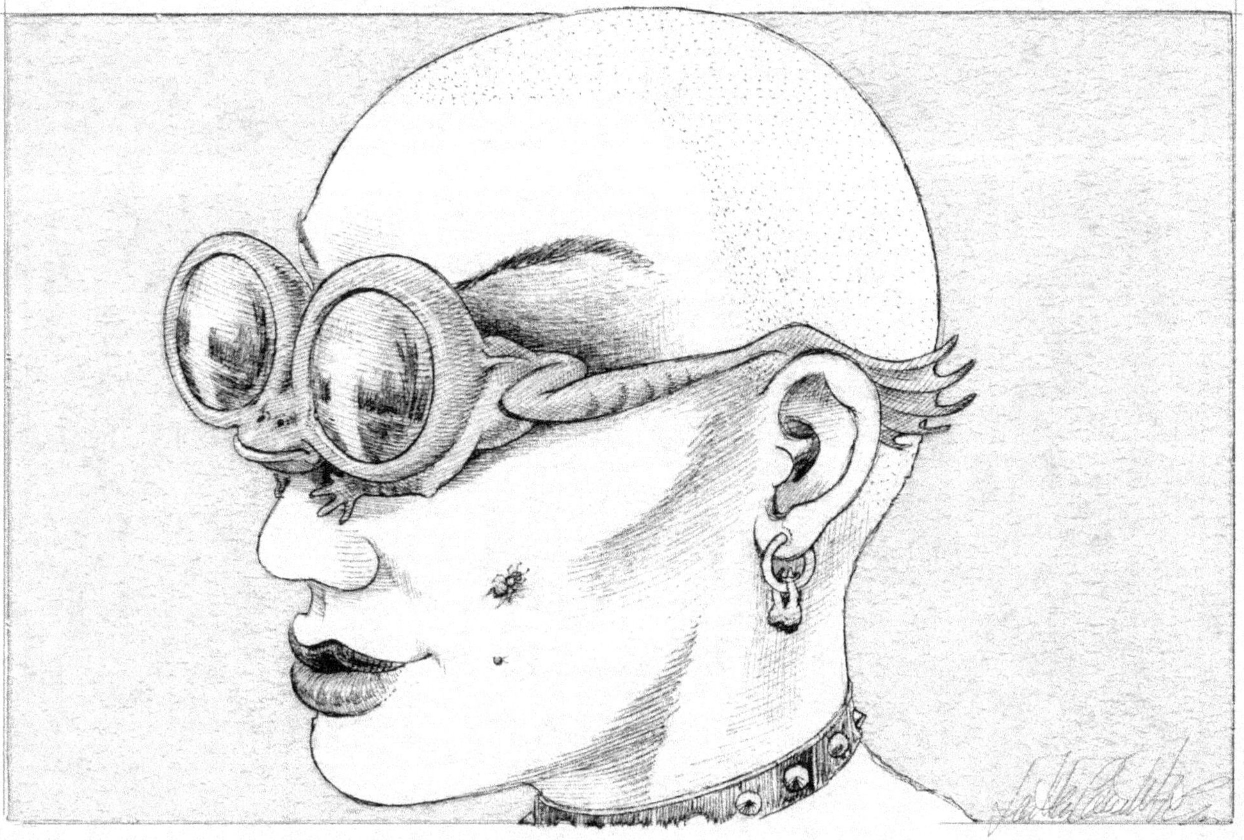

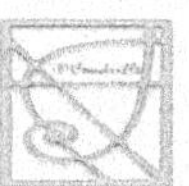

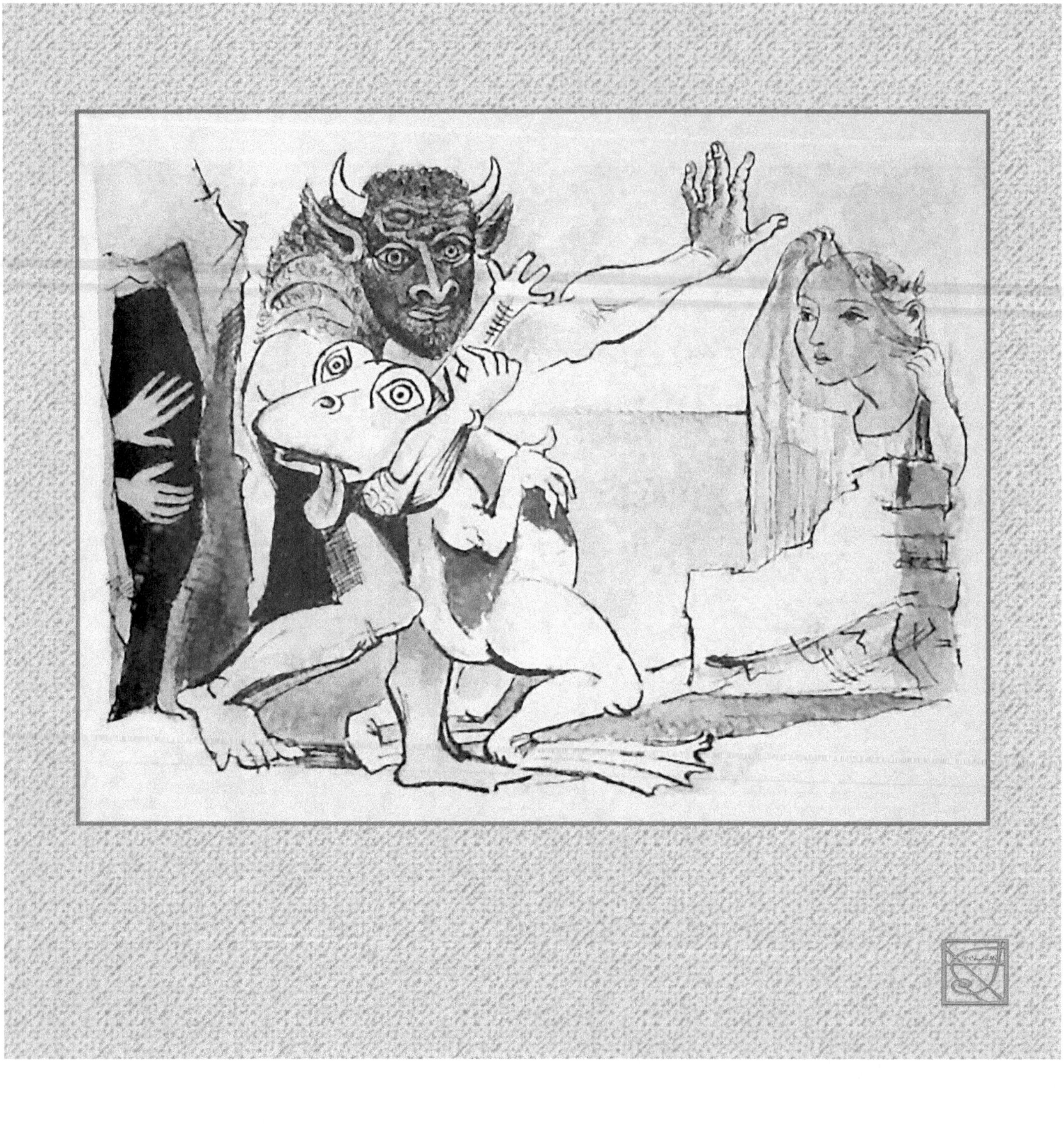

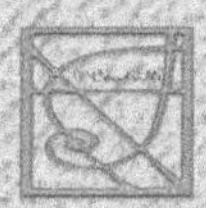

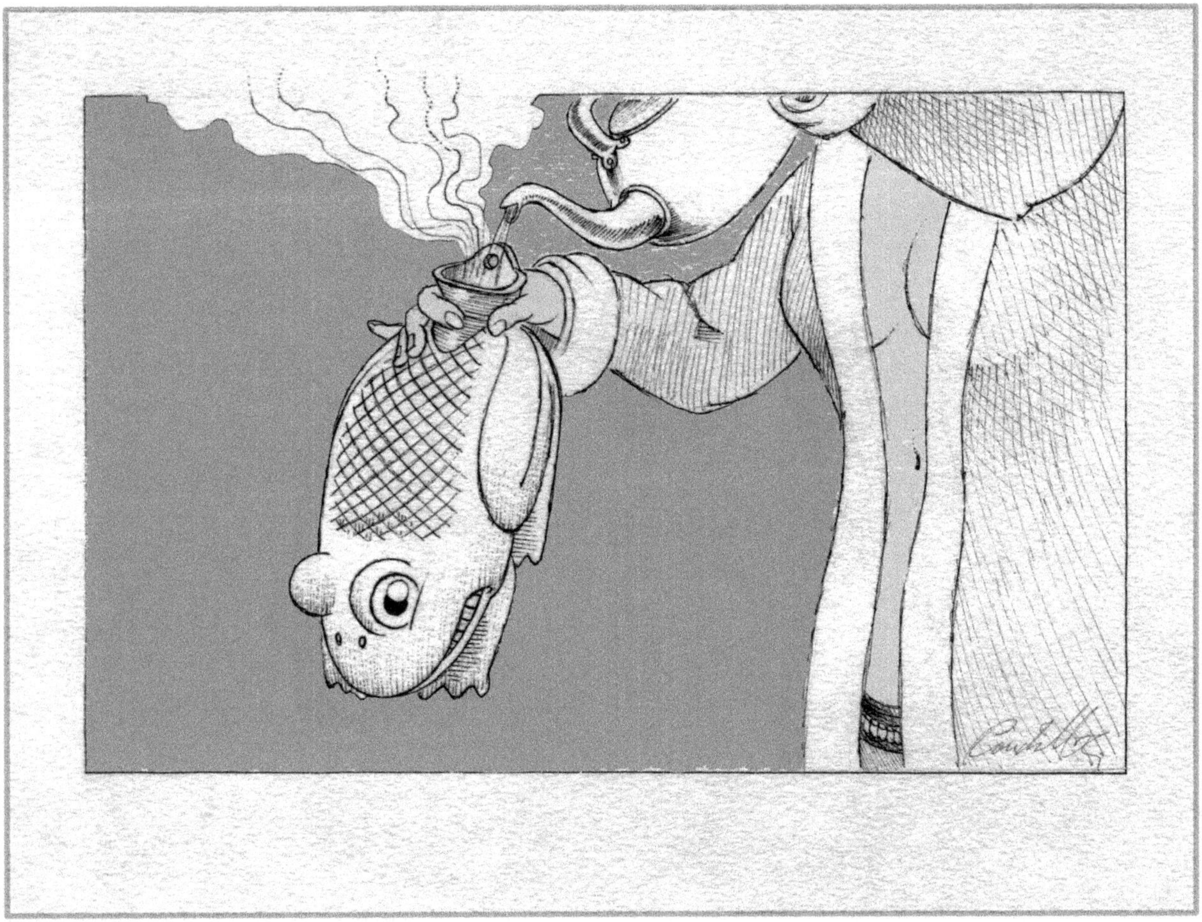

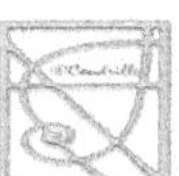

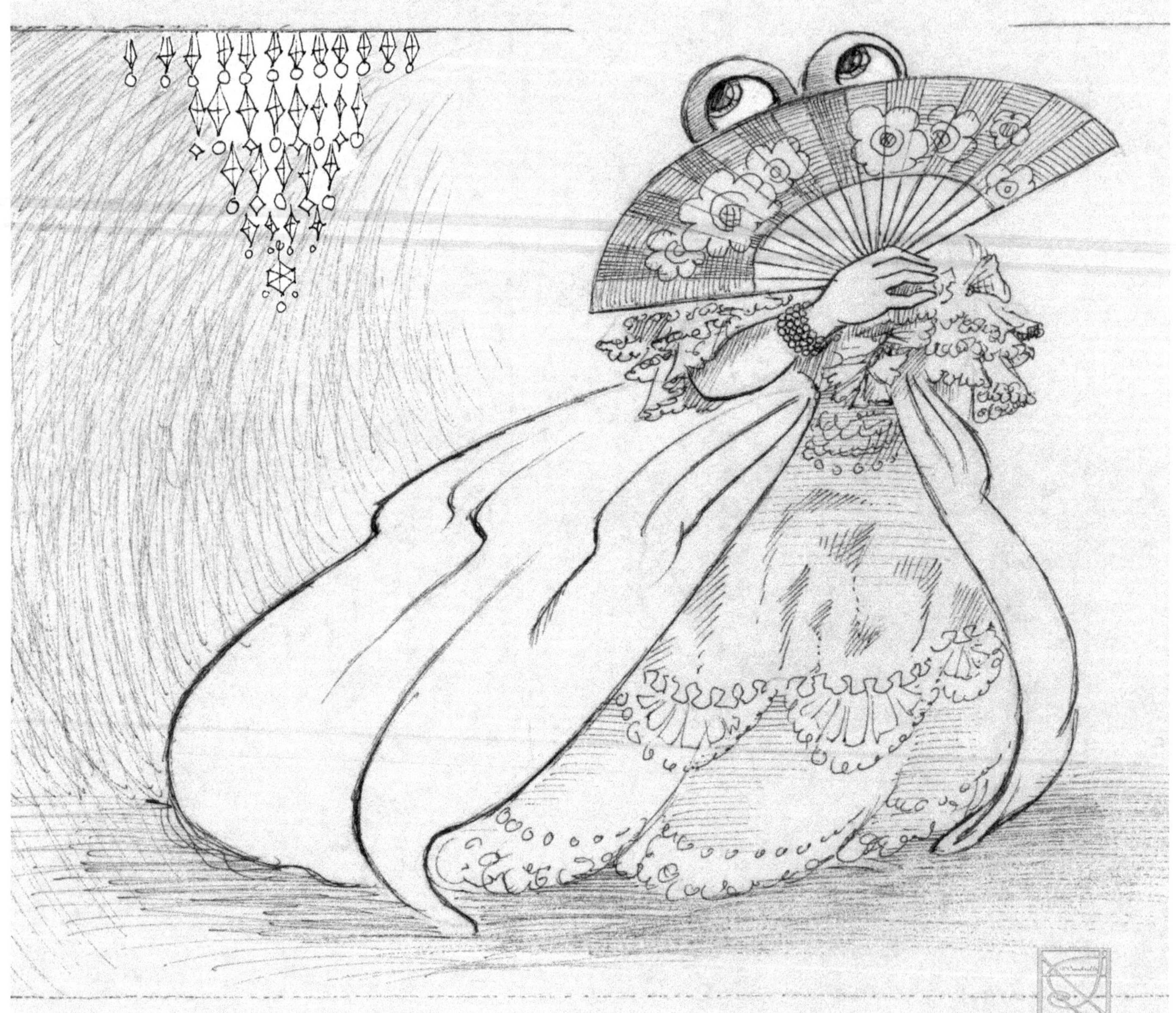

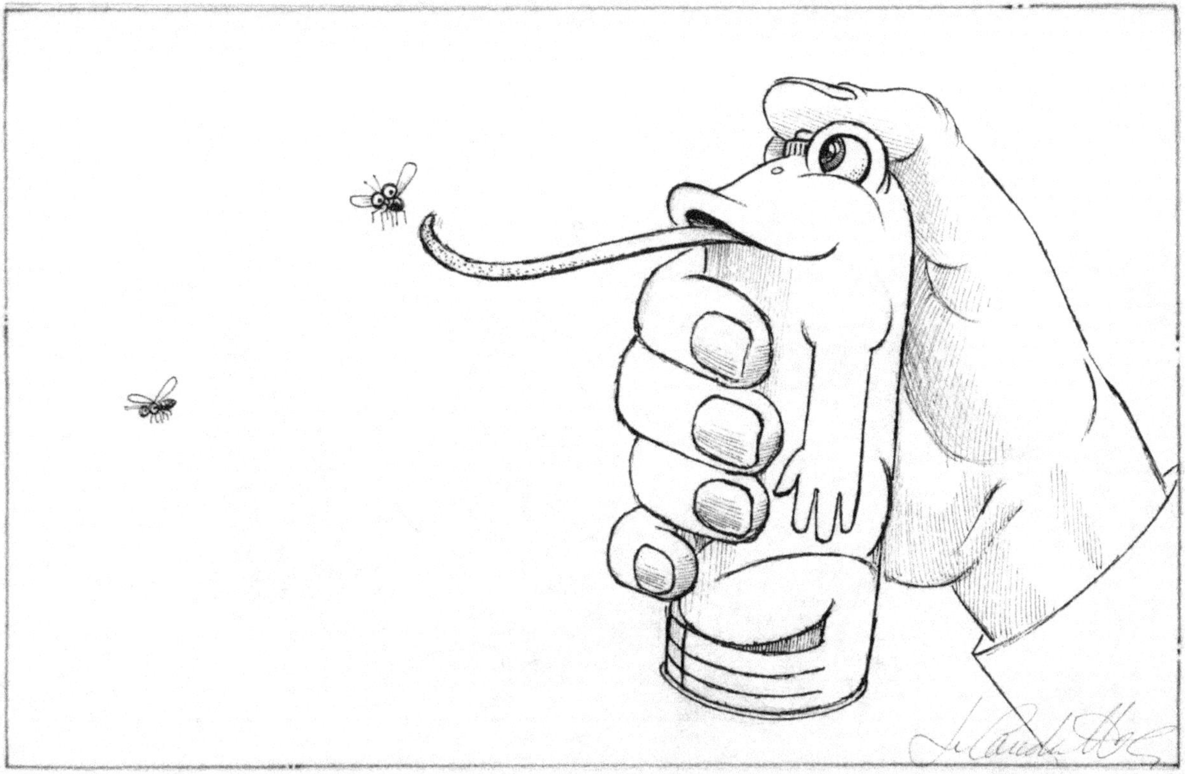

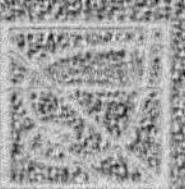

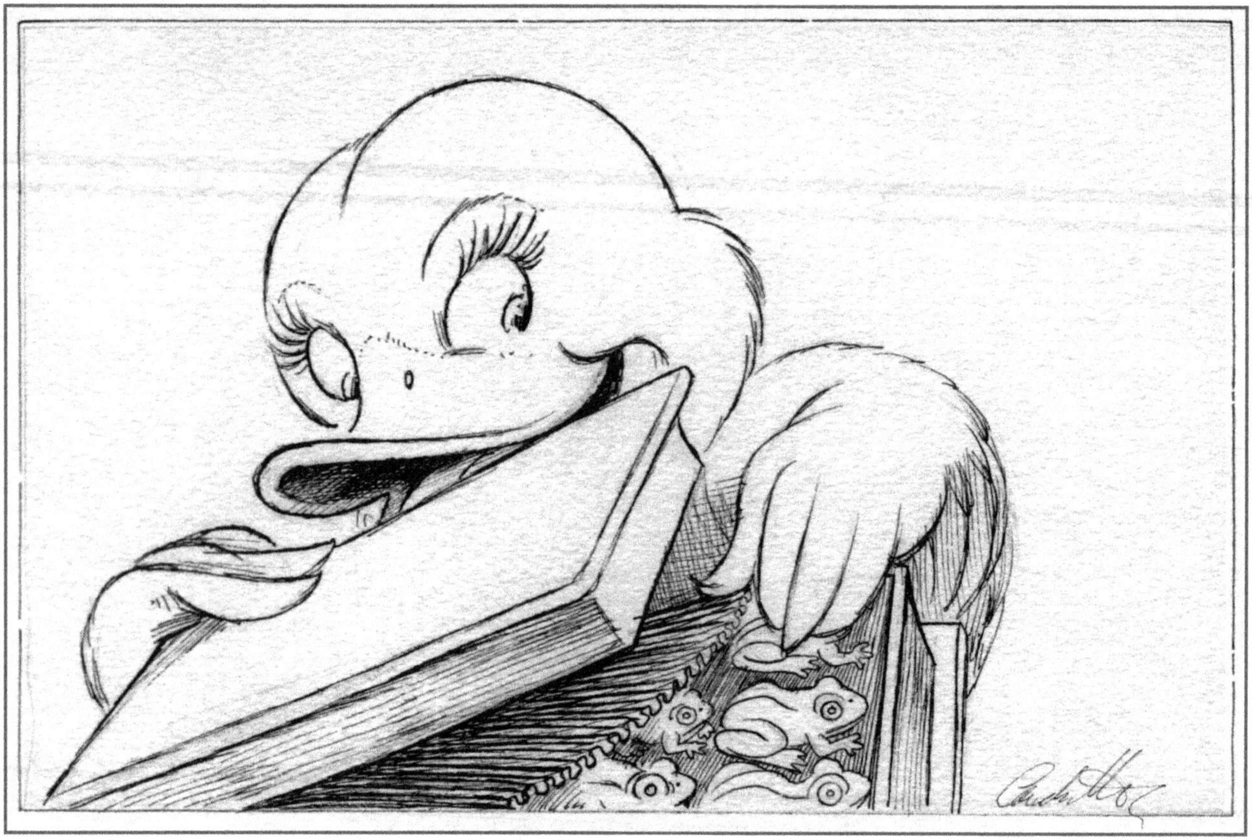

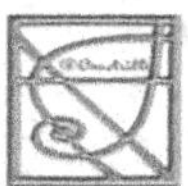

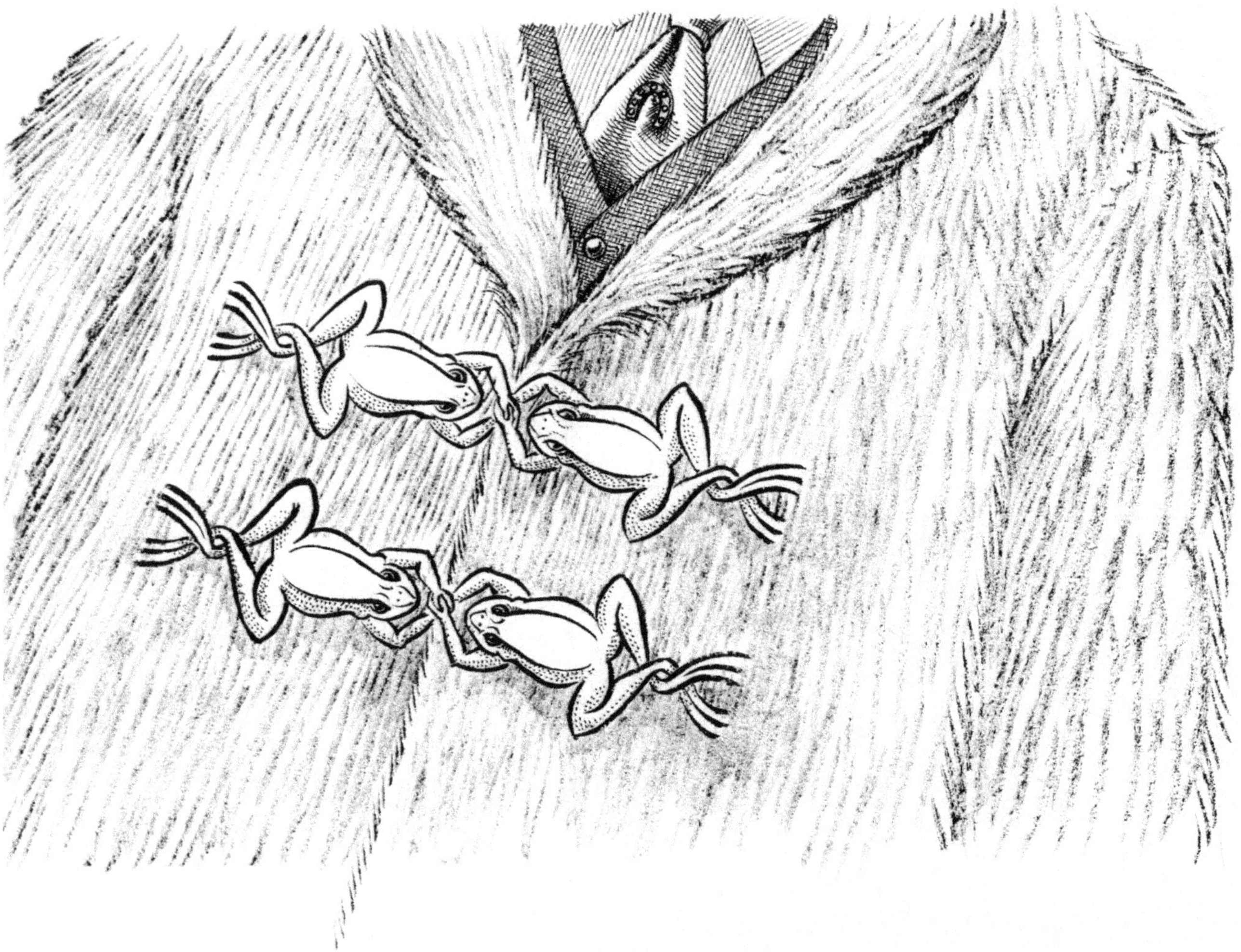

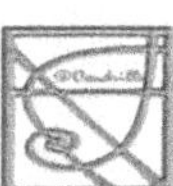

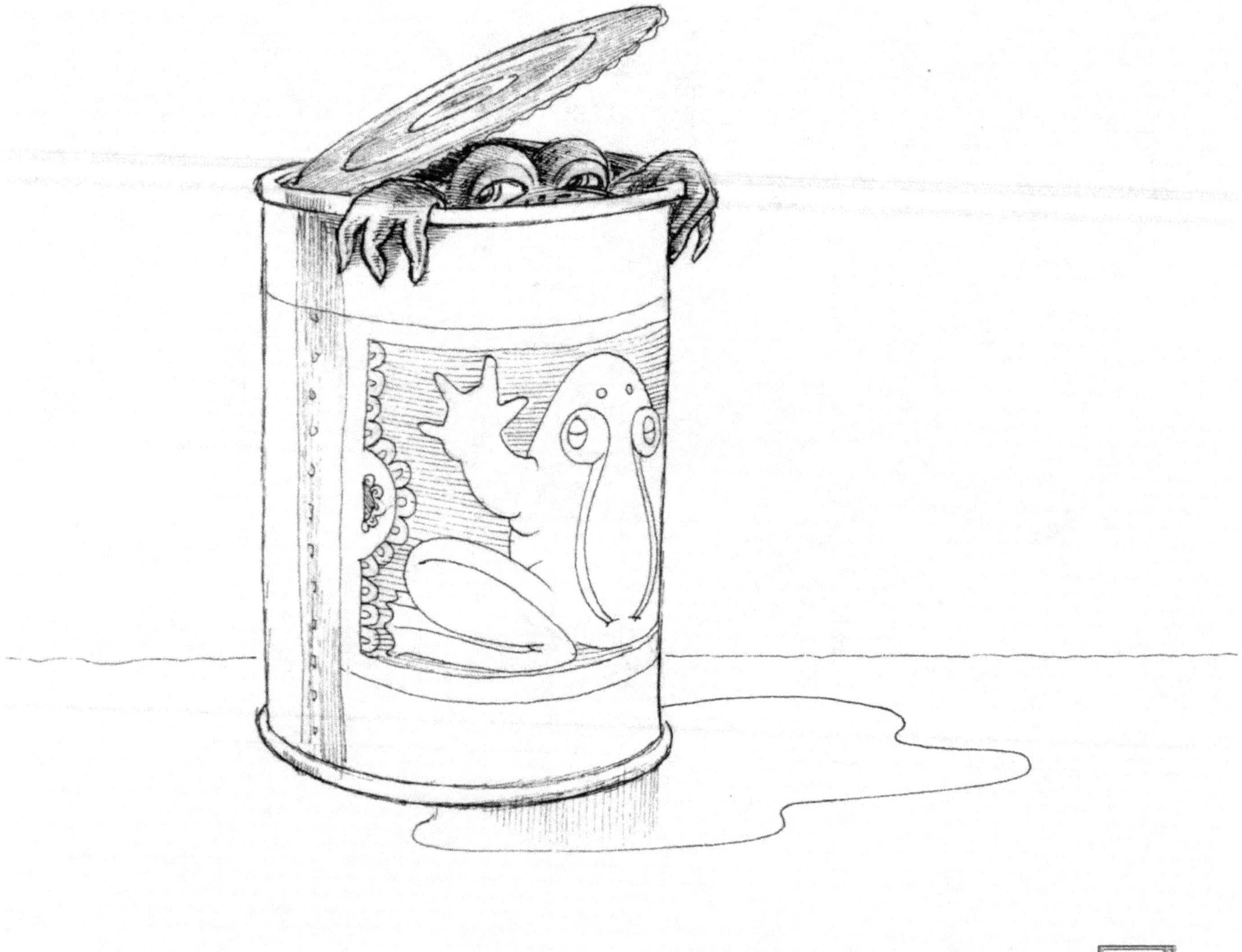

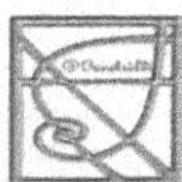

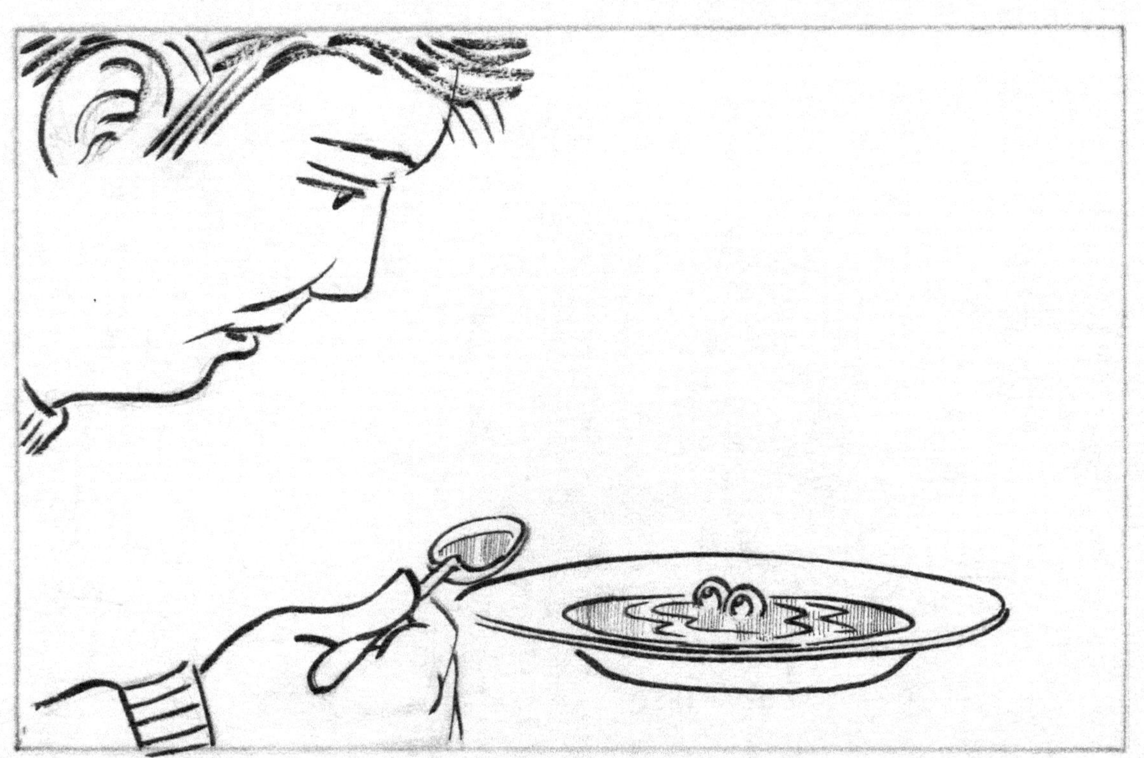

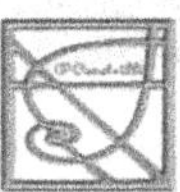

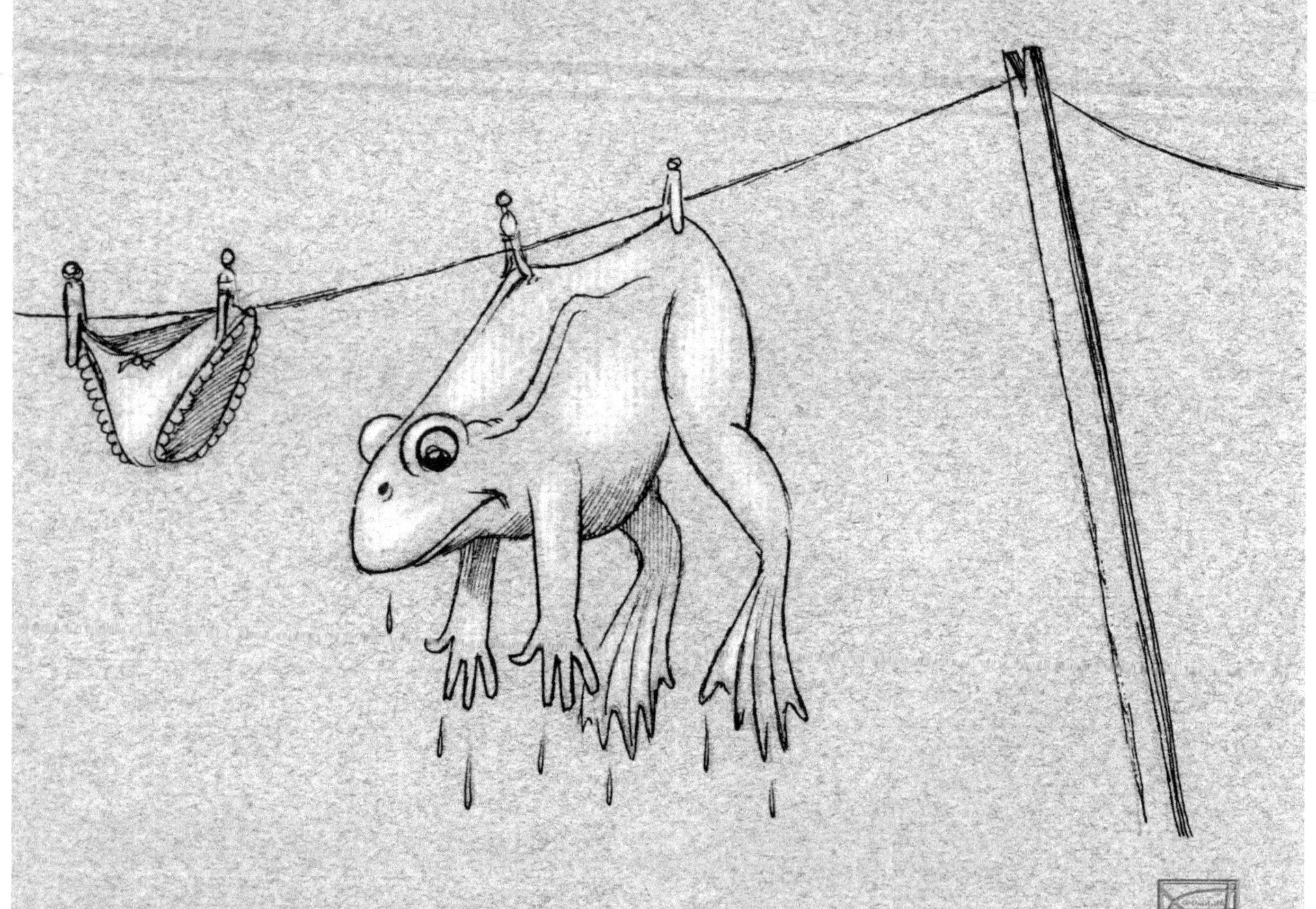

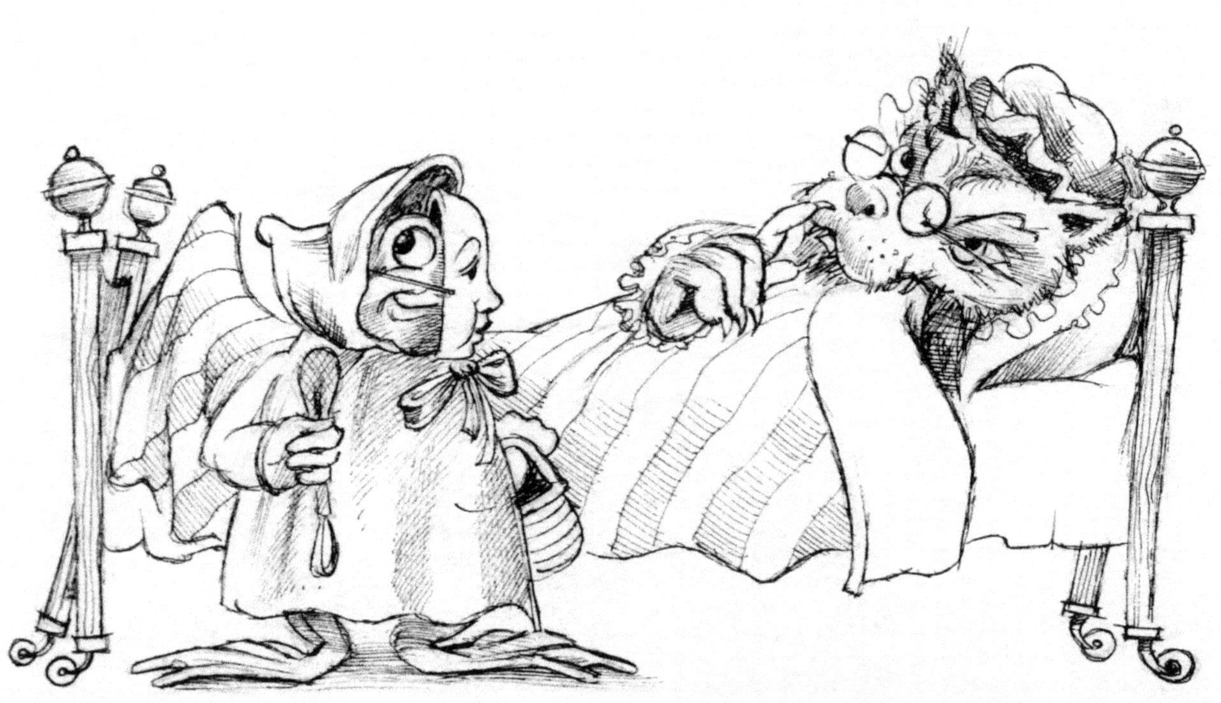
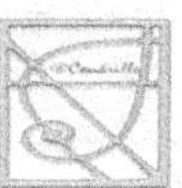

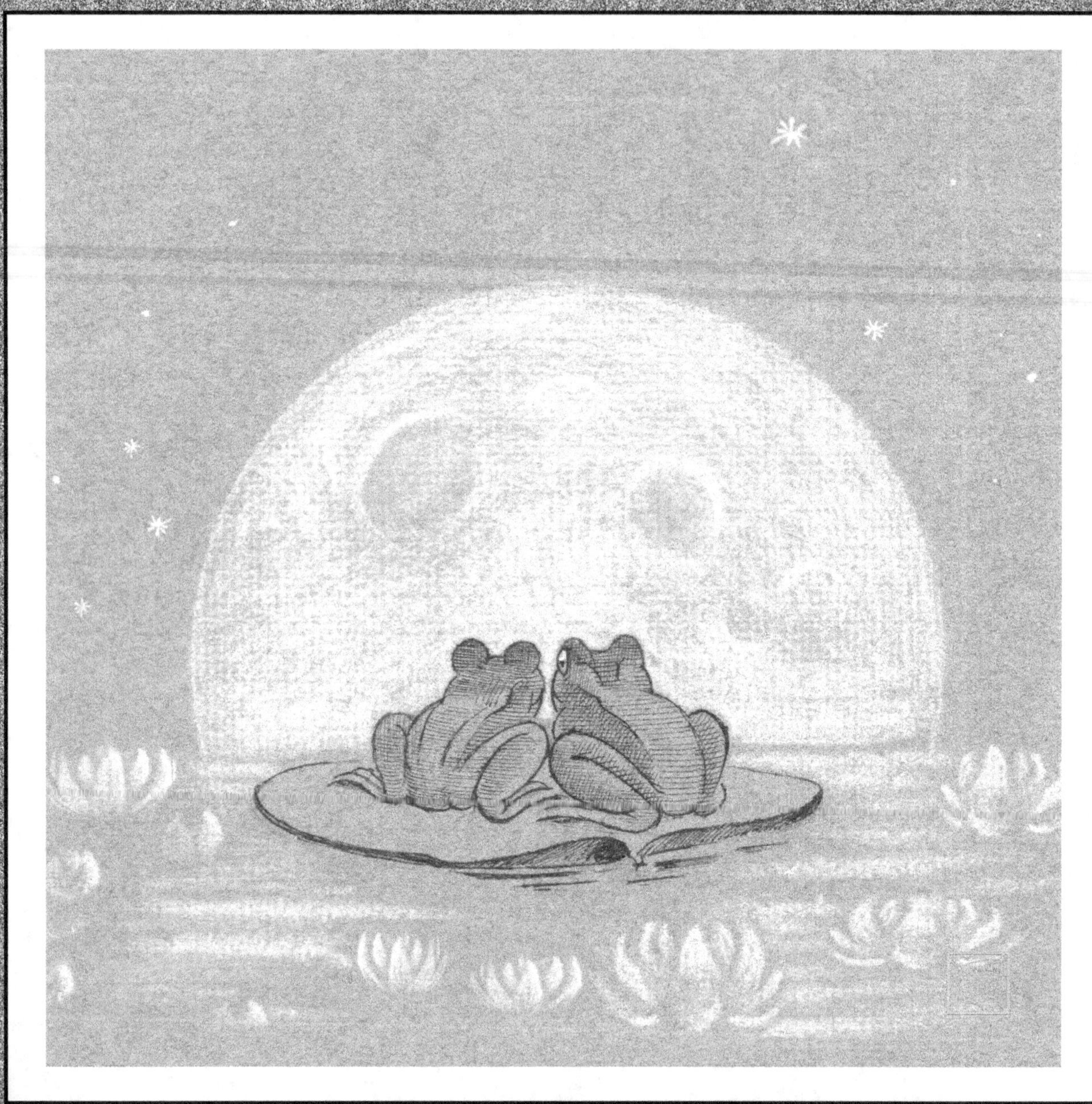

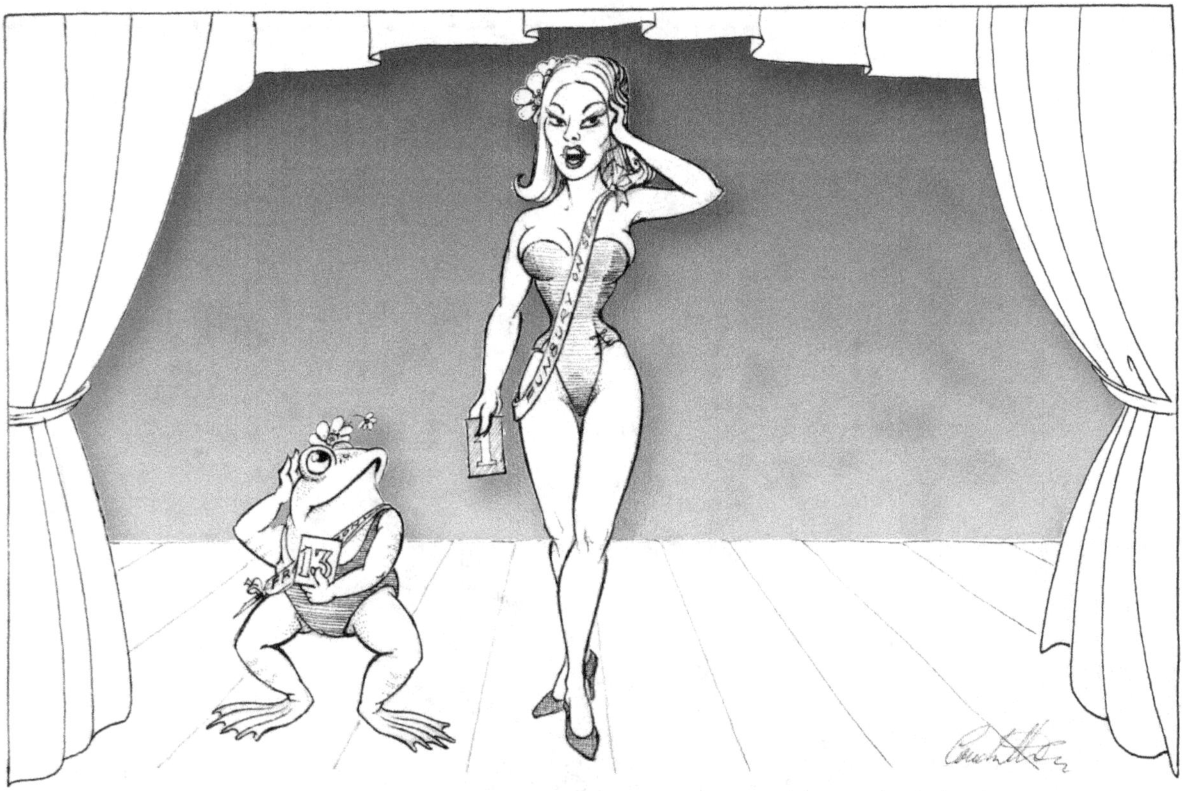

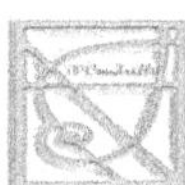
13
1

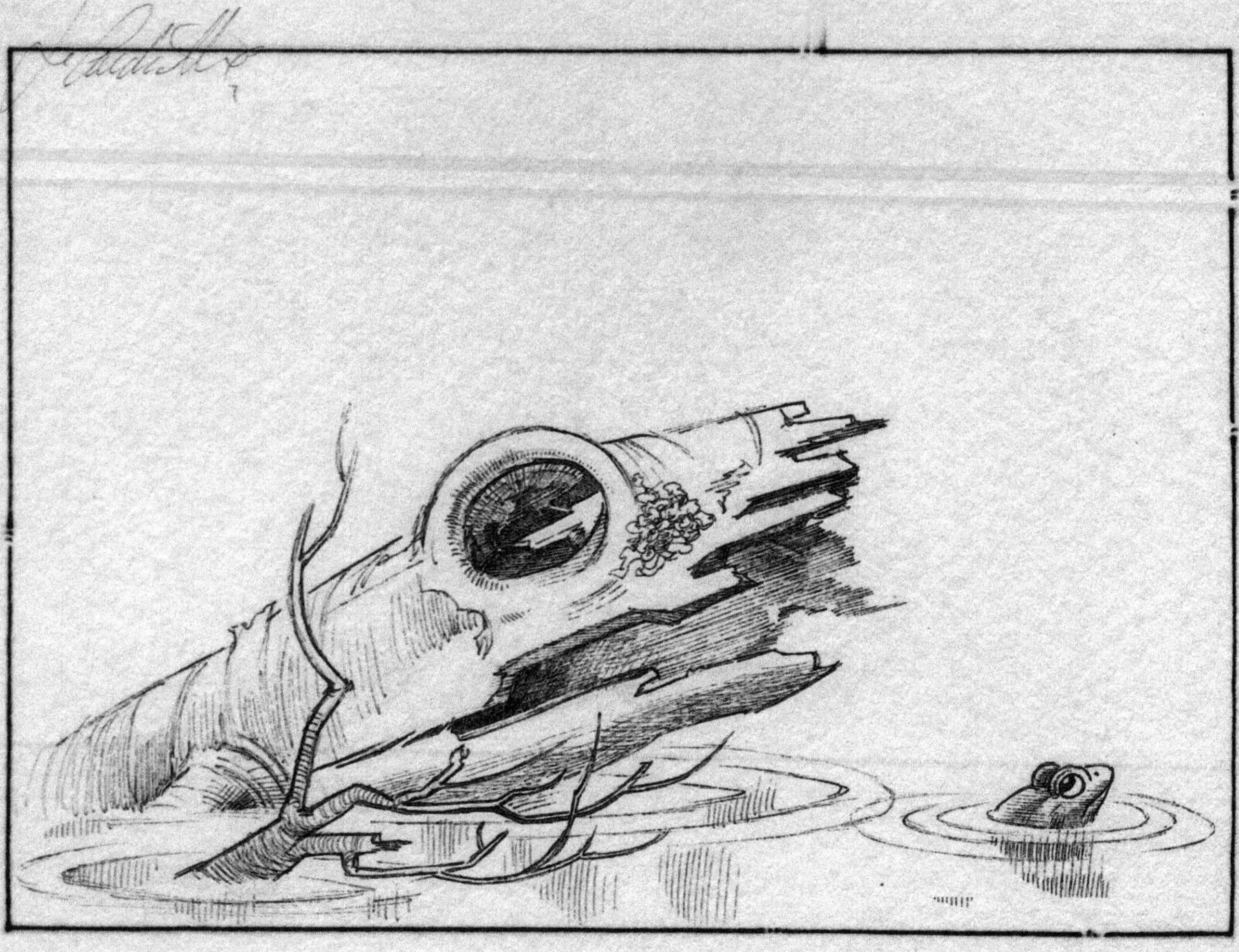

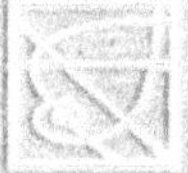

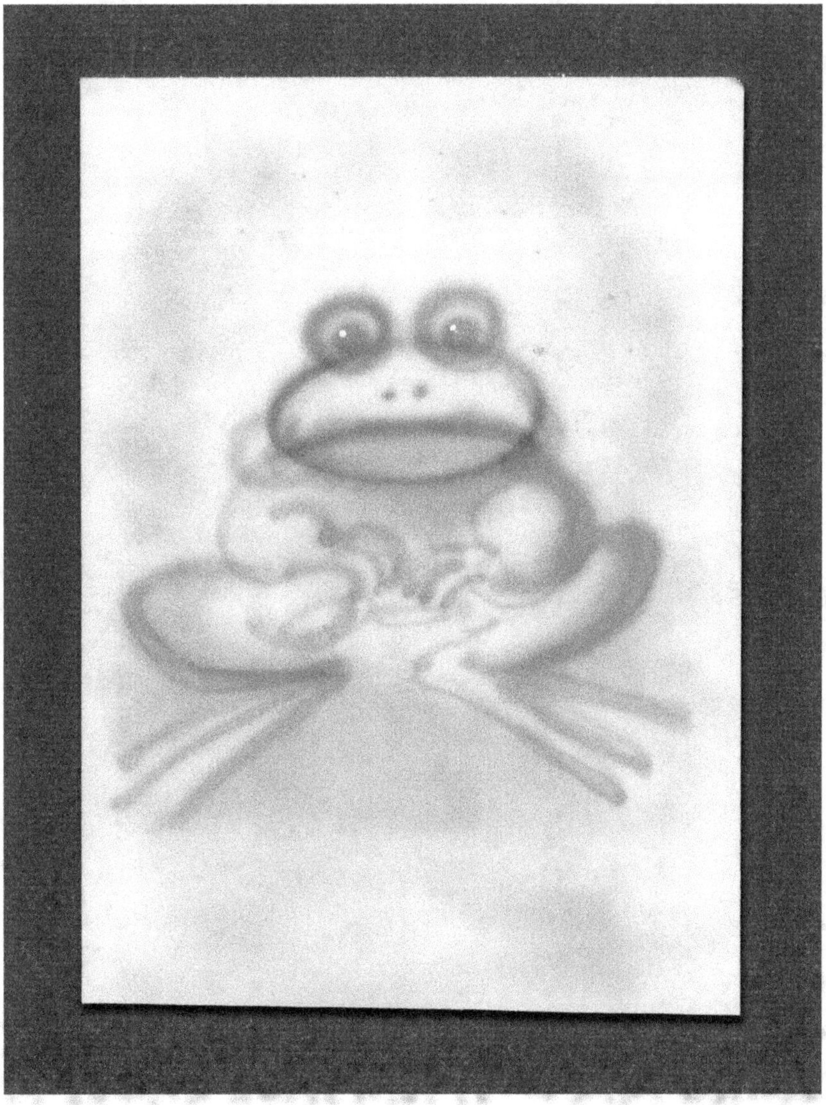

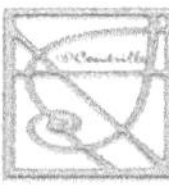

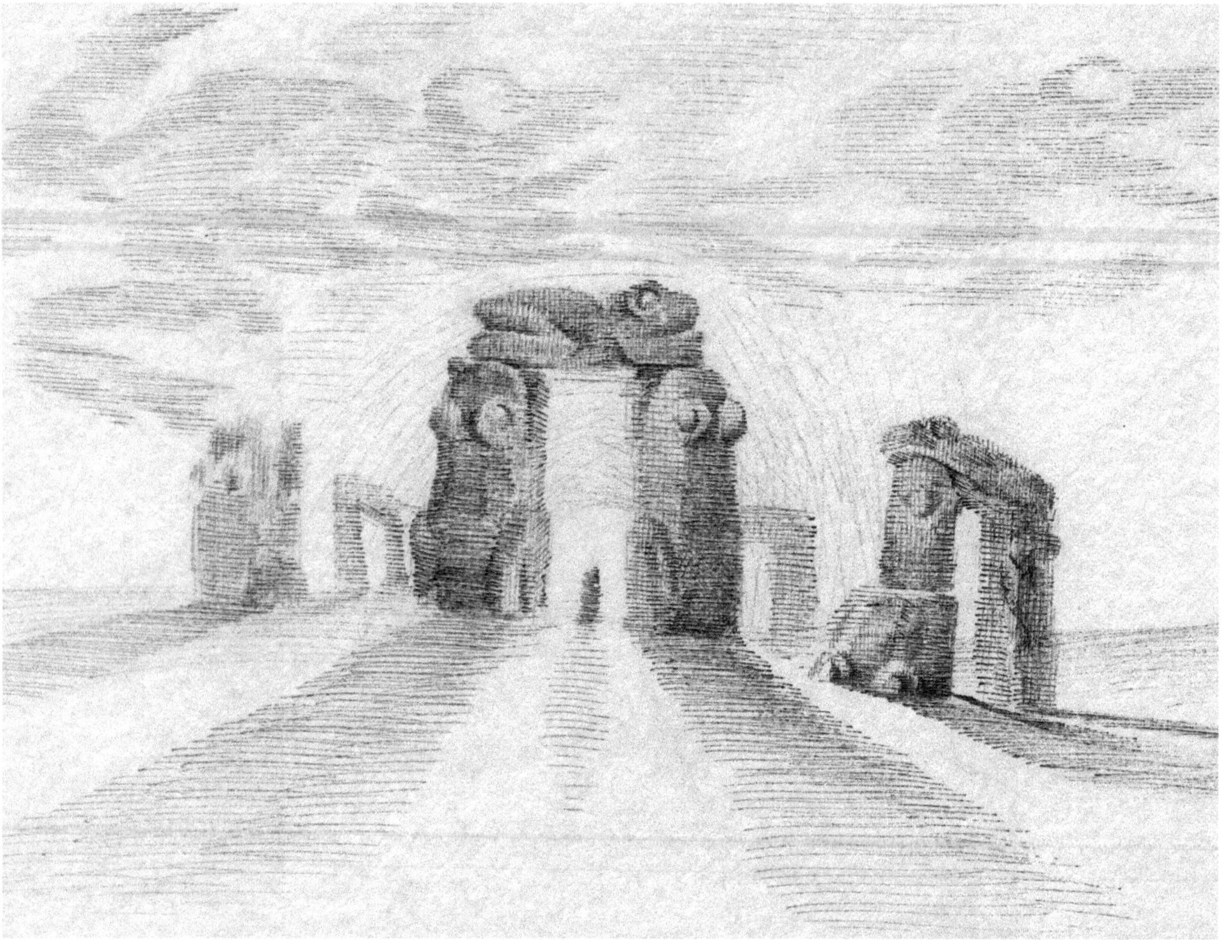

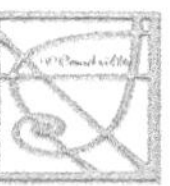

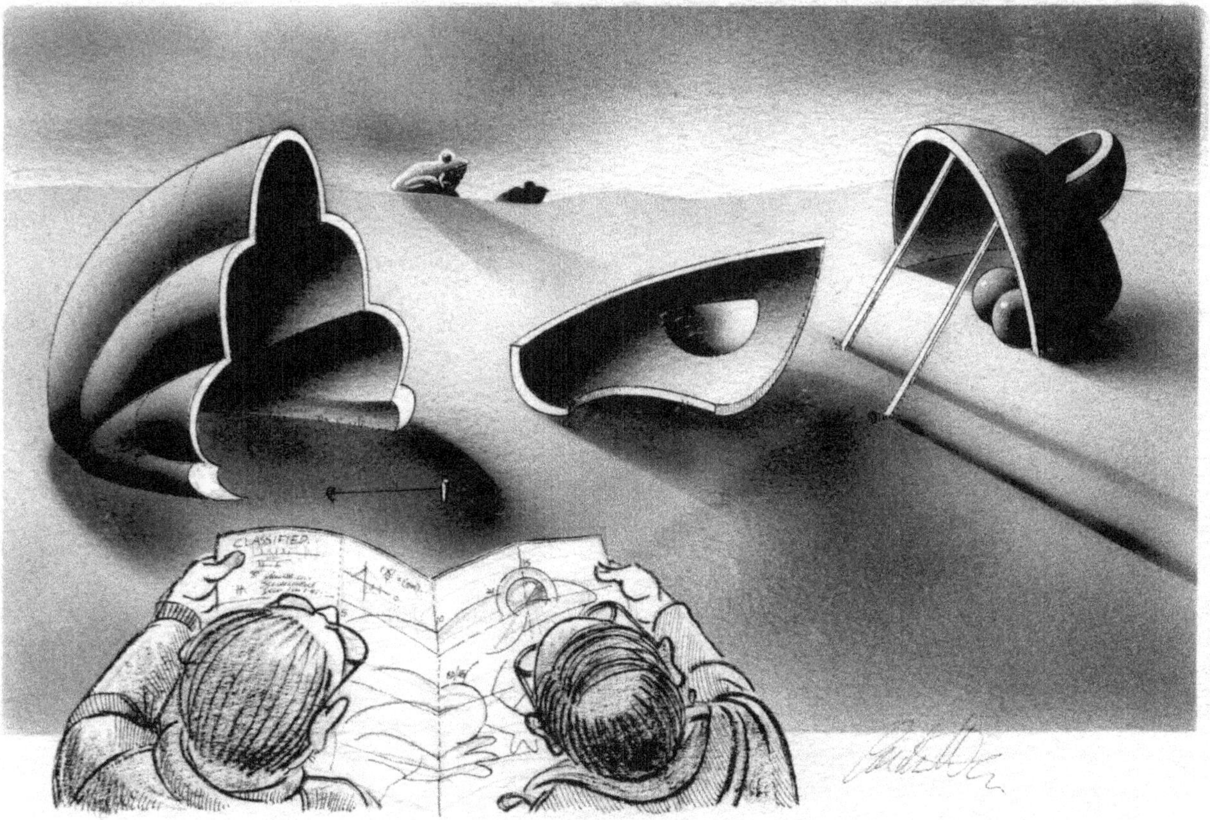

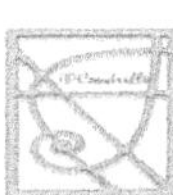

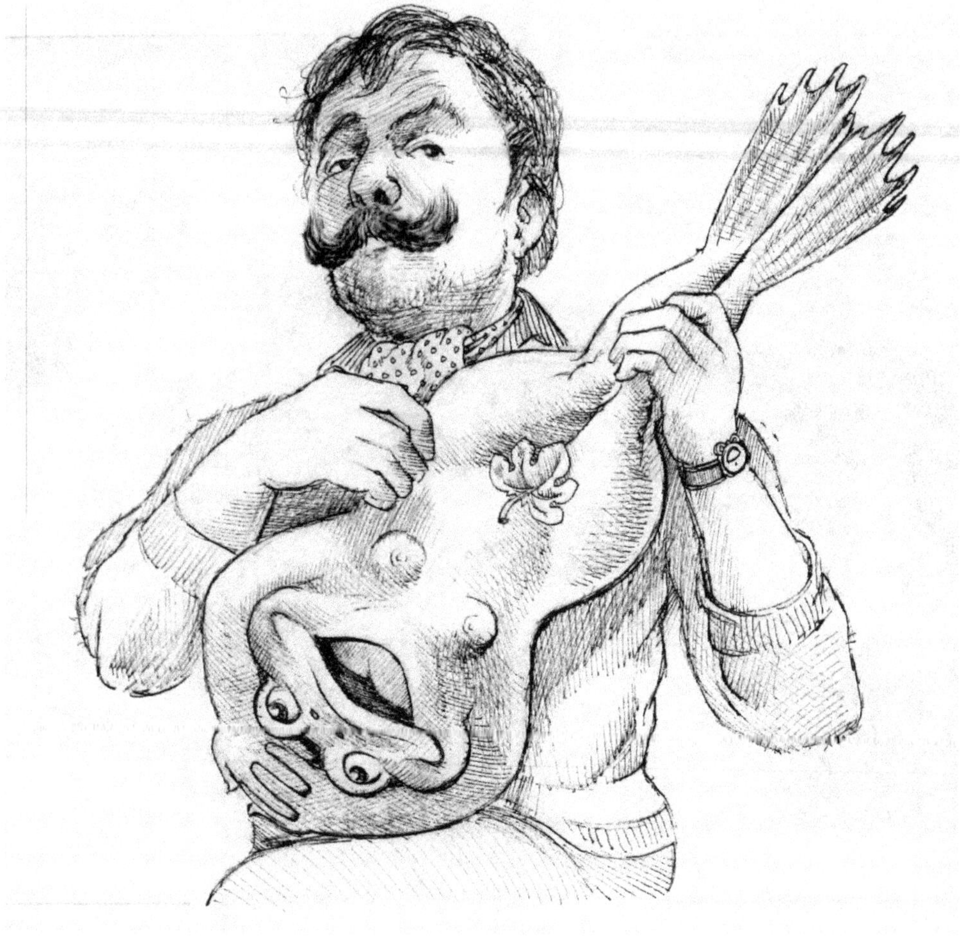

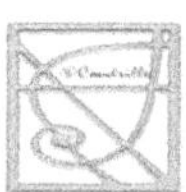

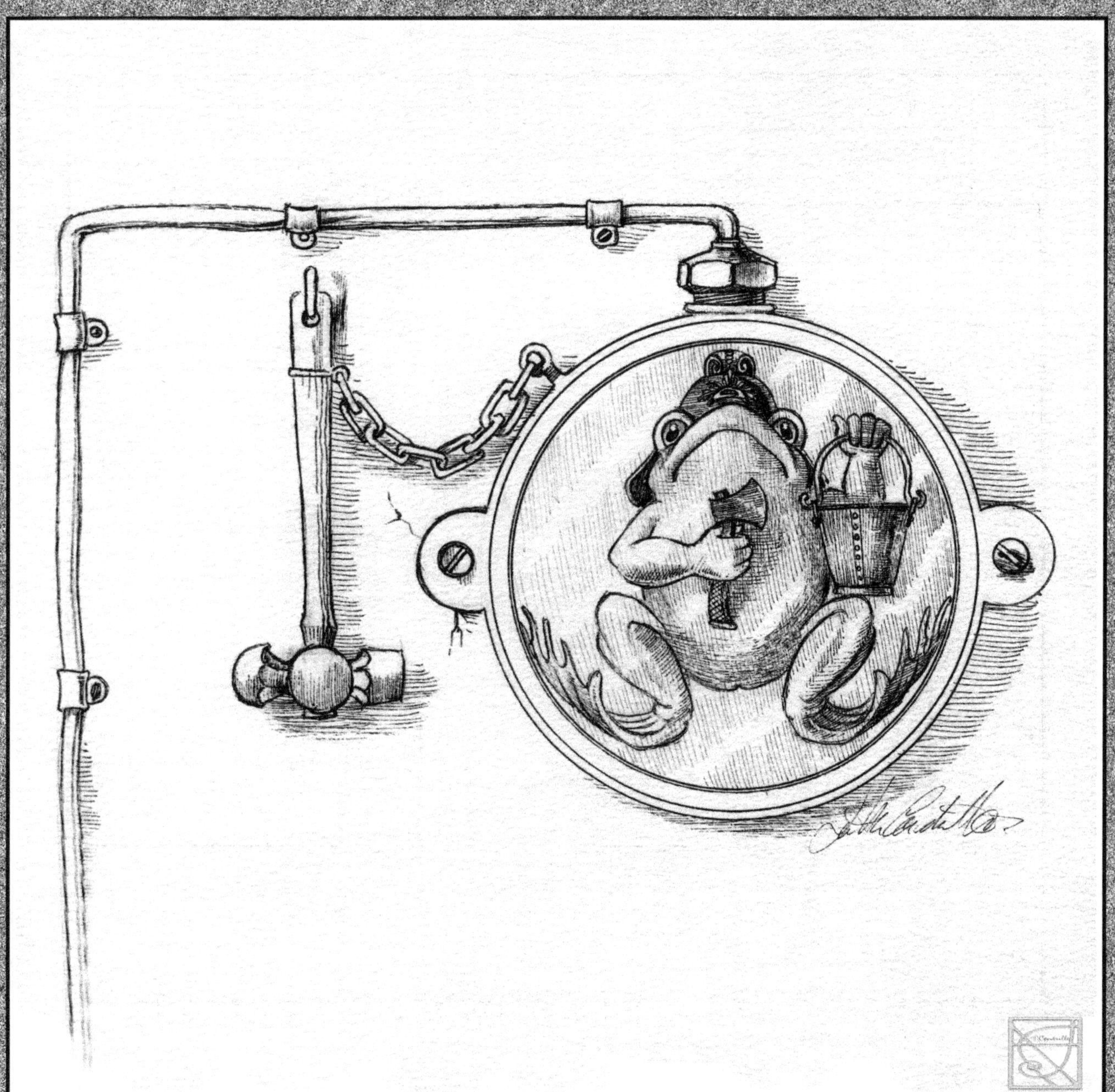

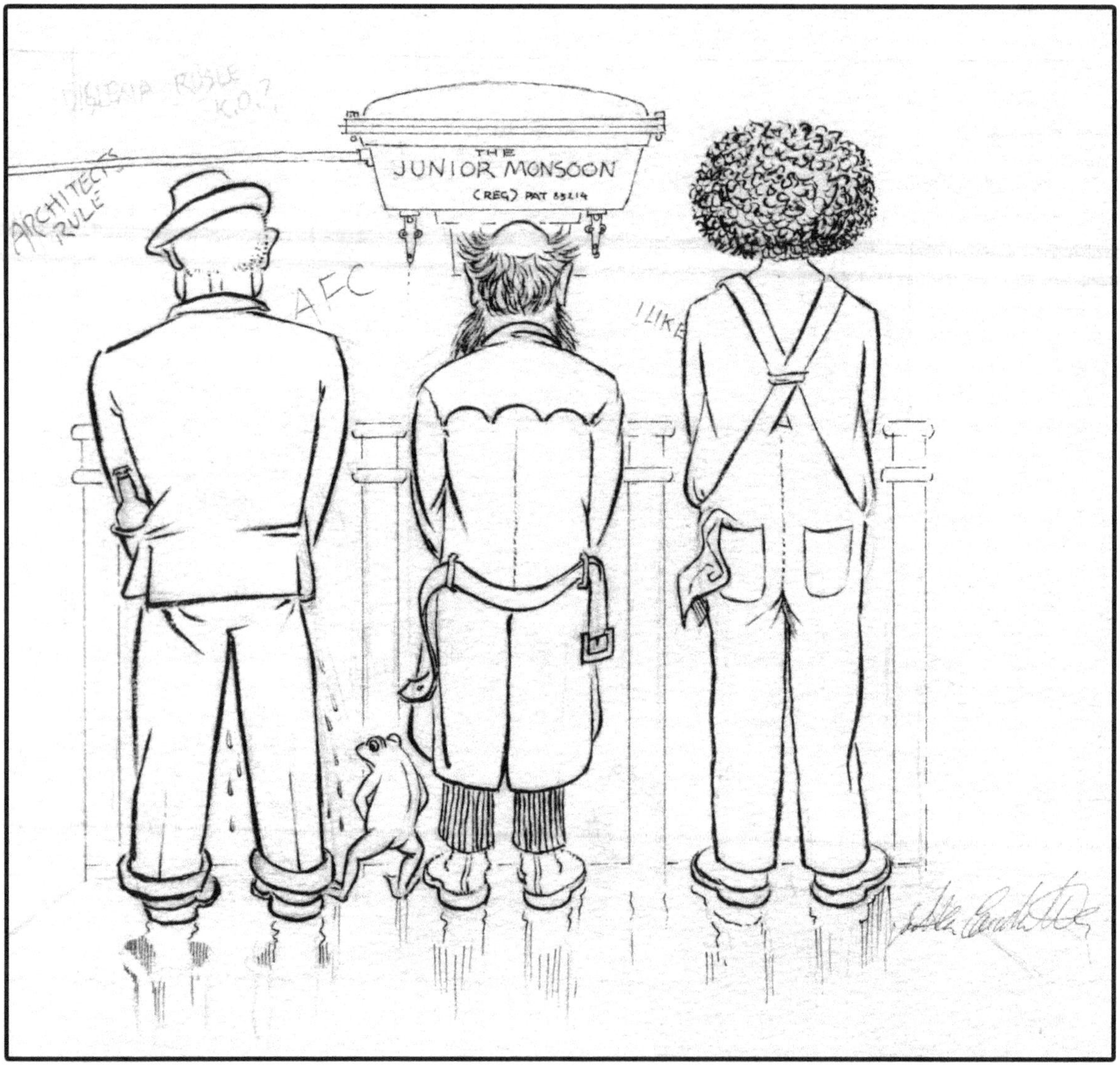

HELENA RUBIE K.O.?
ARCHITECTS RULE
THE
JUNIOR MONSOON
(REG) PAT 33214
AFC
ILIKE

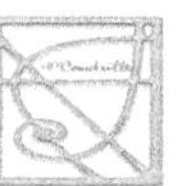

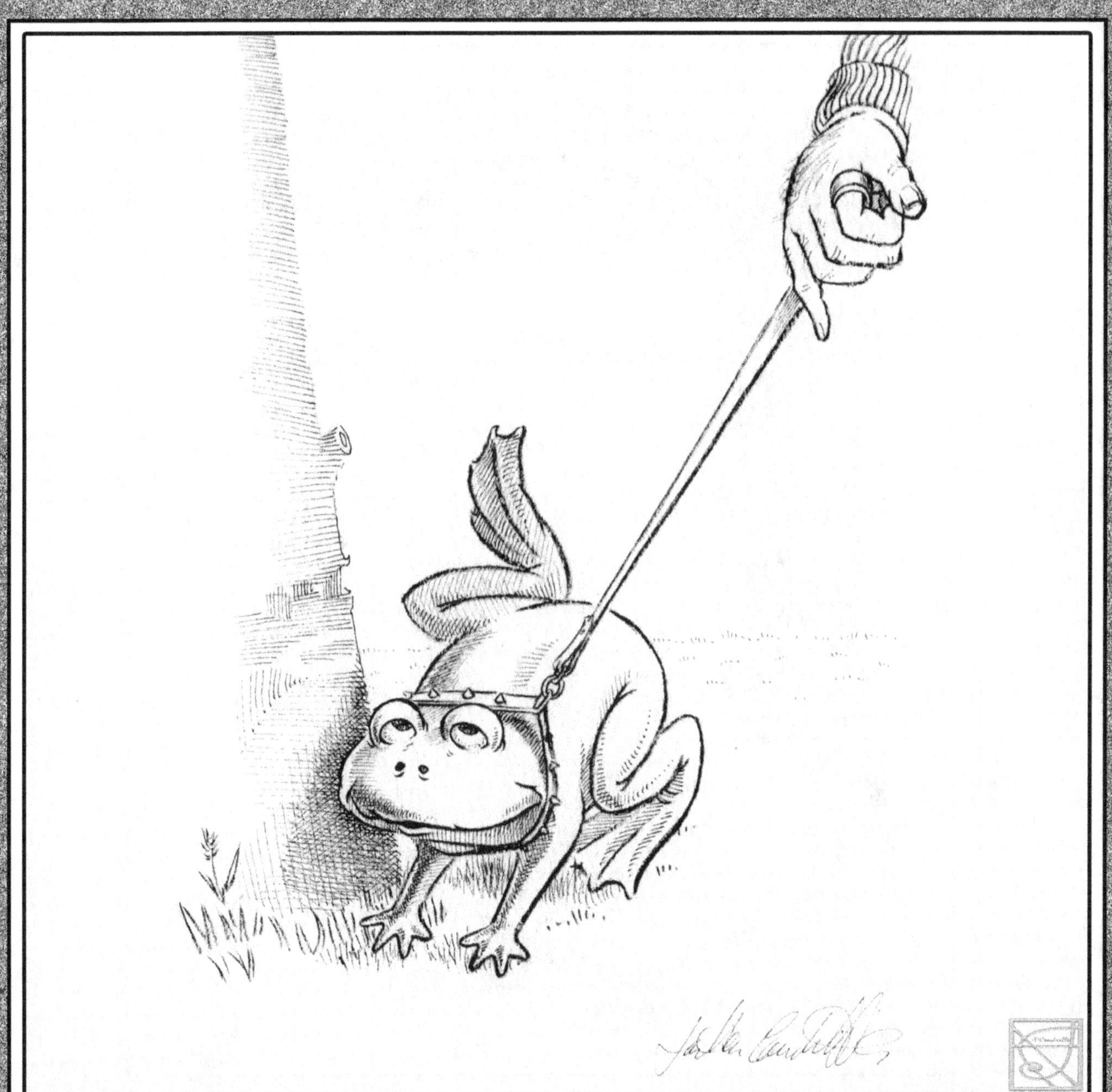

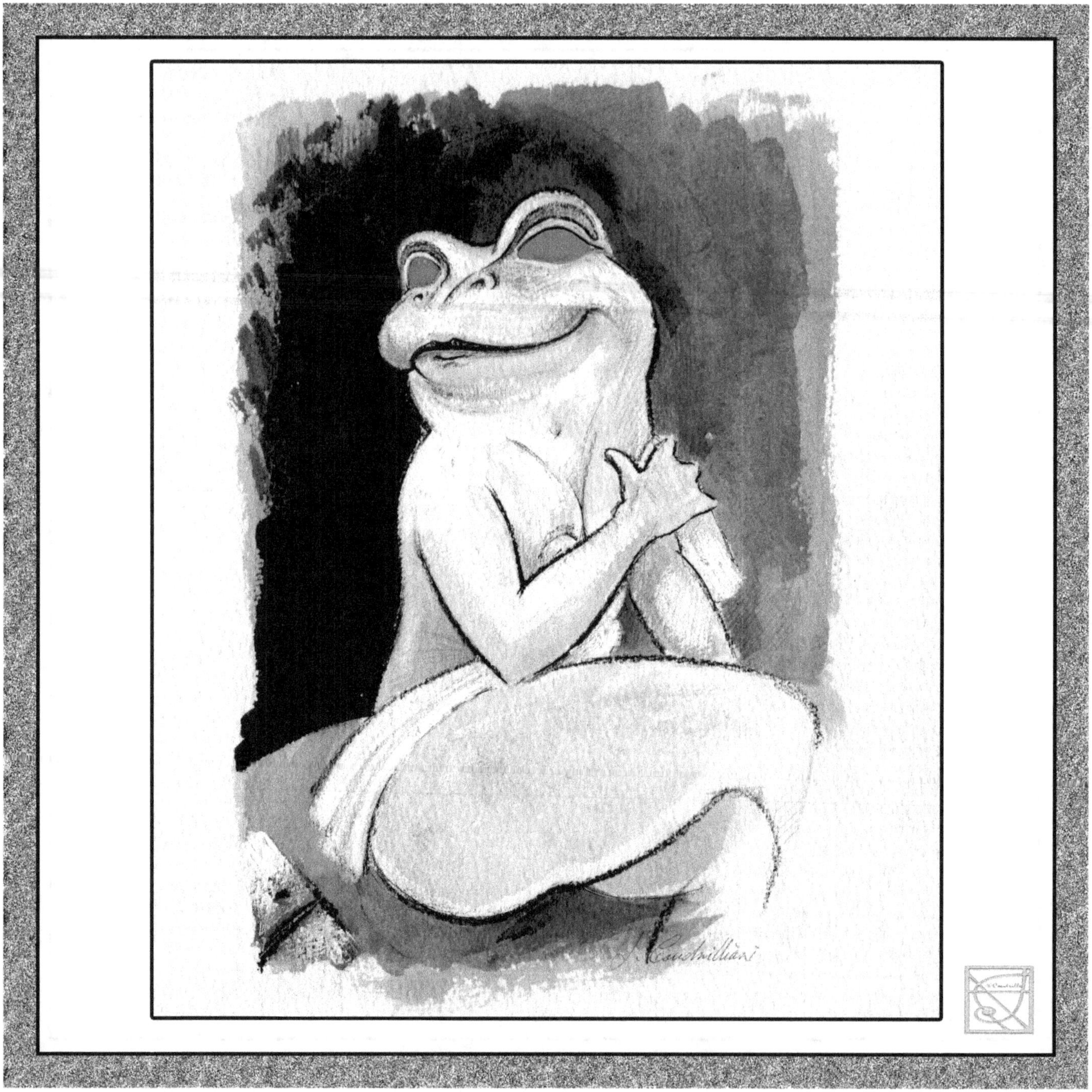

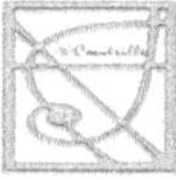

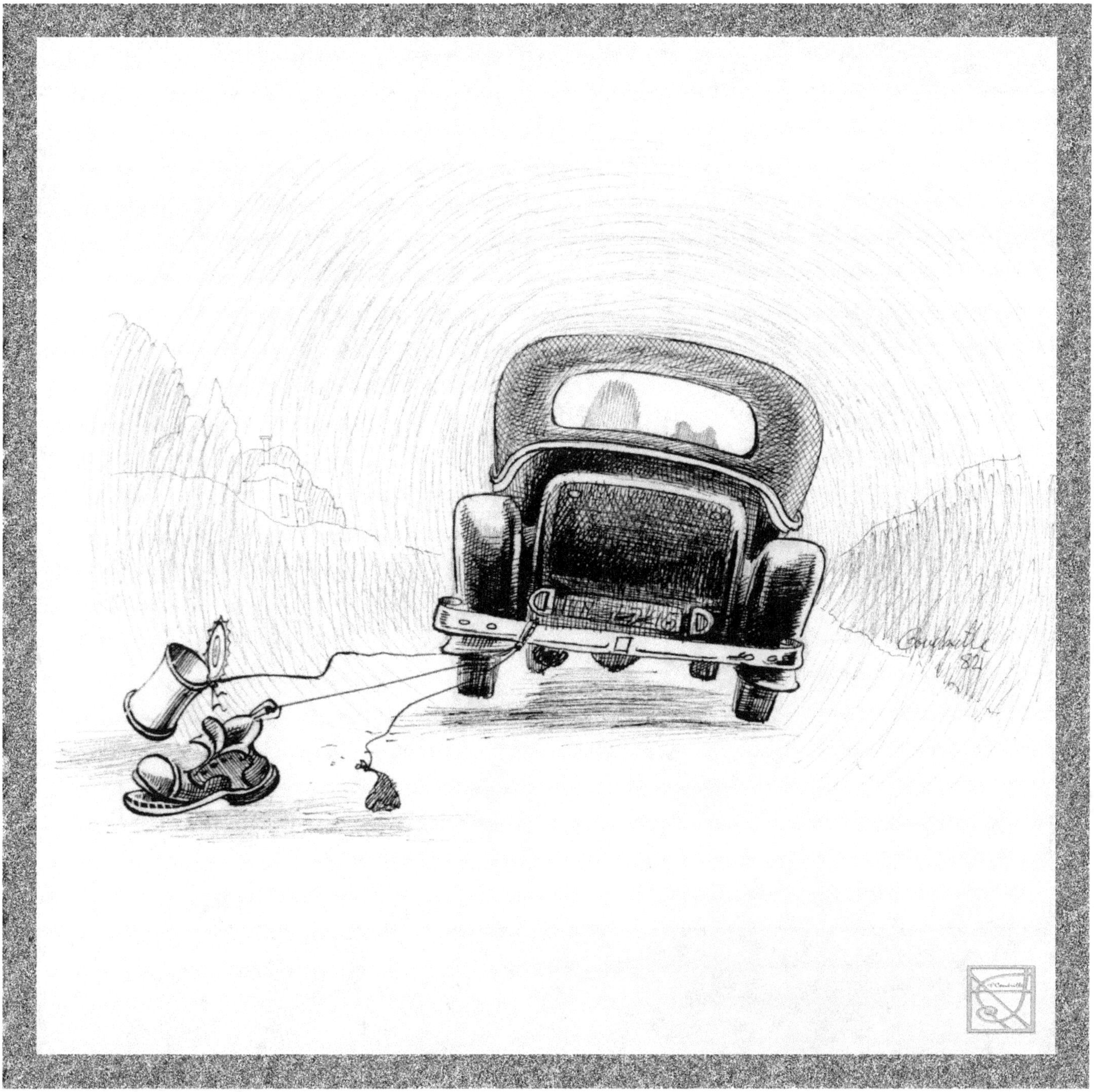

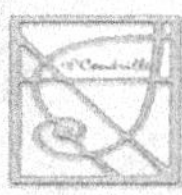

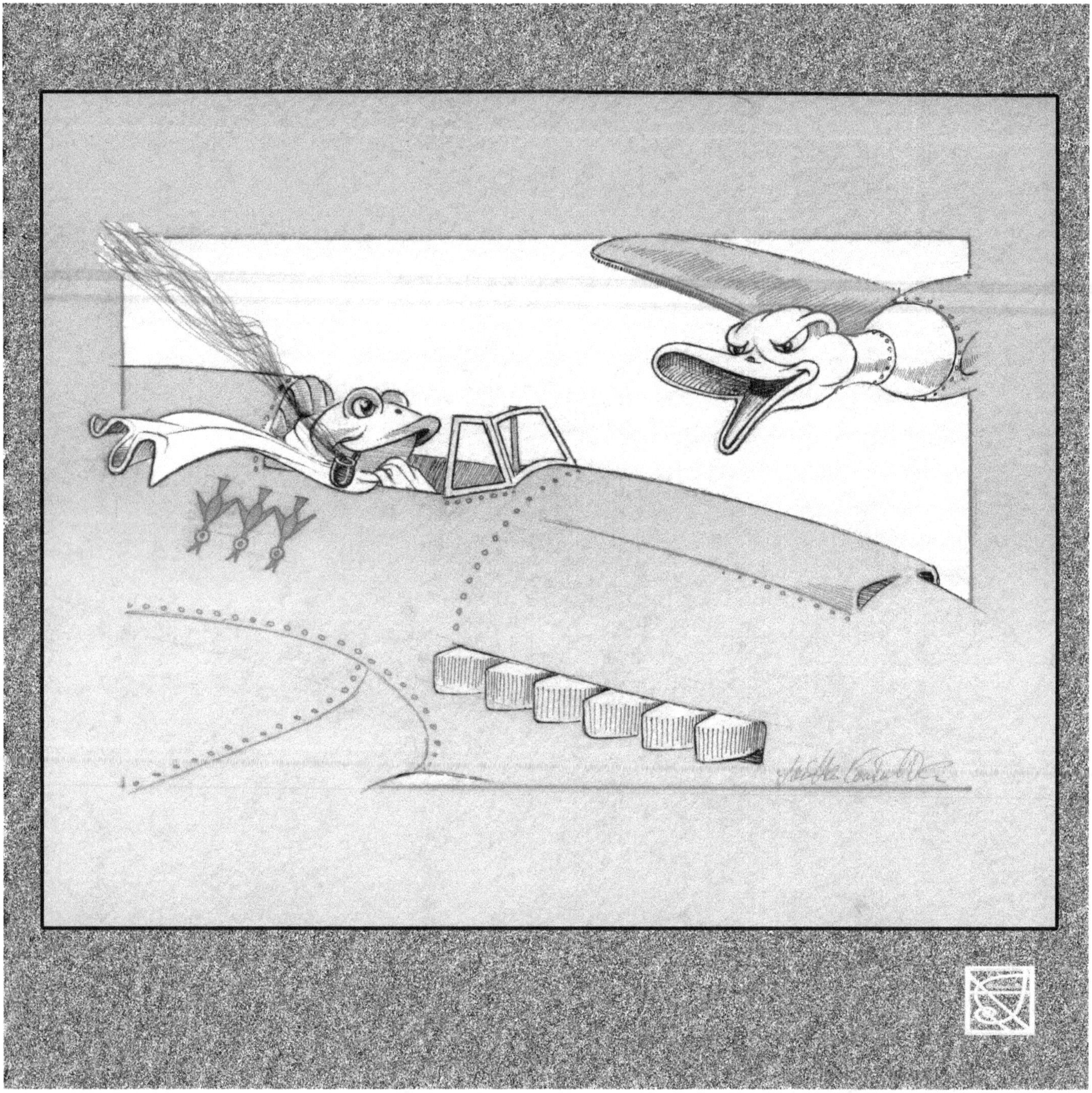

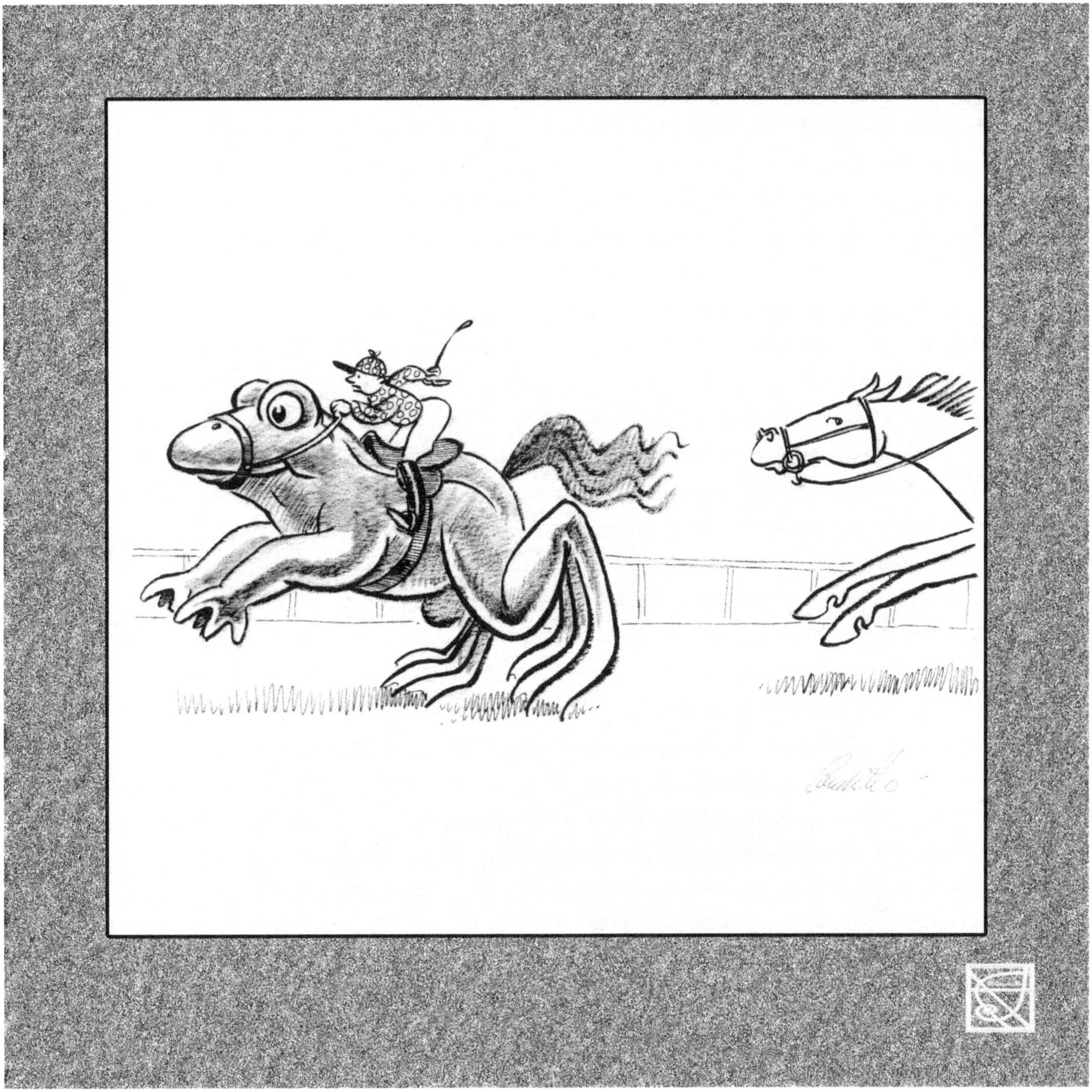

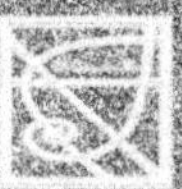

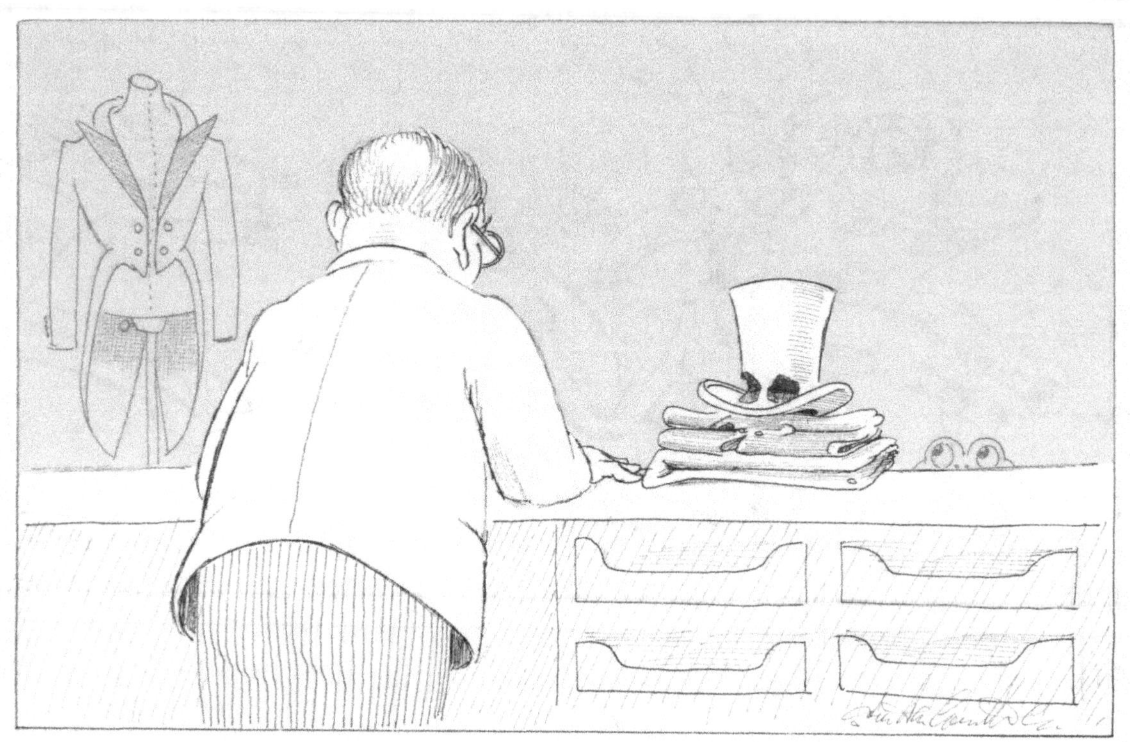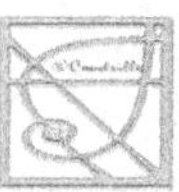

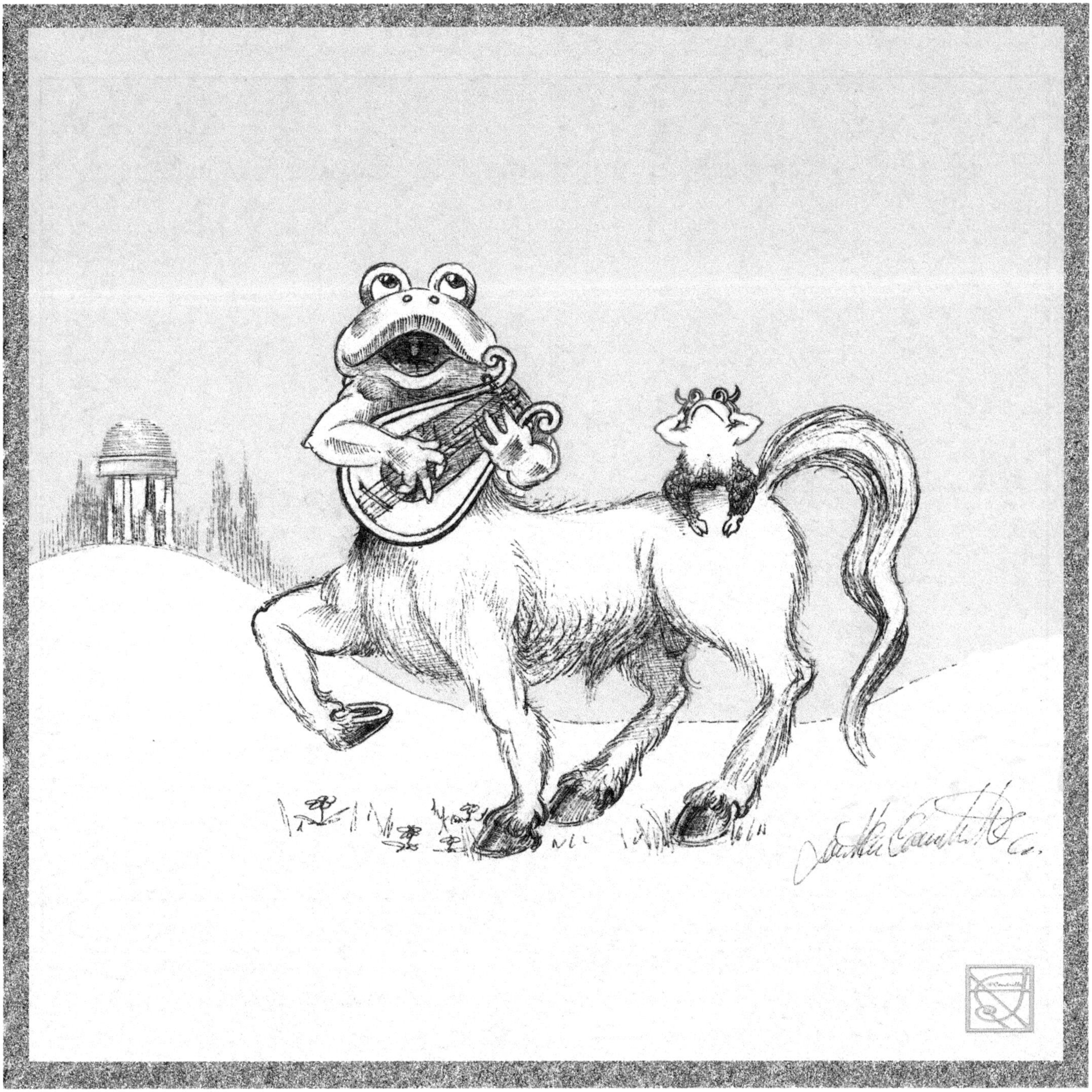

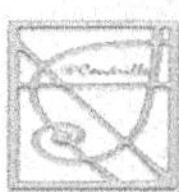

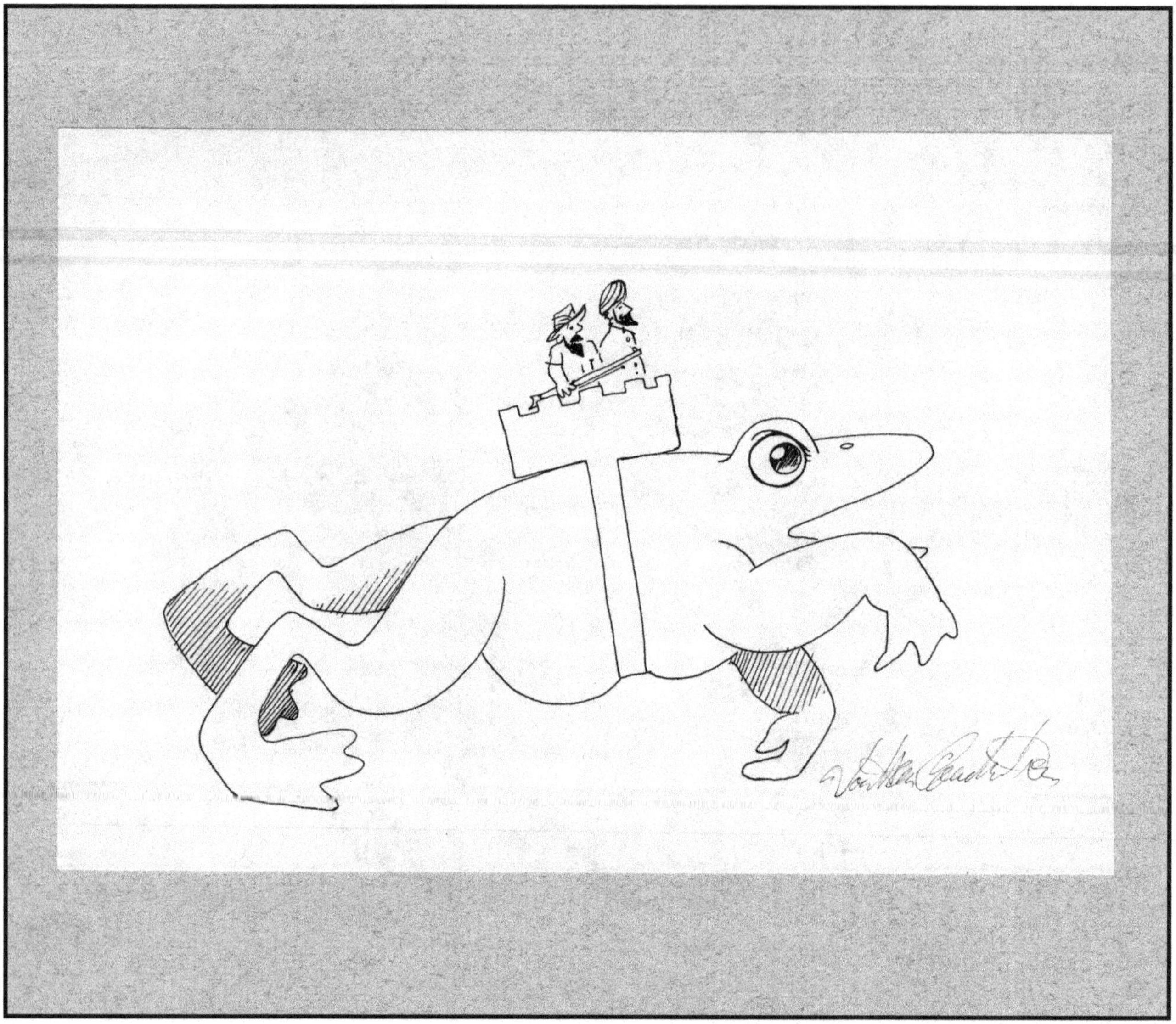

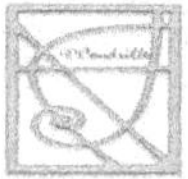

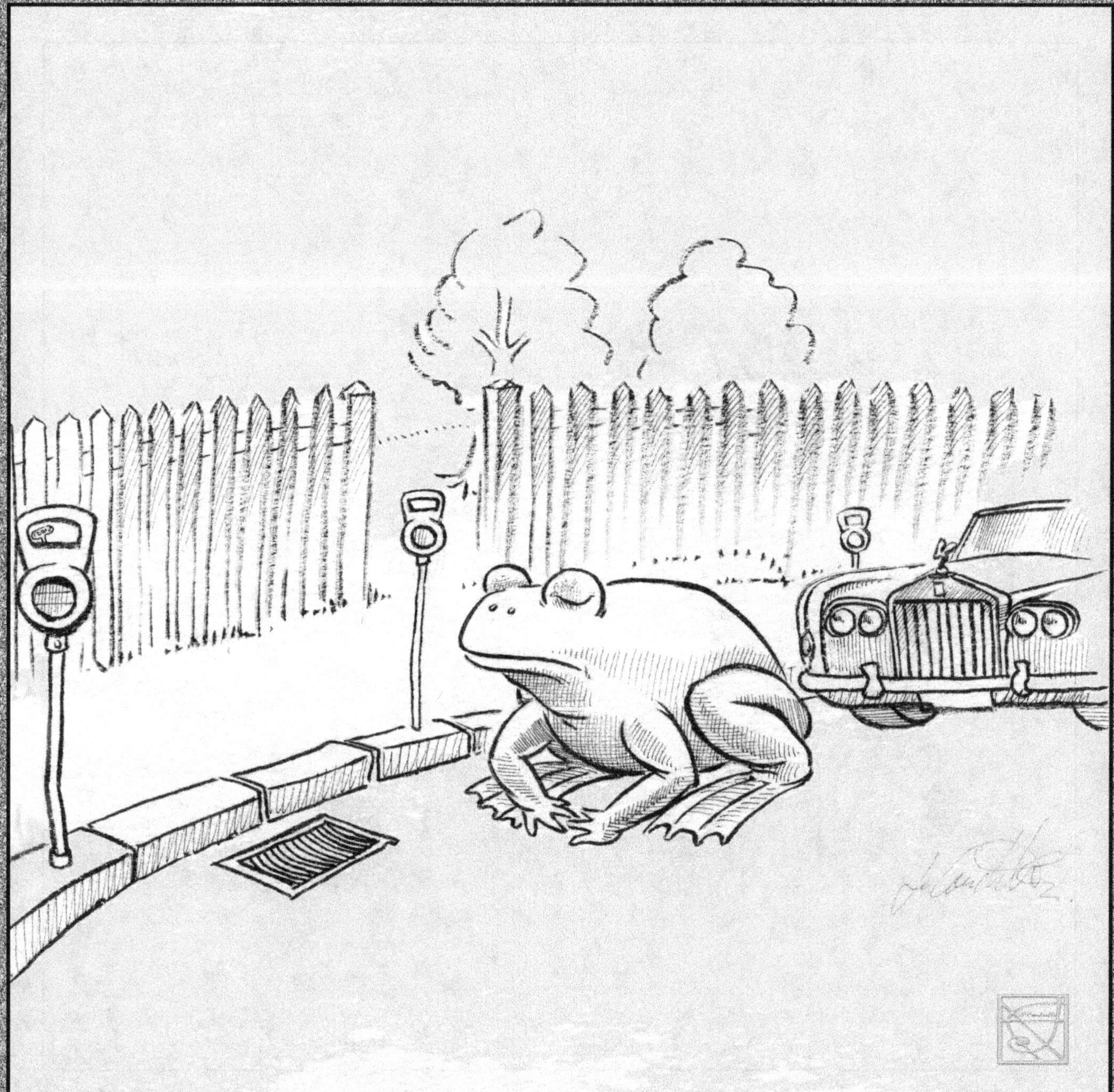

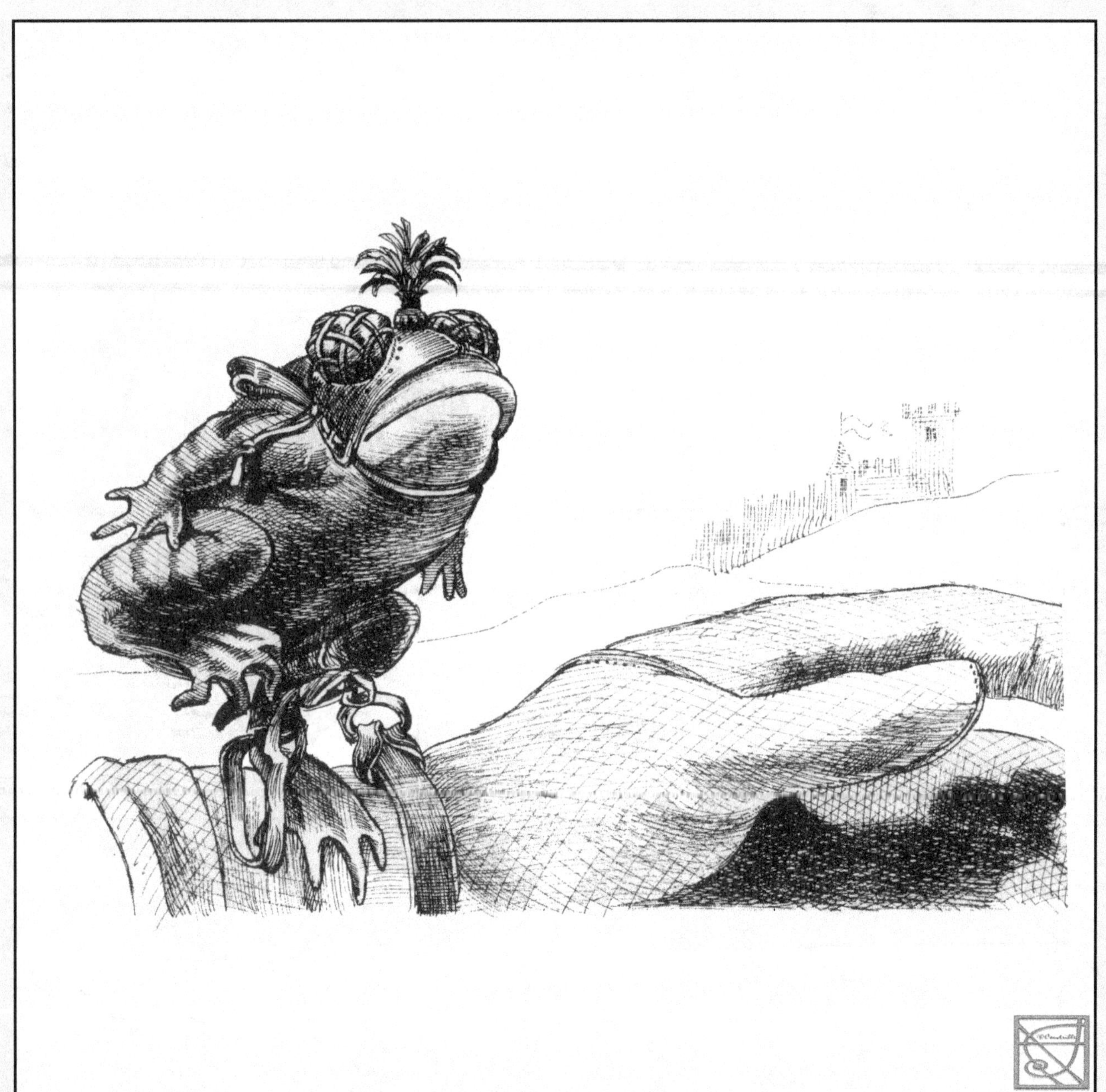

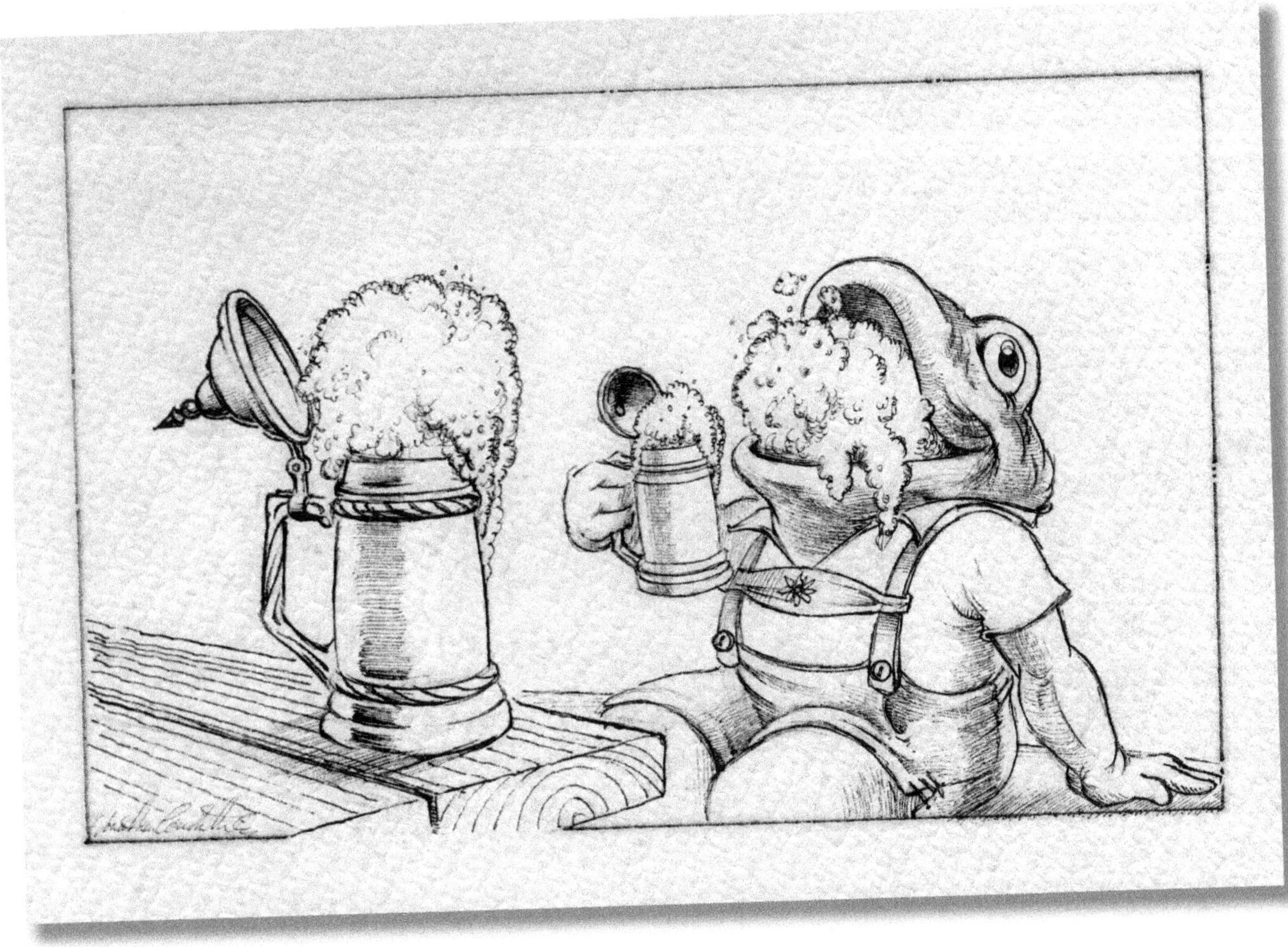

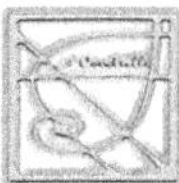

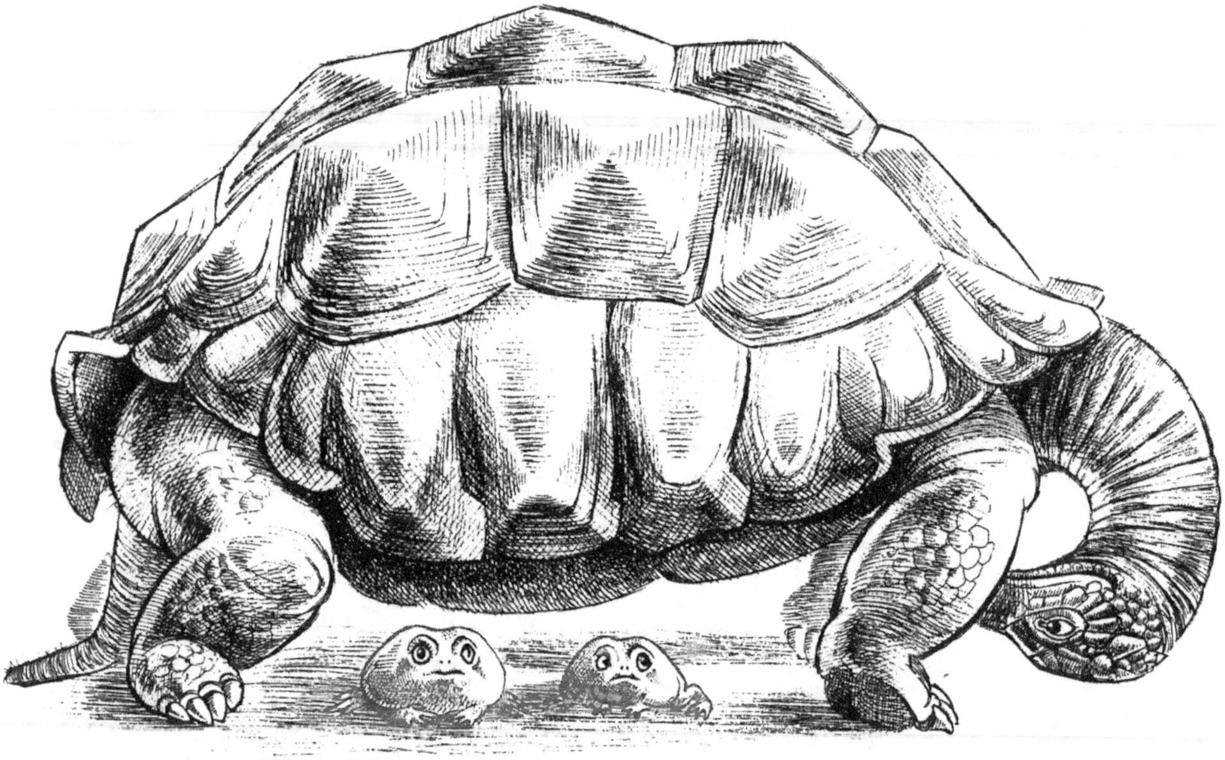

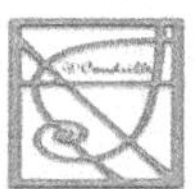

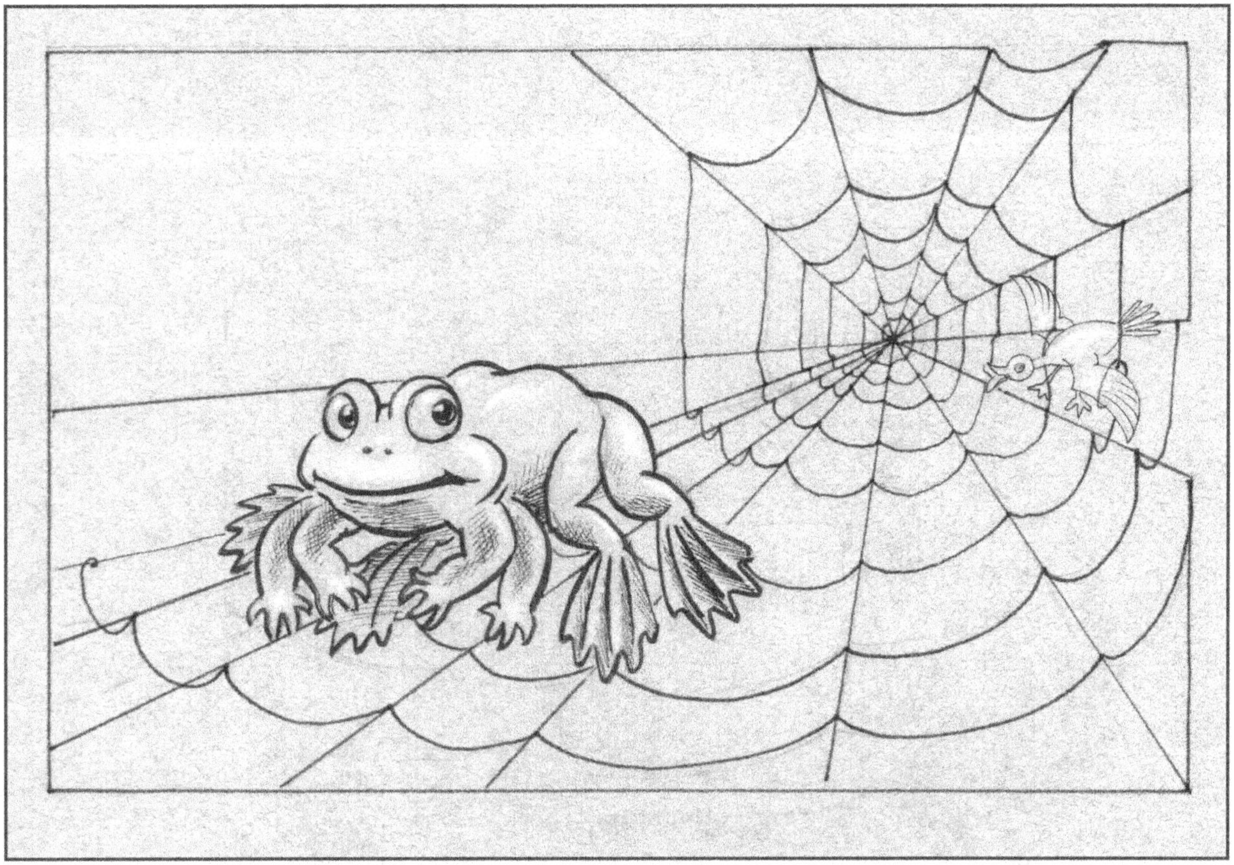

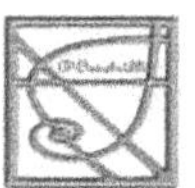

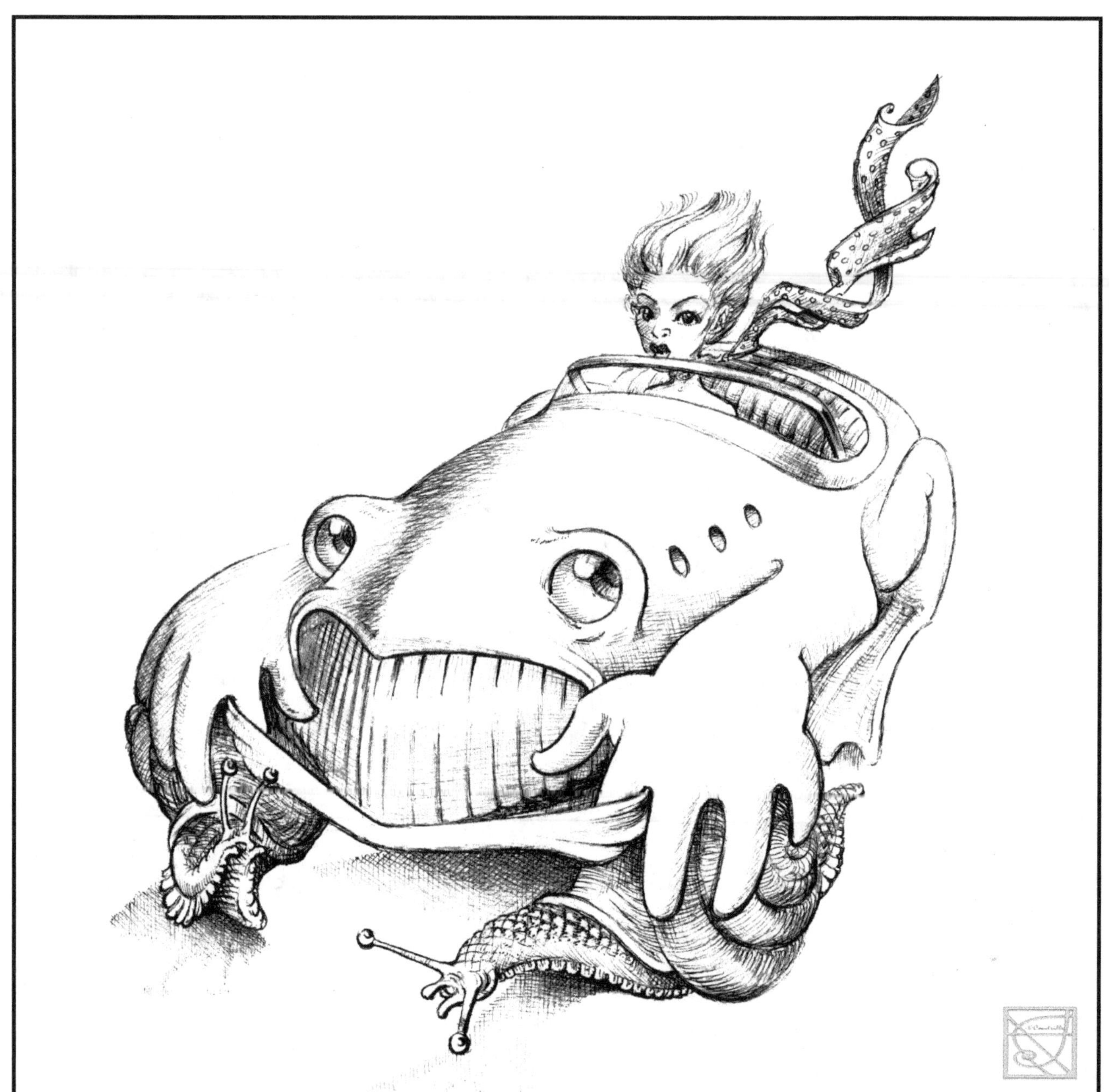

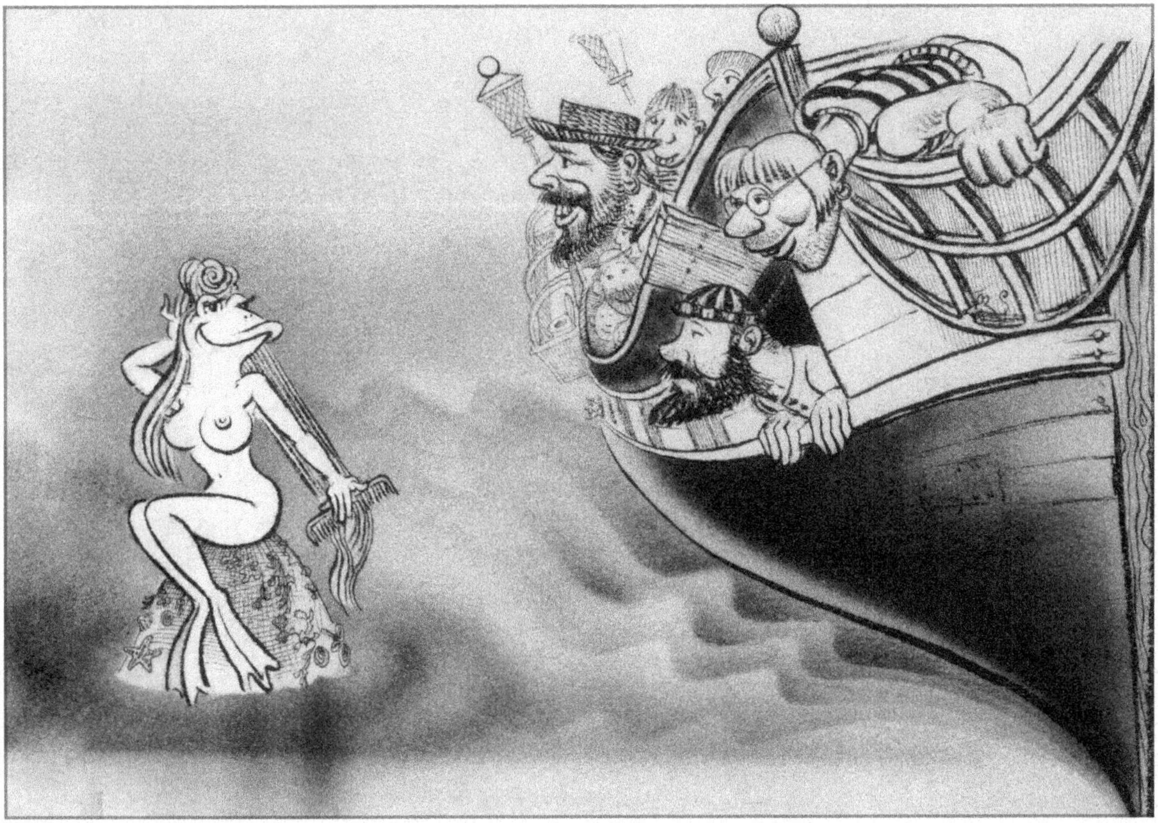

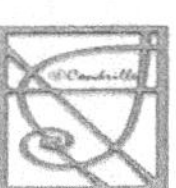

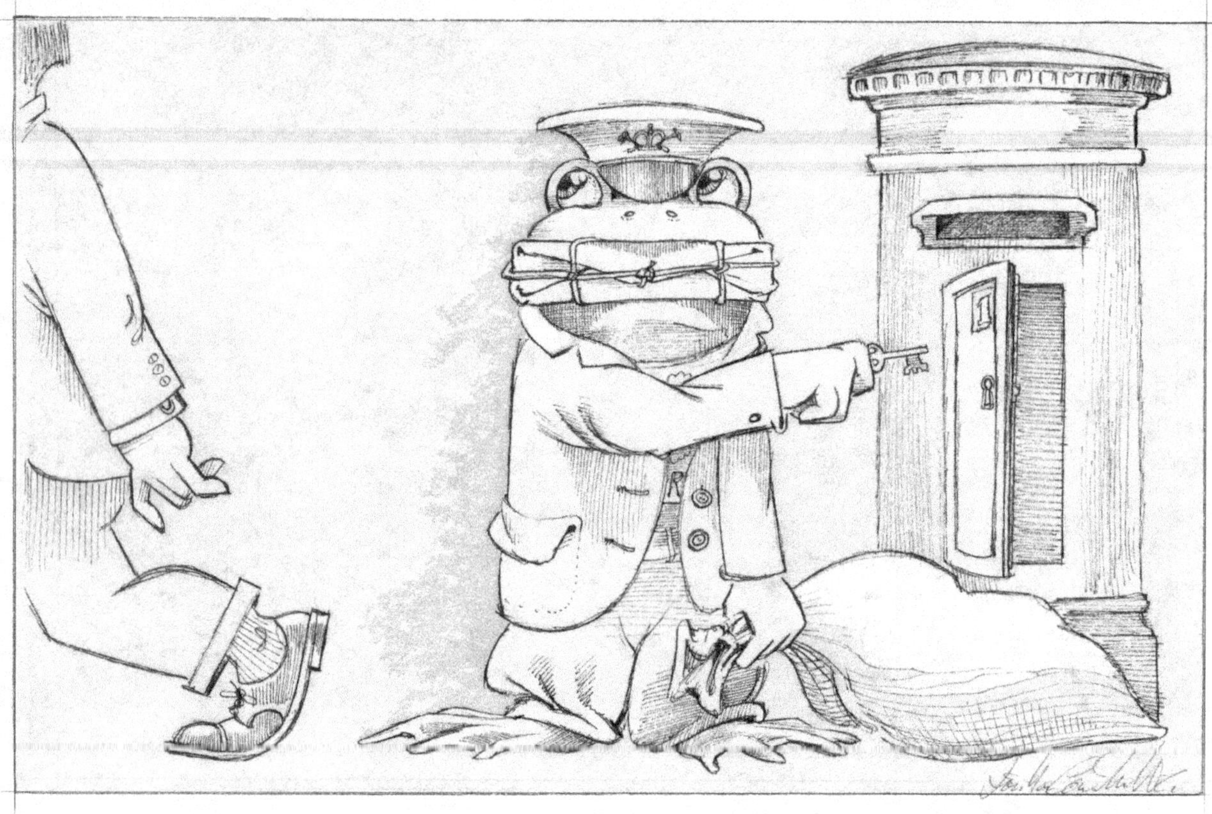

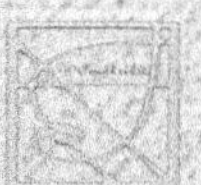

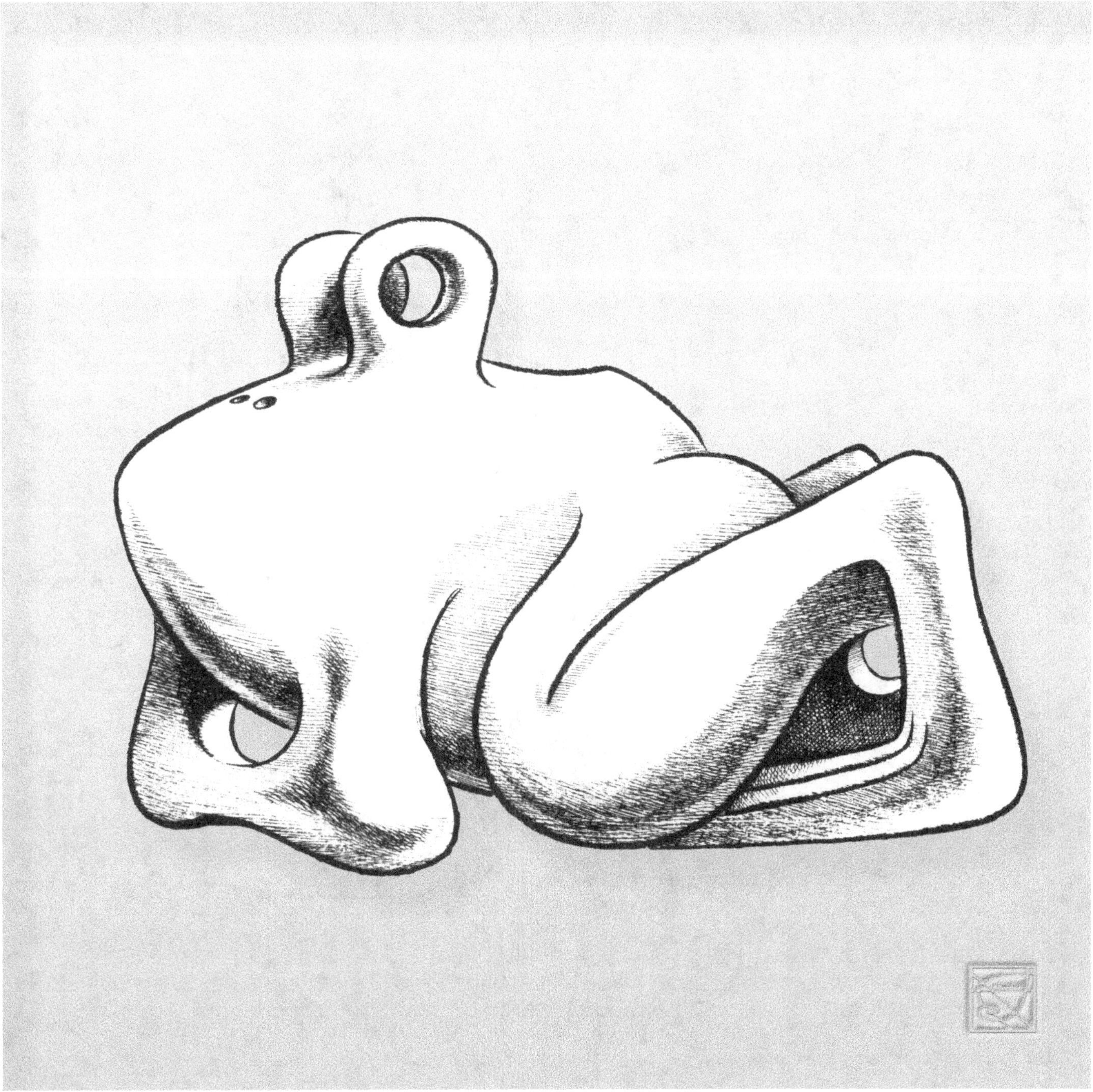

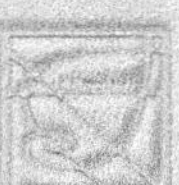

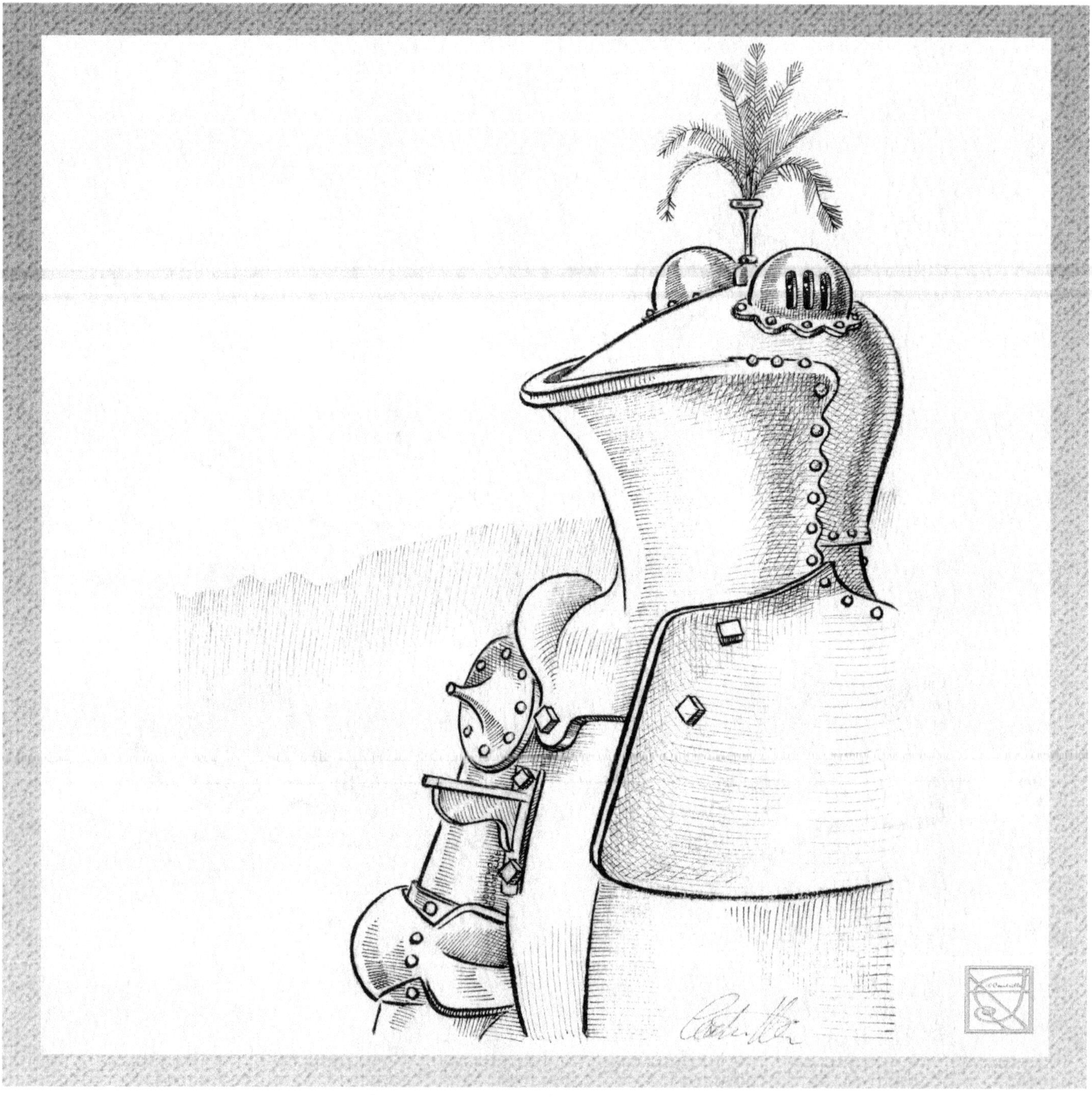

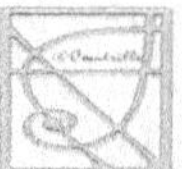

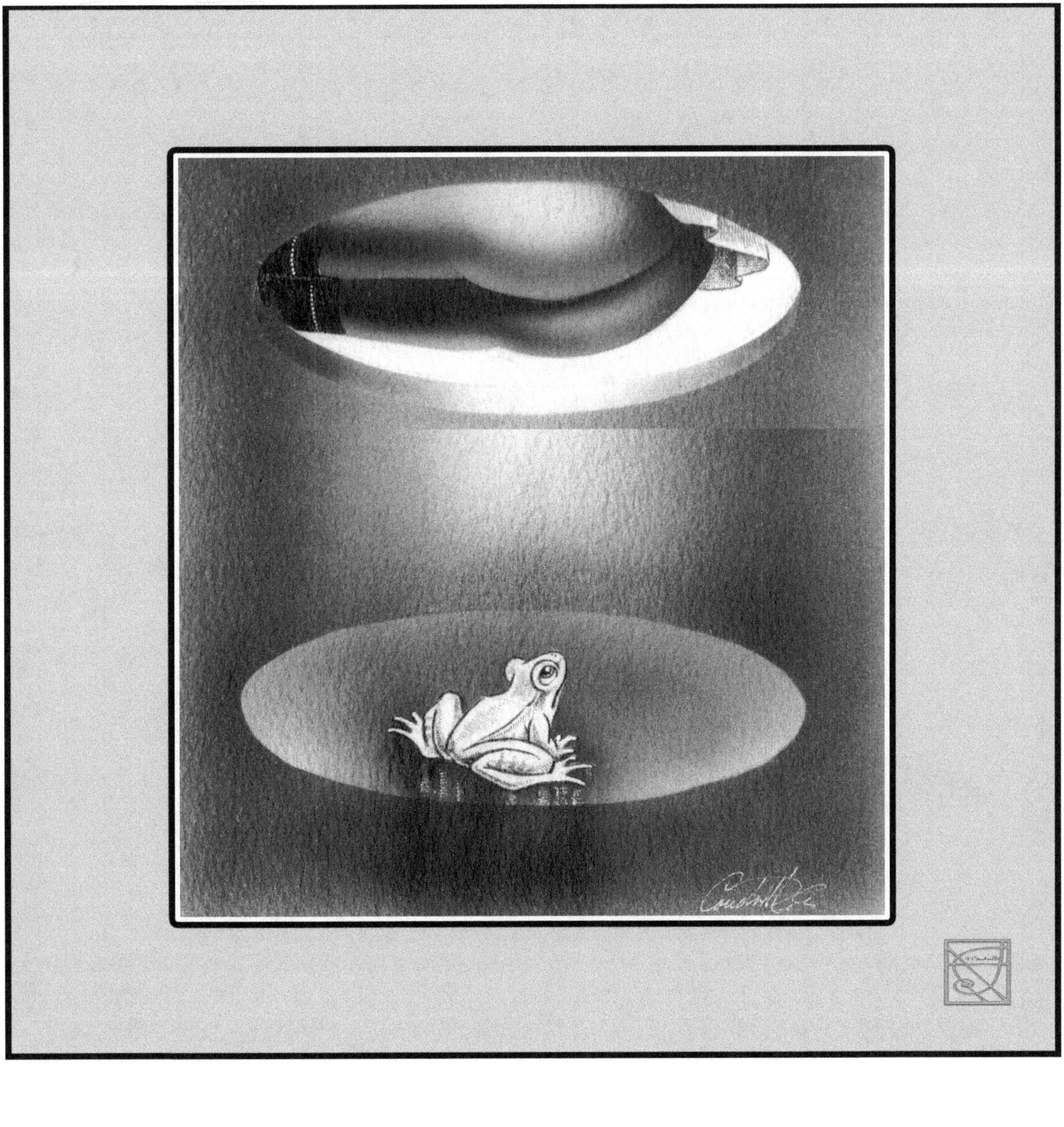

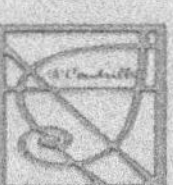

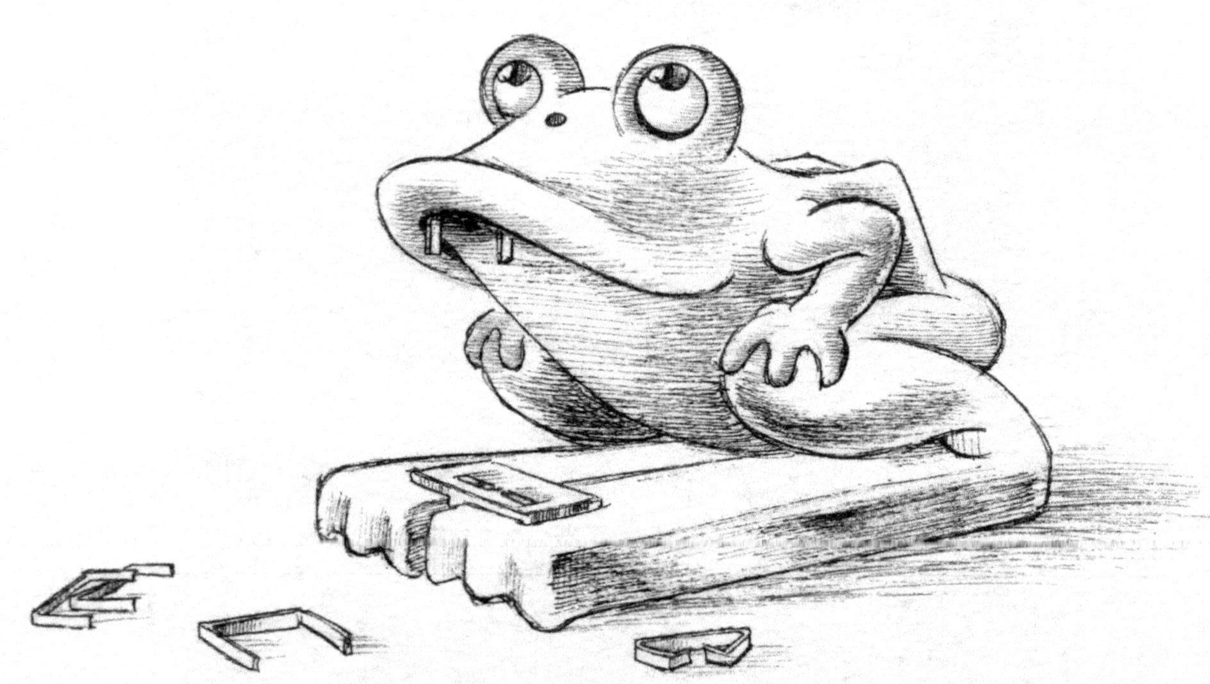
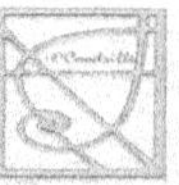

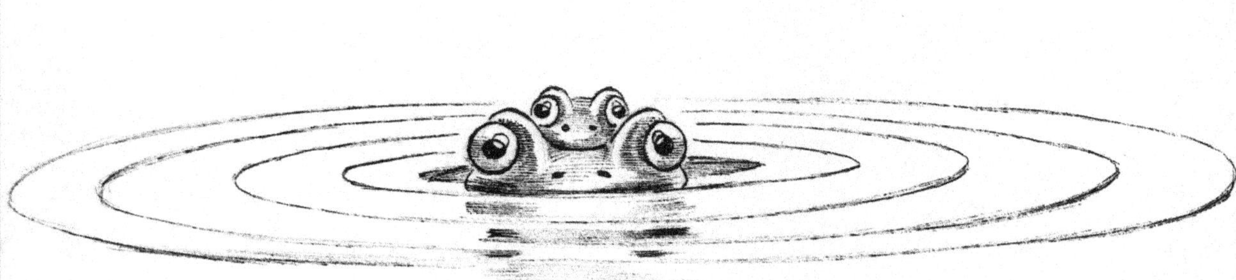
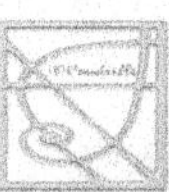

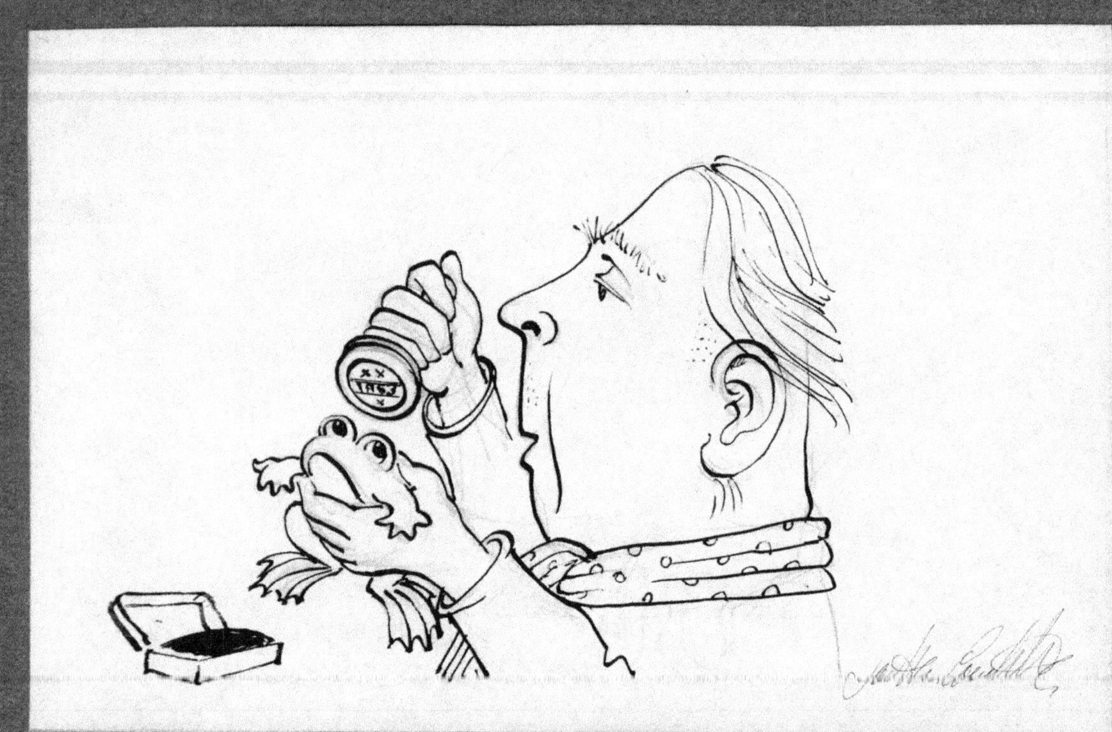
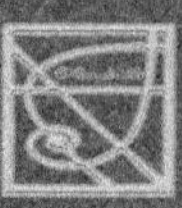

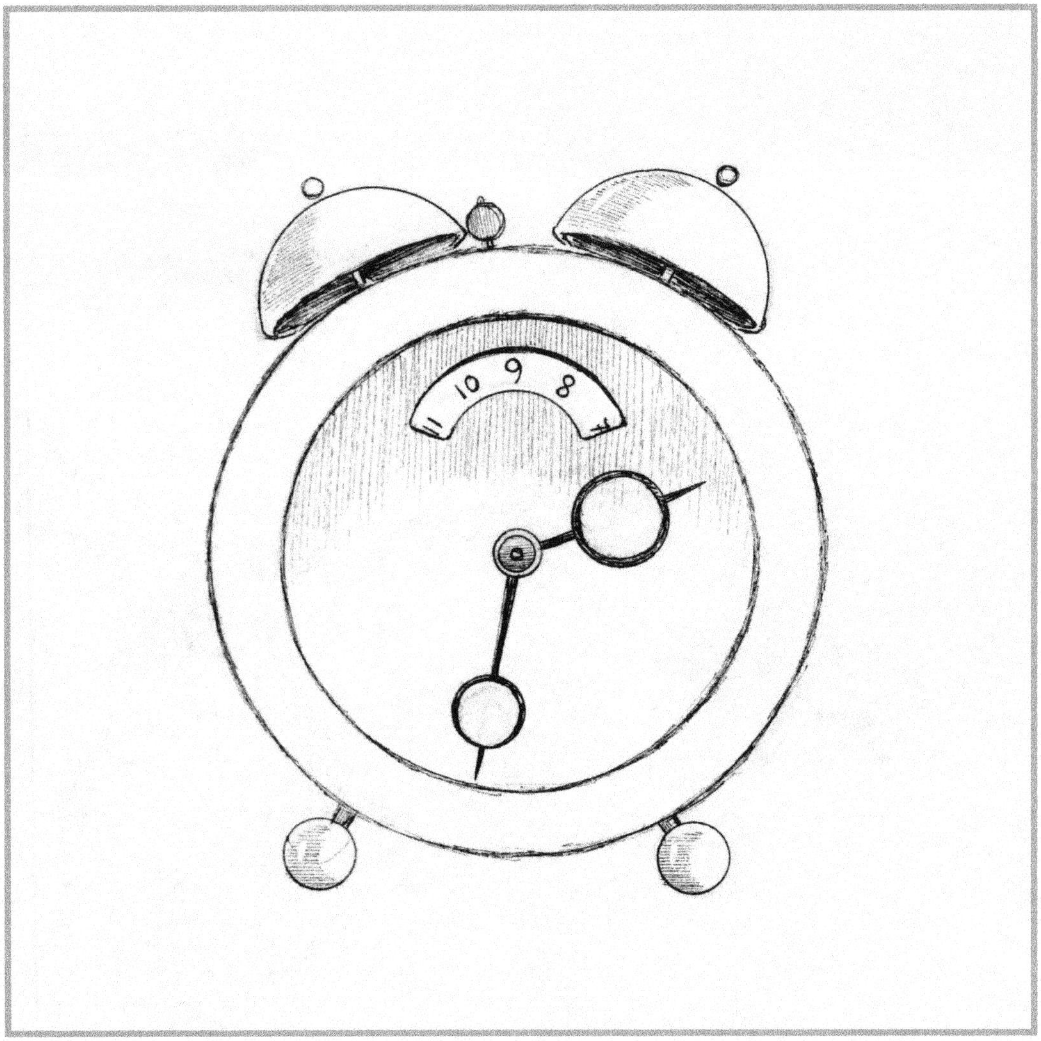

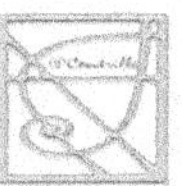

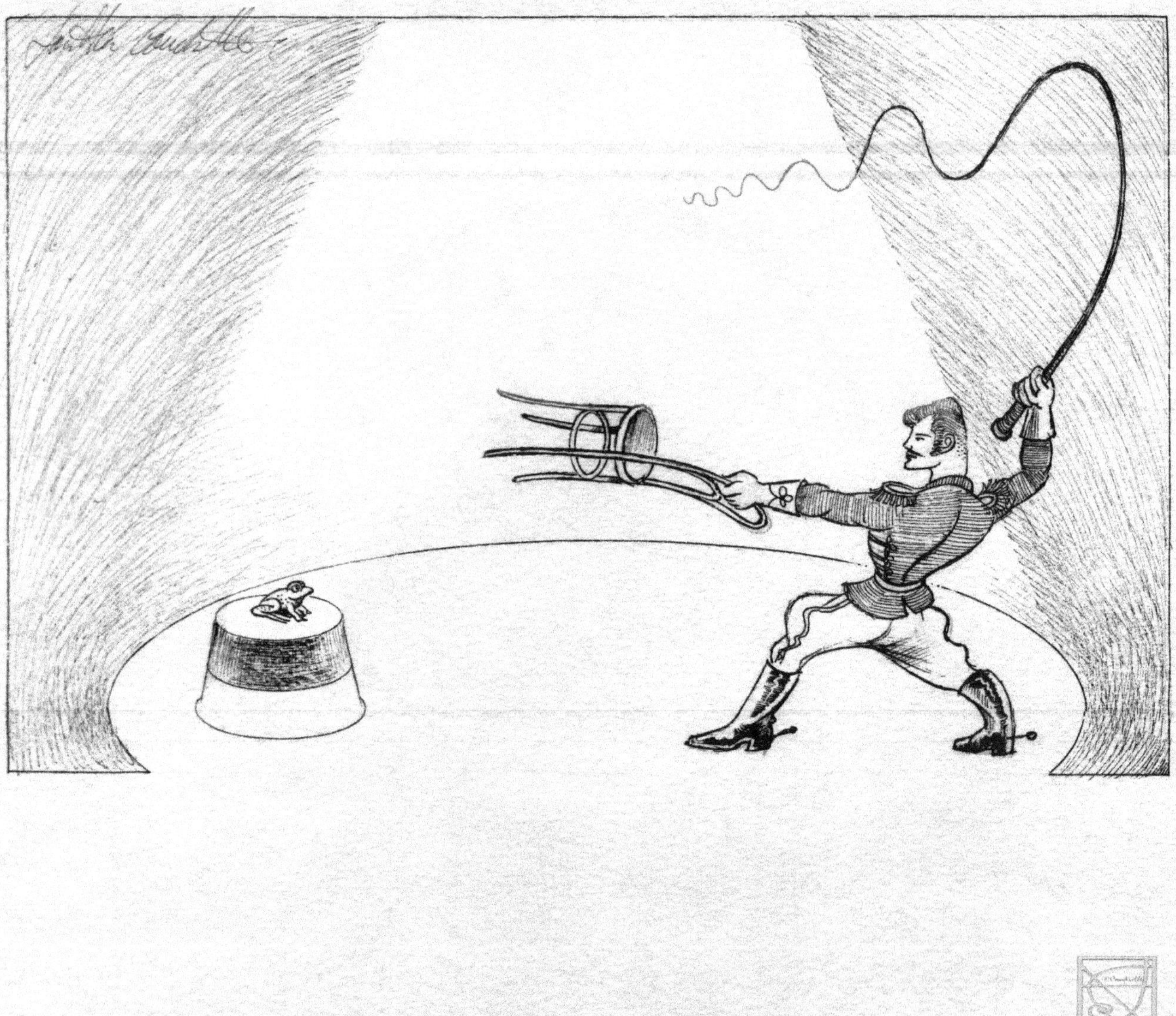

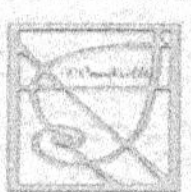

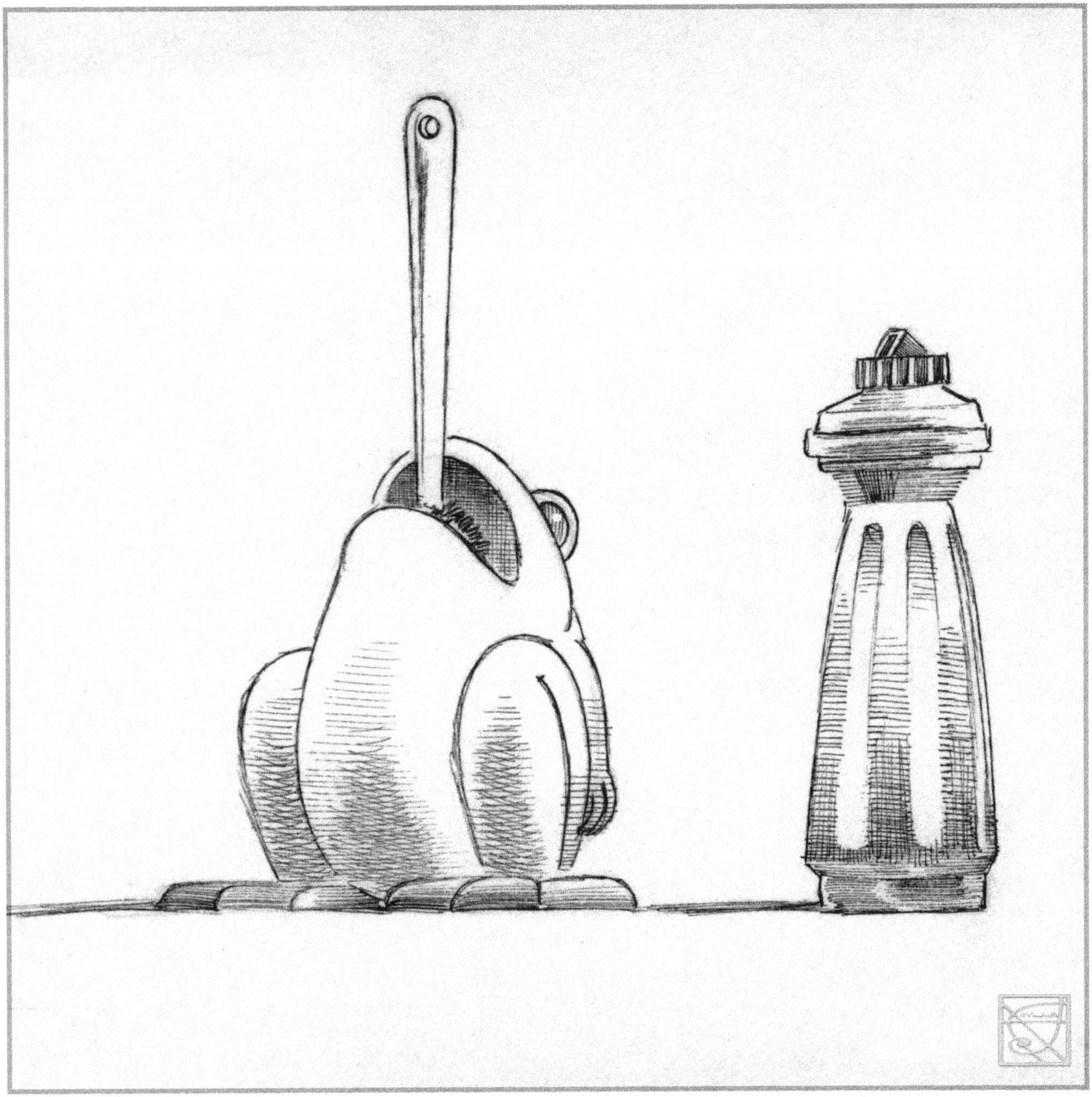

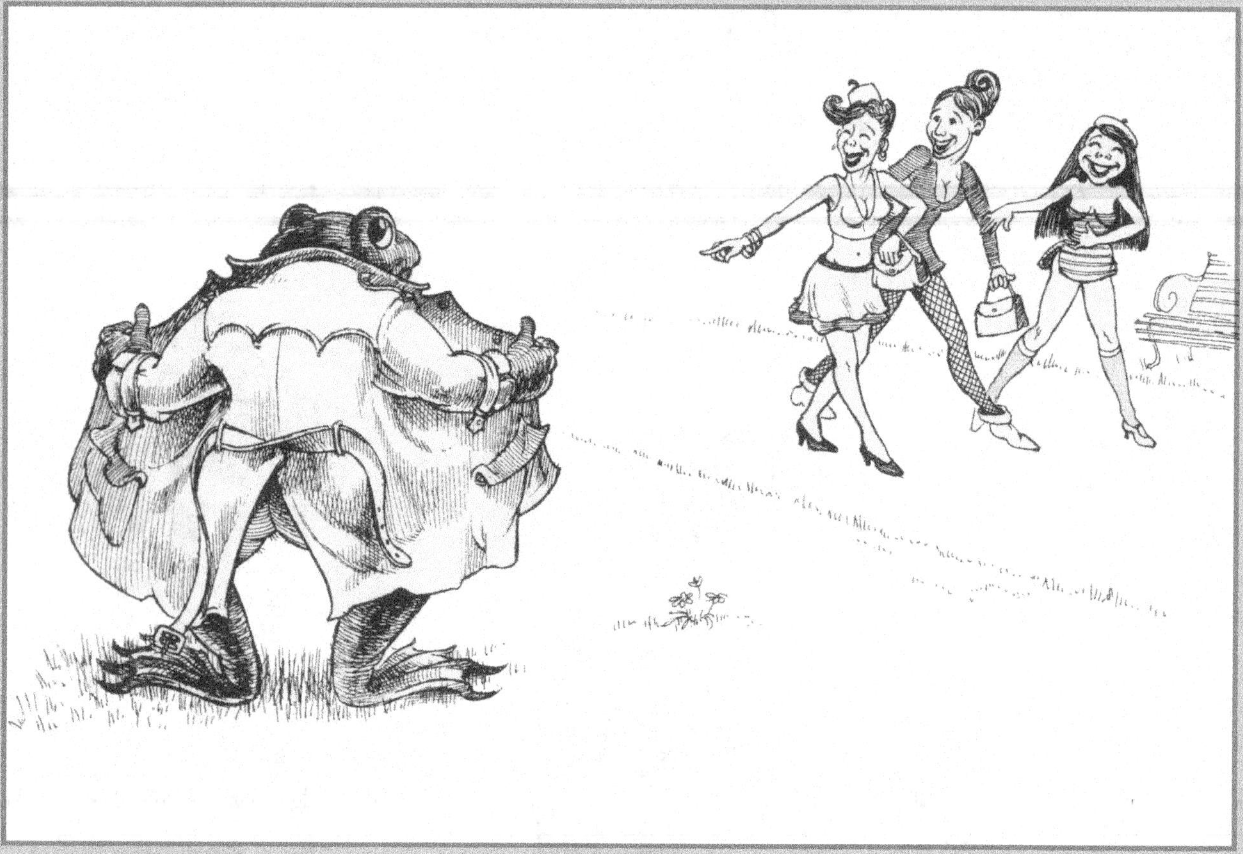

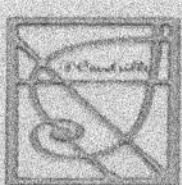

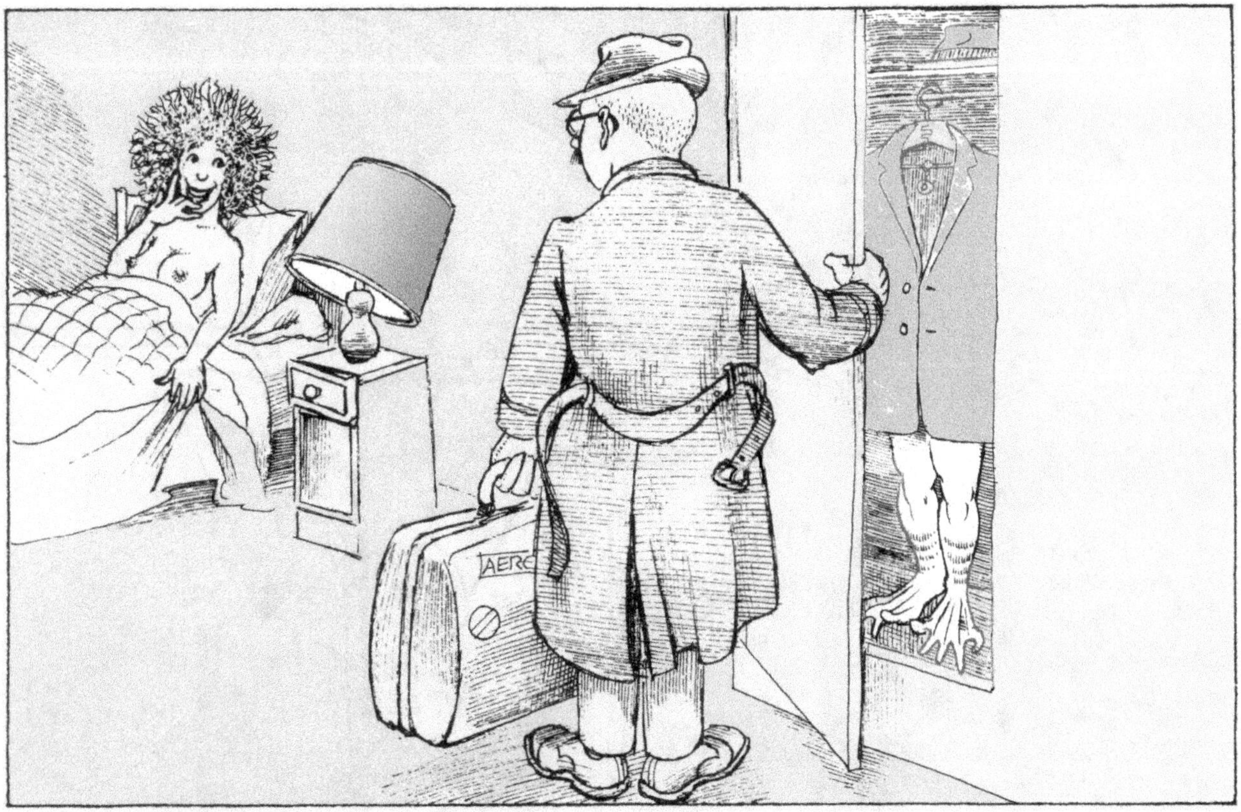

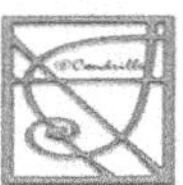

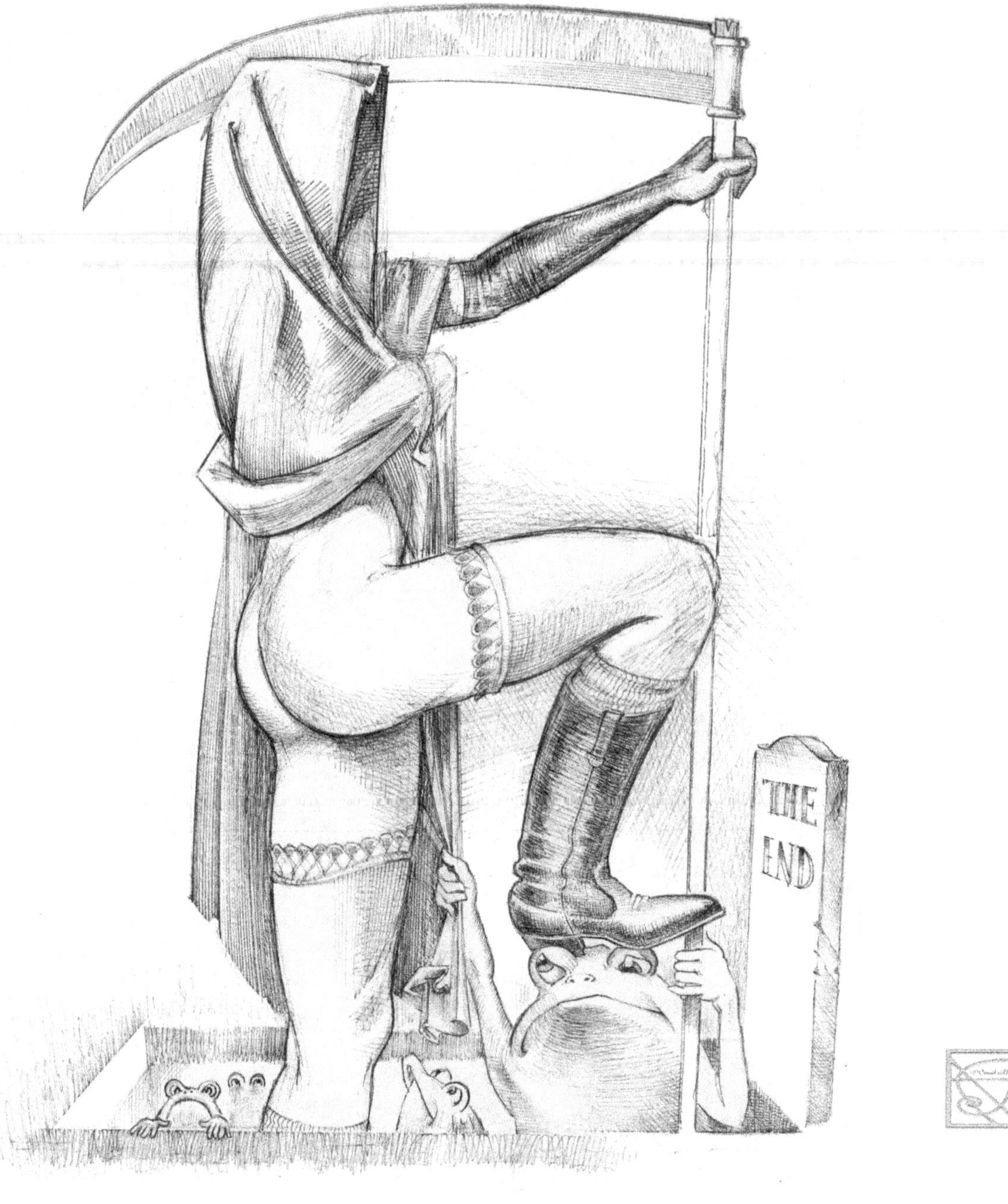

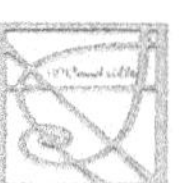

THE
END

Farmer Fisher

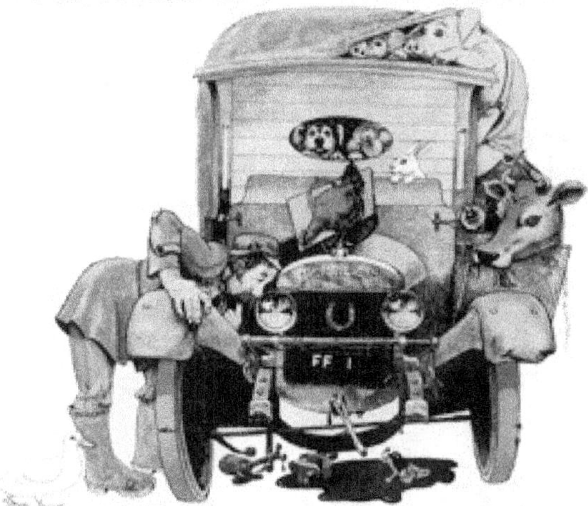

Jonathon Coudrille

Children's Book of the Year 1976

It is quite simply a breathtaking piece of Christmas magic which will stay with your children forever.
RMW (Amazon)

Farmer Fisher's
Russian Christmas

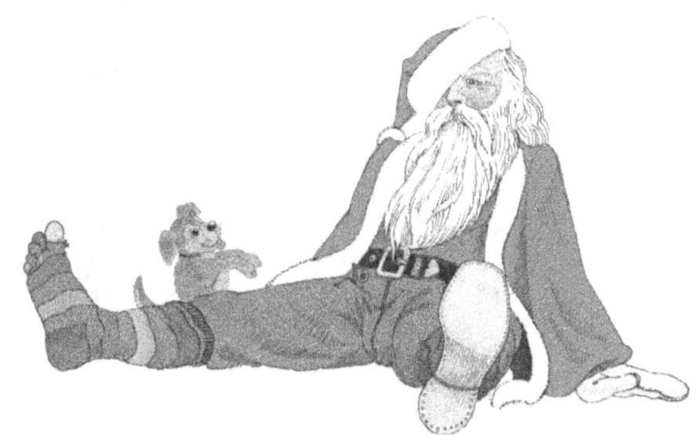

Jonathon Coudrille

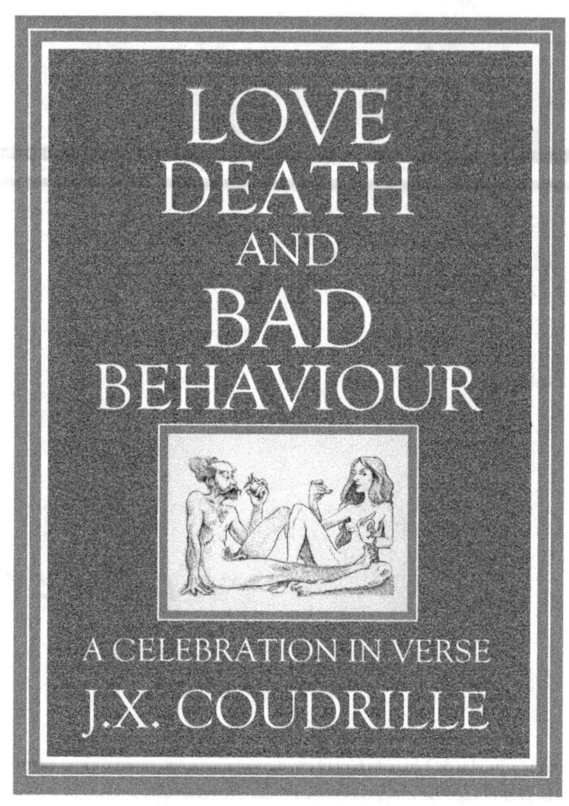

DEDICATED TO HUMAN-KIND AND,
THAT IMPOTENT OLD ASS DEMOCRACY